Let the People Decide

Let the People Decide

The Autobiography of
Dennis Canavan

BIRLINN

First published in 2009 by
Birlinn Limited
West Newington House
10 Newington Road
Edinburgh
EH9 1QS

www.birlinn.co.uk

ISBN: 978 1 84158 839 1

British Library Cataloguing-in-Publication Data
A catalogue record for this book is available from the British Library

Designed and typeset by Iolaire Typesetting, Newtonmore
Printed and bound by MPG Books Ltd, Bodmin

Contents

Part III: Parting of the Ways

Part IV: A Man o' Independent Mind

List of Illustrations

The Bonny Baby competition, Central Park, Cowdenbeath, 1943.

The 7-a-side football champions at the Cowdenbeath Co-operative Gala, 1953.

Mum, Dad, Raymond, Dennis, Kathleen and Ian on holiday at Pettycur Bay, Kinghorn, July 1947.

Dux of St Columba's High School, 1958.

St Andrew's College (Drygrange Seminary) Football Team, 1959.

Dennis John, Ruth, Mark and Paul, 1973.

Taking Parliament by storm. After my election in 1974.

With Henry Dawson, Tony Benn, Caroline Benn, Naida Ferguson and John Robertson, before a public meeting in Bonnybridge, 1977.

On an underground visit to Polmaise Colliery, Fallin, 8 February 1978.

With Mark, Elnor, Dennis John, Paul and Ruth, 1979.

Taking the plunge with the Parachute Regiment for a charity event, Aldershot, 30 November 1981.

With Yasser Arafat in Beirut, c. 1980

Parliamentary charity swim at the RAC club in London, c. 1982.

Parliamentary line-up for the 1984 London Marathon.

Scottish Labour Party 5-a-side football tournament, 1985.

Crossing the finishing line with a personal best time in the 1985 Glasgow Marathon.

With Harry Ewing MP and David Steel MP, signing the Claim of Right at the first meeting of the Scottish Constitutional Convention in the Assembly Hall, The Mound, Edinburgh, 20 March 1989.

Shaking hands with King Juan Carlos of Spain in Madrid, c. 1990.

With Helmut Kohl, Chancellor of the Federal Republic of Germany, in Bonn, c. 1993.

With Boutros Boutros-Ghali, Secretary-General of the United Nations, at the UN Headquarters in New York, c. 1995

Celebrating with Camelon Juniors Football Club when they won the Scottish Junior Cup in 1995.

The Scotland team singing *Flower of Scotland* before playing against England in a parliamentary challenge football match at Upton Park, home of West Ham FC, in 1998.

Evening Times, 7 May 1999.

Daily Record, 7 May 1999.

Daily Record, 14 May 1999.

With John Knox at the assembly Hall on The Mound, where the newly elected Scottish Parliament met for the first time, 12 May 1999.

The Scotland team which beat Ireland 3–2 in the inter-parliamentary football match at Trinity College, Dublin, 24 November 2002.

Bertie Ahern, the Irish Taoiseach, shaking hands with the team captains before the Scotland *v* Ireland inter-parliamentary football match in Dublin, 24 November 2002.

With Adam, after receiving an honorary doctorate from the University of Strathclyde, 4 July 2008.

With Christine and Adam after receiving an honorary doctorate from the University of Stirling, 21 November 2008.

At the Falkirk Wheel with some young supporters during my last election campaign, 2003.

At Lock 16, Forth and Clyde Canal, Camelon.

With a group of pupils at Easter Carmuirs Primary School, Camelon.

With Christine and Adam, 2008.

Foreword

Dennis Canavan's book is a truly extraordinary one, in which political and personal loss are painfully and dramatically relived.

He and I were Labour Members of Parliament together, and he was one of the most thoughtful, independent and courageous of parliamentarians. I visited his home in Bannockburn in 1977 and we were comrades in the campaign committee which became the Socialist Campaign Group of MPs. He foresaw the anti-democratic and centralising tendencies of the party long before the New Labour project and warned against Labour losing young voters over its policies on nuclear weapons and defence in the late 1980s and 1990s. Dennis's career as an MP and MSP, and the disgraceful way that the Labour Party treated him, are well known, and it was the party's loss that he was driven to stand as an independent socialist.

Dennis writes with equal eloquence, emotion and modesty about those events and about the earlier years of his life; describing his upbringing in the mining community of Cowdenbeath, the impact on him of his grandparents and parents, his academic precocity and his wish at the age of 15 to become a priest. Dennis did indeed enter a Catholic seminary at the extraordinarily young age of 16, a life which he left for a teaching career before becoming an MP.

The intelligence, inquisitiveness and humour which informed Dennis's political career are evident on every page of the book. He describes, for example, his father's job as an electrician with the old Electricity Board:

Sometimes the whole of Cowdenbeath would be plunged into darkness and we would be sitting at home in candlelight, watching the flames from the coal fire licking their way up the chimney and telling each other ghost stories. Suddenly the electric lights would go on and we knew that Dad would soon be home. Once he had fixed the high-voltage cable, it was like something straight from the Book of

Genesis: 'Let there be light and there was light.' It was our Dad that dunnit and we saw that it was good.

Dennis's family life encapsulated the history and traditions and ideology of the Labour movement in the twentieth century. He himself was brought up in a row of council houses that was built on top of a pit in Cowdenbeath. The subtle influences at work on him came from Christianity, socialism and trade unionism. In his great-aunt's house, the *Daily Worker* and the *Catholic Herald* would be lying on the table side by side. His Grandfather Canavan was clearly a strong influence, working with the trade union and labour movements and encouraging his grandson to success through education.

While still a very young man, Dennis 'became fascinated by the study of philosophy and it certainly taught me to think critically and, years later, to see through the sophistry and sloppy thinking of many politicians. I am not the sort of guy who instinctively believes everything the teacher or the priest or the politician or the papers tell me and my philosophy course at Drygrange [Seminary] helped to open my mind.'

He put his early training to good effect when he entered the House of Commons. Just one story from his parliamentary career illustrates the point. Dennis was a great friend of Africa (the Africans rather than the despotic leaders of recent years) and, when Nelson Mandela addressed parliament in Westminster Hall in 1996, Dennis found himself seated behind Margaret Thatcher. He tapped her on the shoulder and said he was surprised to see her there. When she sternly asked 'Why?' he said bravely: 'Well, I distinctly remember you describing Nelson Mandela as a terrorist and saying that anyone who believed that the ANC would form a democratic government in South Africa must be living in cloud cuckoo land.' What other MP would have had that courage?

Tony Benn
March 2009

—— ◆ ——

Matters of life and death

When politicians say that they're giving up the job to spend time with the family, a frequent riposte is: 'Aye, right! So what's the real story?' This is my real story. When I announced my retirement in 2007, I was the longest-serving parliamentarian in the Scottish Parliament, having spent twenty-six years at Westminster and eight years at Holyrood. I have never regretted standing for parliament. For me, it was a great privilege to be a representative of the people. I always tried to put people first and, even after I was disowned by the leadership of my party, the people responded by giving me the biggest majority in the Scottish Parliament.

But my many years of parliamentary service, especially at Westminster, meant frequent absences from home and, as a result, my family life suffered. When my youngest son, Adam, was born in 2002, I had already given up my seat in the House of Commons and, although I was still a Member of the Scottish Parliament, I was able to spend more time at home than I had ever managed when I was at Westminster. It was Adam who made me realise how much I had missed during the early years of my older children, and that was brought into sharper focus by a sequence of events which still fill me with indescribable grief.

They say that all political careers end in tears. I never set out to be a political careerist but my career, such as it was, certainly ended in tears, although that had more to do with human tragedy than any political events.

I was 32 when I was first elected to the House of Commons in 1974. I was the proud father of four smashing children: Mark (aged eight), Ruth (aged six), Dennis John (aged three) and Paul (aged two). Ruth, who was ill in hospital at the time, is now the only one of the four left.

The loss of a child is the worst thing that can happen to any mum or dad. You think it should never happen because it seems so contrary to the whole natural cycle of life for your child to die before you. It is almost as if there is a psychological mechanism within you that helps you to cope with the death of a parent, but there is no such mechanism when you lose a child. Losing one child is bad enough, but losing three children almost beggars belief, and I still find it very difficult to fathom. I sometimes waken up in the middle of the night imagining it was all just a nightmare before I have to face the awful truth that it actually happened.

I have heard well-meaning people at funerals trying to console the bereaved with words like: 'I know how you feel but, believe me, time is a great healer.' With all due respect, they don't know how I feel because none of them has lost three children. The passage of time may have helped me to deal with the pain, but it's still there. I am now resigned to the fact that it will be with me for the rest of my life and it feels like a huge void, as if part of my gut has been ripped out and can never be replaced. Not a day goes by without me thinking about my boys and how much I miss them. It must be even worse for Elnor, my former wife, who went through the pain of giving birth to our three beloved sons and then went through the greater pain of watching them die.

Paul was only 16 when he died, a young lad on the verge of manhood. We had been on holiday together in the Algarve during his school holidays in the summer of 1988. He had very blond hair and fair skin and I often wonder if over-exposure to the sun had something to do with his untimely death. He certainly enjoyed swimming and playing on the beach, often without a shirt, although I do not recall him ever suffering from sunburn. Indeed, he hardly had a day's illness in his life until the autumn of 1988.

The first visible sign of anything wrong was when a mole appeared on his upper arm. As it was smaller than a five-pence piece I was not too concerned, but my daughter Ruth wisely persuaded Paul to see our GP, Dr King. He immediately arranged for a biopsy, which revealed that the mole was a malignant melanoma. I had never heard of such a condition before and, when the cancer specialist explained that it was potentially lethal, I thought that he was just describing the worst possible scenario. I never thought that, six months later, Paul would be dead.

Even the medics seemed initially optimistic. They excised the mole and grafted some skin from Paul's thigh onto his arm. Paul then went to Gartnavel Hospital in Glasgow for an operation called isolated limb perfusion, a form of localised chemotherapy which avoids most of the nasty side effects such as sickness and loss of hair. The procedure involved temporarily isolating the affected limb from the rest of the body and then perfusing the limb with chemicals to combat the cancer.

The operation was hailed as a success and the surgeon seemed confident that Paul would make a full recovery. At the turn of the year, he was given the all-clear but, as a safeguard, was advised to have a check-up every six months or so. I have a very vivid recollection of Paul and the rest of the family enjoying ourselves at Ruth's twenty-first birthday party in January 1989.

However, a few weeks later, Paul complained of dizziness and I noticed that he was staggering, as if unable to keep his balance. When this was reported to Dr King, he feared the worst. He told me that Paul's symptoms indicated that the cancer might have spread to the cerebellum, the part of the brain that controls balance. The cancer specialist at Stirling Royal Infirmary made immediate arrangements for me to take Paul to the Southern General Hospital in Glasgow for a brain scan, which confirmed Dr King's worst fears. Paul had several brain tumours, which were inoperable. We were told that he had only weeks to live.

I shall never forget Paul's courage when he was told that he was going to die. There were no tears, no self-pity, only a stoic acceptance of his fate. I resolved there and then to spend as much time as possible with him. I told the whips' office in the House of Commons that I would be taking indefinite leave of absence. Michael Cocks, the Chief Whip, was very considerate and I received messages of sympathy and support from other parliamentary colleagues. Most people were very understanding, but there was one notable exception.

The Shadow Secretary of State for Scotland at that time was Donald Dewar, and the Scottish Labour whip was Allen Adams, MP for Paisley North. Allen informed me that, when he told Donald that my son was dying, Donald replied: 'Oh no! That's all we need. He was mad enough before but I shudder to think what he'll be like now!' Donald's off-the-cuff remark revealed an attitude towards me which was to have future repercussions, but more of that later.

Throughout Paul's illness, I found the support which the whole family received from Strathcarron Hospice to be invaluable. As Constituency MP I had been involved with the hospice since its inception. I well remember the inaugural meeting when the principal founder, Dr Harold Lyon, outlined his vision of a hospice to care for terminally ill people in the Forth Valley area. I was delighted when the chosen location for the hospice turned out to be a large house on the outskirts of Fankerton, near Denny, in my constituency. I was involved in various fund-raising projects, including the annual Strathcarron 10km 'fun run'. In fact, Paul had also taken part in the 1988 fun run to help raise funds for the hospice. Little did we realise that, a few months later, Paul would be a patient, at that time the youngest patient ever admitted to Strathcarron.

The advice we received was that Paul should try to live as normal a life as possible for as long as possible. That meant staying at home rather than being an in-patient at the hospice, so that he could be with his family and friends. We had some great times together and Paul never complained. When I asked him if he would like to go on holiday, he chose to go to the west coast of Donegal for a few days.

Shortly after he returned home, Paul's mobility deteriorated rapidly and I used to take him around in a wheelchair to ensure that he got some fresh air and the opportunity to meet other people. The Macmillan nurses from the hospice visited him regularly and were very supportive of the family. When Paul became confined to bed, the nurses came on a daily basis and Ruth, my daughter, cared for him continuously. Eventually, however, we were advised that the hospice was the best place for the palliative care which Paul required and he spent the last few days of his life at Strathcarron. Keith O'Brien, Archbishop of St Andrews and Edinburgh, now Cardinal O'Brien, visited him in the hospice. Paul did not know what he had done to deserve such a distinguished visitor but I think that he was even more impressed when Tommy Burns and Andy Walker of Celtic Football Club called in to see him just two days before he died. Tommy and Andy were brilliant ambassadors, whose charisma and compassion inspired all around them. It was a cruel irony that, 19 years later, Tommy Burns died of exactly the same condition as Paul.

Paul's funeral service was from the Church of Our Lady and St Ninian, Bannockburn, the same church where he had been baptised only 16 years before. A packed congregation heard Cardinal Gordon Joseph Gray paying tribute to a courageous young man who, like his biblical namesake, had run the race to the finish.

When Paul died, I thought that that was the worst experience of my life and that nothing as painful as that could ever happen to me again. I knew within my heart of hearts that I would never get over it completely but I tried to be positive by reminding myself that I had three other healthy children. You never know what's round the corner.

My oldest son, Mark, had graduated from Strathclyde University with an Honours degree in Engineering. After graduating, he did a fair bit of globetrotting, and his successful career took him to responsible positions in places as far afield as the USA and Australia.

When he returned to Scotland with his wife, Sandra, they seemed intent on settling here, especially after the birth of their son, Tommy. However, it came as no great surprise when they decided to move to Australia, as that was Sandra's home and Mark had obviously enjoyed his time there. With his CV, he had no problem finding a good job and the future looked bright.

In autumn 2004, I was delighted when Mark and his family returned to Scotland for a break. But it turned out to be a heartbreak. Shortly after their arrival, Mark told me that he had amyotrophic lateral sclerosis. When I confessed that I didn't know what he was talking about, he explained that it was a form of motor neurone disease. I had heard of MND but knew little about it. At that time, the only unusual thing I noticed about Mark was that he was sometimes rather unsteady on his feet. That in itself did not seem too alarming but, the more I learned about MND, the more I realised how serious it was.

The next time I saw Mark was about six months later, when I visited him in Australia. I was shocked. He needed crutches to enable him to walk and he had lost a considerable amount of weight. I knew that time was running out for him and, on my return to Scotland, I was deeply depressed, especially as my brother, Ian, was also terminally ill with pancreatic cancer. Ian died in August 2006, just a few days after his sixty-sixth birthday. One of the pall-bearers at his funeral was my son, Dennis John. Four months later, he too died of cancer.

I still find it all too difficult to comprehend. Like his younger brother Paul, our Dennis had never had a serious illness in his life before being struck down by cancer. Some of the symptoms were very similar to those which Paul had in the later stages of his illness, after the cancer had spread to his brain: lack of balance causing him to stagger. A brain scan revealed a massive malignant tumour. He was operated on by Professor Ian Whittle, one of the best brain surgeons in the country, and the operation to remove the tumour was technically a success. For weeks, Dennis John was a patient in the

Western General Hospital, Edinburgh, and I would visit him several times a week, usually en route to the Scottish Parliament or on my way home. After the operation, there was a problem with infection – which came as no great surprise to me, because I had observed that parts of the hospital were filthy.

Dennis John made sufficient progress to begin a course in radiotherapy and he was allowed home, provided he attended hospital on a daily basis for the treatment. I would usually drive him and his partner, Alison, to the hospital and, on the days I could not manage, I would arrange for another driver. On the final day of his radiotherapy treatment, my good friend, Tommy Canavan, drove Dennis John and Alison to the Western General because I had urgent business at parliament.

About lunchtime I received a phone message from Tommy's wife, Maria, advising me to contact the hospital immediately. Dennis had suffered a cardiac arrest during his radiotherapy treatment. The medical staff managed to resuscitate him and put him on a ventilator. The family took it in turns to organise a bedside vigil round the clock. We hoped and prayed and waited but, after a week, it was obvious that he was never going to regain consciousness. When the doctors explained the situation at a family conference, we unanimously came to the conclusion that there was no point in keeping the ventilator going indefinitely. Dennis died peacefully on 22 December 2006 and I felt privileged to be with him, holding his hand while he passed away.

It was the saddest Christmas of my life and I knew that Christmas would never be the same again for Dennis John's two sons, Ciaran (aged nine) and Calum (aged eleven). As the funeral directors were closed over the Christmas break, we had to wait a whole week before the funeral could take place. For most families, the festive season was a time of joyful celebration. For the Canavan family, Christmas 2006 was a time of indescribable misery. I dreaded the thought of having to tell Mark, whose condition had deteriorated to the extent that he was literally speechless. When I eventually plucked up the courage to phone him, he was unable to respond in words but I could hear him bursting into tears. I too was overcome with grief, but I knew that I had to keep going. Making the funeral arrangements helped to concentrate my mind but, after it was over, I was plunged into a very, very deep depression.

Even before Dennis became ill, I had been thinking about retiring from full-time politics. I was approaching the age of sixty-five and, in December 2006, I told my two employees, Anne and Maureen, that I would come to a decision over the Christmas–New Year break. Under the circumstances, it was a difficult time to come to a rational decision on anything because I could hardly think straight. I kept thinking about poor Mark on the other side of the world and how long he had left. I had to get out there to see him as soon as possible and, after many sleepless nights, I decided that I would announce my retirement by means of the following open letter to my constituents:

Dear Constituents,

After a great deal of reflection, I have now come to a decision not to stand this year as a candidate for re-election to the Scottish Parliament.

This year I shall be 65 and I have had the honour of being a representative of the people for a third of a century. During that period, I have been fortunate in enjoying good health but sadly that has not been the case for some of my children.

In 1989, when I lost my son, Paul, at the age of 16, I thought that was the worst thing that could ever happen to anyone. But recently my family has been hit by more devastating events.

As you may be aware, Paul's brother, Dennis, died last month and my oldest son, Mark, is on the other side of the world suffering from motor neurone disease, for which there is no known cure. If you believe in the power of prayer, please use it and let us all hope that scientific research will find an answer soon.

Such family circumstances fill me with regret that, because of my job, I did not spend enough time with my children at an earlier stage in their lives and I feel that I should now compensate in some way. My youngest son, Adam, who will be starting school this year, is a healthy, happy child and I sometimes wonder what I would do without him.

I am blessed with a loving daughter and five wonderful grandchildren. Over the last few months, I have learned a lot about the value and real priorities of life and today Adam and I are leaving for Australia for two weeks to spend some time with Mark and his family.

I would like to thank all my constituents, particularly those who have faithfully supported me over the years. It has been my privilege to serve you and, on my return from Australia, I shall continue doing so to the best of my ability until the dissolution of parliament.

I released the letter to the press on 23 January 2007, the day that I left for Australia, in the hope that I would manage to escape without being pestered by media demands for further comment and interviews. However, by the time Adam and I arrived at Glasgow Airport, we were met by a BBC TV crew along with some press reporters and photographers. Adam was in his element posing for the cameras and I did a long interview with Catriona Renton of the BBC who, by coincidence, had previously worked for me as a researcher at the House of Commons. My partner, Christine, told me afterwards that the interview received positive media coverage, as did the following extracts from the Scottish Parliament Official Report:

> THE FIRST MINISTER (Jack McConnell): I do not intend any disrespect to any distinguished members who will retire this May but, given Dennis Canavan's family circumstances, it is appropriate today to record our appreciation of his work over a very long career. In 1979, Dennis Canavan was the first parliamentary candidate I ever voted for. In my view, he was an outstanding parliamentarian over a long period, both as a Labour representative and as an independent member. As I am sure everyone else does, I wish him a long and happy retirement with his family and I hope that they enjoy it as much as he will. [Applause]

> NICOLA STURGEON: I echo the First Minister's comments about Dennis Canavan. Dennis is a man of principle. He has had an incredibly difficult time of late. I know that we all wish him and his family the very best for the future.

As things turned out, Mark did not have much of a future at all. When I visited him at his home in Sydney, I found it very difficult to control my emotions. He was in a wheelchair and had lost so much weight that he was scarcely recognisable. His physique was skeletal, his speech was nonexistent and his mobility was virtually zero. Nevertheless, he was able to communicate using a tiny device attached to his baseball cap which enabled him to use his neck muscles to operate his computer keyboard. It was a vivid demonstration that his power of intellect was as strong as ever and that is one of the most important things to realise about motor neurone disease: the mind is still there, even when the body is wasting away.

Despite the sadness and the worry, we managed to have some very enjoyable times together. Mark and Sandra invited some friends to their home for a Burns Supper with poetry, songs and lots of fun. Children can also be a godsend in such a situation. Mark's son, Tommy, is just a year older than my youngest son, Adam, and the two boys were like long-lost brothers, playing together and getting up to all sorts of mischief. It brought back memories of Mark as a child, playing with his younger brothers and sister.

I could not help admiring Mark's attempt to smile in the face of adversity. His faith was indestructible and that seemed to give him the strength to keep going. Every week, he would go to a meditation session held in the crypt of St Patrick's Church near Sydney Harbour. I went with him once but I do not think that I got anywhere near the level of spirituality that Mark experienced.

When the time came for us to leave, I knew that it would be my final farewell. If Adam had not been with me, I think I would have broken down. As soon as I got back to Scotland, I told Elnor, Mark's mother, that Mark did not have long to go. We made plans for her to visit him in April but, during the second week of March, we received a phone call from Sandra telling us that Mark had been admitted to hospital. Elnor got the next available flight and reached Mark's bedside a few hours before he died on 19 March, the Feast of St Joseph, who is the patron saint of a happy death. Death can never be happy for those who are left behind. I still find it all too difficult to comprehend but I am convinced that Mark is now at peace with his brothers. If anyone ever asks me where God was when my sons died, my answer is: 'God was with them and they are now with God.'

I flew out to Australia for Mark's funeral. Without Adam it was a long and lonely journey. The Requiem Mass was held in Rookwood Cemetery on the outskirts of Sydney in the chapel of the Sacred Heart. The name struck a chord with me because Mark had been baptised in the Church of the Sacred Heart in Edinburgh. The Requiem Mass was a simple but very moving service. Elnor and I read the lessons and Mark's five-year-old son, Tommy, read a prayer. I felt so proud of him, and I wonder what the future holds for him.

When I am in the depths of my depression, I try to count my blessings. I have a loving daughter, five wonderful grandchildren and, of course, Adam and Christine. They all enjoy good health and I pray that that will continue for many years to come.

My experience of life and death has taught me many things about the real value and meaning of life. There are few things in life that are certain, but death is one of them. As a result, we all have a limited time on this earth. Time is therefore one of the most precious gifts we have and some of the most important decisions we have to make in life involve the allocation of time, especially the sharing of our time with other people. I remember Mark and me discussing some family problem that I had not initially been aware of until years after it had first become manifest to him as a child. When I asked Mark: 'Why did you not tell me at the time?' he replied: 'Dad, you were never there.' He did not mean to hurt me but I have felt it in my gut ever since.

I wish now that I had spent more time with my children when they were younger but I realise that I cannot turn the clock back. I console myself with the fact that Adam has given me another chance to enjoy the company of a child and I honestly don't know what I would do without him. The loss of three children has given me a deeper realisation of what a priceless gift a child is. I also treasure my five marvellous grandchildren, all of whom have lost their father. If I wallowed in self-pity it would not do them any good, and would just worsen my depression.

Being bitter or looking back in anger would be self-destructive. It would be false and foolish of me to say: 'Je ne regrette rien.' We all make mistakes and part of what life is about is learning from our mistakes. If I had my life to live over again, I would do some things differently, but I have never regretted the time that I have spent trying to help other people and trying to make the world a better place. In the final analysis, I have always been content to let the people decide whether those efforts were worthwhile and this book relates the story of my efforts and the verdict of the people.

It is dedicated to Mark, Dennis John and Paul.

Part I

— ♦ —

Never Forget Whence You Came

CHAPTER ONE

Roots

One of the earliest influences on me as a child was my paternal grandfather, Frank Canavan. He was born in Carrickmore, County Tyrone, Ireland, in 1879. Carrickmore is just a small village about ten miles from Omagh, the scene of the biggest atrocity of the Troubles, when 29 people were murdered by a bomb planted by the so-called 'Real' IRA, a few days after the signing of the Good Friday Peace Agreement in 1998.

Carrickmore became famous, or infamous, during the Thatcher regime, when a BBC *Panorama* team filmed an IRA 'take-over' of the village. It seemed a rather stage-managed propaganda stunt designed to show that the area was a Republican stronghold where the writ of the British Government did not run. When Margaret Thatcher found out, she was absolutely livid and ordered Willie Whitelaw, the Home Secretary, to get on the blower to the BBC Chairman, Sir Michael Swann. Two senior members of the BBC editorial staff were severely reprimanded and nearly lost their jobs.

All that was over a century after my grandfather was born, but it shows that my family history would no doubt have been very different if Grandad had stayed in Carrickmore. In 1884, his family left Ireland and headed for Scotland. They were what nowadays we would call economic migrants. Grandad was the youngest of eleven children and he was only four years old when they arrived in Cowdenbeath, Fife. Why Cowdenbeath? His father and older siblings would be looking for work and Cowdenbeath at that time had a thriving coal industry. My great-grandfather got a job with the Cowdenbeath Coal Company at eight shillings (40p) per week, but his stay in Scotland was short-lived. He died in 1888, when my grandfather was only nine years old.

Grandad started school in Cowdenbeath and left at the age of ten. The law would not allow anyone as young as that to work underground. So he got a job for a couple of years with a local ironmonger before starting at No. 7 pit at the age of 12. I remember No. 7 pit very well. It was right in the town centre, adjacent to Central Park, the home of Cowdenbeath Football Club, nowadays known as the Blue Brazil.

Grandad worked in the mining industry for about a quarter of a century and, when the First World War broke out, he served in the army. After being demobbed, he returned to work in the coal industry but he soon realised that to continue in that job would be a suspended death sentence. For health reasons, he left to work as a school janitor and attendance officer. He spent much of his life working to help other people, mainly through the Labour and Trade Union Movement and later in local government. In his spare time, he studied legislation on a wide range of subjects including employment, health and safety, workers' compensation, education and pensions. He used that knowledge to win many benefit claims on behalf of his fellow workers and their families. He had a reputation for being a champion of the underdog: the poor, the sick, the disabled, the unemployed, the homeless and the dispossessed.

He was also a baillie and a Justice of the Peace but, when he sat on the judicial bench, his justice was always tempered with mercy. I used to wonder how Labour people could sit in judgement of their neighbours. Grandad would reply that, if all the judges were Tories, the prisons would be full of working-class people. The Labour magistrates tended to use non-custodial sentences.

Grandad also had a vision thing about education, which he saw as the key to the liberation of the working class. It was probably his influence on both my parents which made them encourage their children to stay on at school and, if we wanted, to go on to college or university.

He also had strong religious beliefs. I would describe him as a devout Catholic, but not sanctimonious and certainly not sectarian. In fact, he was ecumenical and maybe his ecumenism was more geological than theological because it was probably hewn at the coalface. When people are working together in cramped, dangerous conditions, they know the meaning of things like solidarity and comradeship and the common humanity which binds us together, transcending religious and ethnic differences. If the roof is threatening to come down on top of your head, it does not matter a damn whether the guy next to you is a Prod or a Tim. You're all in the same boat and the crew must pull together for survival.

Grandad was a man who respected people of different religious and political beliefs. That was an important example which I have tried to live up to all my life. Most of his colleagues in the Labour and Trade Union Movement would be Protestants and some would have no religion at all. The Communist Party was so strong in our area that the neighbouring village of Lumphinnans was called Little Moscow and the local MP was a Communist, Willie Gallacher. Most of the Communists were atheists, but not all of them. My Great-Aunt Susie lived in Lumphinnans with her three sons and, when we visited her, I would sometimes see the *Daily Worker* lying by the fire alongside the *Catholic Herald*.

Years later, when I told one of my university contemporaries that I hailed from Cowdenbeath, he said: 'Cowdenbeath? Is that where all the posh folk vote Labour to stop the Commies winning?' Another student tried to wind me up by saying: 'Can anything good come out of Cowdenbeath?' I cheekily replied that someone had once said the same about Nazareth.

Grandad was a practical man as well as a man of principle. He had a good working relationship with people of different beliefs and often they all worked together for the common good. As a result, he won huge respect right across the political spectrum and, shortly before he died, he was given the freedom of the burgh of Cowdenbeath. At the freedom ceremony, he received a scroll stating that he was made 'an Honorary Burgess of the Burgh in recognition of his unfailing and devoted interest in all matters relating to the welfare of the citizens of Cowdenbeath'. I am proud to say that the framed scroll is now on display in my home, where it hangs on the wall near the entrance to my study.

When I was in my early teens, Grandad asked me to help him write down a few notes about his life experience, particularly his record of public service. He was a modest man who would have thought 'memoirs' too pretentious a word for his literary effort. He could no doubt have managed well without my assistance but he may have felt that I had a greater mastery of the English language just because I was in the A class at High School, whereas he had left school at the age of ten. Years afterwards, I suspected that he may have had an ulterior motive. Maybe he wanted me to continue his work in some way. Whether that was his intention or not, helping Grandad with his 'memoirs' kindled in me an interest in politics as a means of helping other people, and he certainly was a great inspiration to me.

Grandad married Helen Ferris, a native of Cowdenbeath.

Although she was of Irish Catholic stock, Grandma also had a Calvinist streak in her. I don't know quite where it came from but I suspect that it had something to do with following the customs of her Protestant neighbours in order to avoid causing them any offence. In the early 1950s, council 'parkies' used to go round the public parks on a Saturday night to lock up the roundabouts and swings to stop the children playing on a Sunday. My brother, Ian, and I had a couple of old rusty second-hand bikes which were stored in Grandad's garden shed because we had no shed of our own and the air-raid shelter in our garden was filled with my father's electrical contraptions. When Ian and I wanted to go cycling we had to go down the road to Grandad's and ask for the key to the shed. Normally that was no problem, because Grandad's house was only about 100 yards away. However, on a Sunday, there was a huge problem because Grandma apparently thought it was a sin to cycle on the Sabbath. Ian and I therefore hatched a plan whereby I would distract Grandma with a prolonged conversation, maybe about the content of the priest's sermon that morning, while Ian would surreptitiously get the key to the shed and release the bikes.

Grandma also strongly disapproved of Sunday football, but then, so did the Scottish Football Association and continued to do so until long after Grandma died. During the 1960s, I played for Edinburgh University on a Saturday and I sometimes played for a team called Dunfermline Celtic on a Sunday. If the SFA bigwigs had found out that I was playing Sunday League Football, they could have banned me from playing for the university and Grandma would probably have approved.

Grandma, despite her eccentricities, was a very kind woman who treated her grandchildren with great affection. I often wondered why she did not have more children of her own. My father was an only child and that was very unusual at that time amongst the working class, especially Catholic families. My father sometimes spoke of a wee sister who had died shortly after birth and I wonder if Grandma perhaps had a health problem which prevented her having any more children.

When she died in 1954, it was my first experience of death at close hand. I had previously been an altar boy at Requiem masses and accompanied the priest to the cemetery for the final graveside service, so I never felt that I was sheltered from the reality and inevitability of death. But I felt very sad when Grandma died because she was very special and my brother Ian was so upset that he burst into tears.

Grandad described Grandma's death as the saddest blow in his life. He was so devastated that he was never quite the same man again. He came to live with us for a while and, every Sunday morning, he and I would go to first Mass at 8 o'clock. After Mass, we would walk to Kirk o' Beath Cemetery and stand for a few minutes in silent prayer by Grandma's grave. I would look up sometimes to see a tear in Grandad's eye and it would take him a while to resume conversation on the way home. I sometimes used to think that all he wanted was to follow Grandma and be reunited with her, but he did recover to some extent. We had some happy times together and some great conversations before he eventually passed away in 1966 at the grand old age of 87.

My father, Thomas Canavan, was in some respects like his father in that he believed in Christian and socialist values. He was an active member of the Labour Party and of his trade union but he never stood for public office. Perhaps he had seen that being an elected representative can cause problems for family life, because people would frequently come knocking at his father's door asking for help and, if the problem was of a confidential nature, he and his mother would have to retreat to the kitchen because it was only a small council house.

Shortly after Dad left Beath High School at the age of 14, he started as an apprentice electrician. He would have been able to earn more money by working down the pit, but his father would no doubt have warned him about the dangers and the health risks. At that time many miners' sons became miners themselves but my grandfather's vision was that no one should be forced to work down the pit. Young people should be given the freedom to choose, and education was the means of delivering that freedom. In the early part of the twentieth century, an electrician was at the cutting edge of technology and Dad would not have had any problem finding a job in Scotland. However, he seemed to have an adventurous streak in him and, shortly after completing his apprenticeship, he decided to seek his fortune in the USA.

He was at a party at a friend's house in New York when he met my mother, Agnes McCusker. Agnes was also born in Cowdenbeath, the second oldest of eight children. Her big sister, Isa, had been in my dad's year at school. Their mother, Agnes Horsburgh, had married Thomas McCusker, son of Patrick McCusker. The McCuskers were a Catholic family of Irish descent and the Horsburghs were a Salvation Army family. Agnes Horsburgh was by all accounts a very saintly person. By contrast, Thomas McCusker, my maternal grandfather, had the reputation of being a violent drunkard and to this day nobody in the family knows what became of him.

My mum had left school at the age of 12 to work in a local factory. She then worked 'in service' in Edinburgh. She was employed as a housekeeper and cook in a doctor's house, which was probably a haven of peace compared with the over-crowded house and bullying father she had left behind.

In 1926, the year of the General Strike, Mum came to a bold decision. She was determined to see if there was a better future on the other side of the Atlantic. At the age of 19, she sailed from Greenock and landed in Canada with the princely sum of £5 in her pocket. She had no problem finding work in Toronto because she had excellent references from her former employers, and she sent such glowing reports back to her family in Scotland that they all decided to join her. They emigrated in stages, with the older members of the family going out first to be followed later by their mother and the younger children.

However, there was a problem. The family did not want to take their violent father with them, and they knew that he would physically prevent them going if he found out. Their mother, Agnes, and the younger children therefore had to go into hiding before catching the boat from Greenock to Canada. The entire family resettled permanently in Canada or the United States with the singular exception of my mum. She had been the trail-blazer for the whole family but she was the only one who returned to Scotland. To this day, all my first cousins are resident in either Canada or the USA.

After working in Toronto for some time, Mum decided to move south, perhaps illegally, to New York. That was where she met my father, and they fell in love. Dad persuaded Mum to return to Scotland to get married and they tied the knot in Our Lady and St Bride's Catholic Church, Cowdenbeath, next-door to St Bride's Primary School, where they had both been pupils. I think that Mum was under the impression that they would return to America one day, but that day never came. They stayed for a while in the Methil area of Fife, where Dad had a small shop, but that did not last long. I think that Dad would have been too averse to risk-taking to have been a successful entrepreneur. He seemed to think that there was something intrinsically evil about borrowing money. Getting into debt was immoral, a sign of weakness. Even respectable debts like mortgages were anathema and he would never enter into any hire purchase agreements, which he described as the never-never schemes. His motto was: 'Never a borrower nor a lender be.' If Dad had been Chancellor of the Exchequer, there would have been no credit crunch. There would have been no credit, full stop. I wonder whether Dad would have allowed Raymond and me to go to university if there had been student loans instead of grants, with students incurring debts of five-figure sums in order to get a degree. He would certainly have abhorred such a culture of debt and the fact that young people are now graduating with such millstones round their necks

After a few years running his own business, he reverted to his trade as an electrician and, when the Second World War broke out, he served the war effort at Rosyth Dockyard, then worked with the Electricity Board (now Scottish Power) until he retired. He would often work long hours of overtime, especially when there were power cuts during the winter. Sometimes the whole of Cowdenbeath would be plunged into darkness and we would be sitting at home in candlelight, watching the flames from the coal fire licking their way up the chimney and telling each other ghost stories. Suddenly the electric lights would go on and we knew that Dad would soon be home. Once he had fixed the high-voltage cable, it was like something straight from the Book of Genesis: 'Let there be light, and there was light.' It was our Dad that dunnit, and we saw that it was good.

My eldest brother, Raymond, was born in 1936 and, by the end of the war, Mum and Dad had three more children: Ian, born in 1940, myself in 1942 and Kathleen in 1944. Mum knew then that returning to America was no longer on the agenda, but I think that part of her heart was still there. All her family were on the other side of the Atlantic and, when her mother died, she did not even manage to get to the funeral because she was pregnant with Raymond at the time.

When Mum was in her 80s, she was still so active that we sometimes called her Super Gran. Although she did not have the confidence to fly across the Atlantic on her own, I would occasionally take her with me when I was travelling to Canada or the USA on parliamentary business. I would leave her at her sister Molly's house in up-state New York, or at her niece Bunty's in Toronto. After completion of my series of meetings, usually in New York and Washington DC, I would return to collect her and sometimes managed to stay on a few days. On one occasion, her other surviving sister, Minnie, flew over from California to join us for a family reunion. Mum could blether away all day with her sisters and her niece as if they had never been parted. Sometimes I would try to imagine how different life would have been if Mum and Dad had returned to America, but I am glad that I was born and brought up in Scotland.

Life for me began in a one-bedroom council house in Cowdenbeath. Although very small, it was a fairly good standard of house for the time. It was what some people referred to as a Wheatley house, named after John Wheatley, MP for Glasgow Shettleston, who was Minister for Health in the 1924 Labour Government and is best remembered for his Housing Act. He saw council housing as a means of eradicating the slums and sub-standard dwellings which were home to millions of people throughout Britain.

Although West Fife did not have slum areas on the scale of the Gorbals, some of the housing conditions were nevertheless deplorable. Even as late as the 1950s, when I was delivering newspapers to the miners' rows in Lumphinnans, the stench was sometimes so nauseating that I had to hold my nose before opening some of the doors to throw in the paper. But to their credit, most of the occupants of such sub-standard housing managed to maintain high standards of cleanliness despite the fact that they had no bathrooms or inside toilets.

When Grandad was a member of Cowdenbeath Town Council, the council took full advantage of the Wheatley legislation to begin a programme of council house building. Many other local authorities did likewise in the 1920s and 1930s. Unlike some of the council housing which was thrown up by dud architects in the 1950s and '60s, most of the Wheatley houses are still with us, a testimony to the skills of the building industry and the vision of some politicians in those difficult years between two world wars.

Our family home was in Rosehill Crescent, Cowdenbeath. Because of subsidence caused by coalmining, the houses in that street were later demolished, but there are many similar houses throughout Scotland still standing to this day.

My two older brothers had been born in maternity hospitals, Raymond in Kirkcaldy and Ian in Dunfermline. There was no National Health Service at that time. My mother paid a weekly subscription to a lady called Mrs Eggo, who owned a billiards saloon in Cowdenbeath and was also collector for the doctor, the weekly subscriptions presumably being some kind of medical insurance cover for our family. As far as I know, my mother had not suffered any complications with her two previous births. When my turn came, the GP must have concluded that a home birth would probably be safe enough, because I could not imagine my mother going against the doctor's advice. And so I was born in the bedroom at 69 Rosehill Crescent on 8 August 1942.

CHAPTER TWO

A not so bonny bairn

My earliest clear recollections of childhood are of when I was about three years old, but, in later life, my mother told me about a much earlier auspicious event in my life, of which I was unaware until well after I had started school.

She was rummaging through some family photographs one day, when she came across one of a 'bonny baby' competition held at Central Park, home of Cowdenbeath Football Club, but this was no mere sporting occasion. The year was 1943. The war meant that league football was suspended and the line-up on the photograph was a team of Cowdenbeath mums proudly holding up their offspring for judgement.

'Who won the competition, mum?'

'We did, son.'

I could not believe it. The obvious 'winner' was a little girl who was a dead-ringer for Shirley Temple. She was a wee stoater with beautiful ringlets down to her shoulders. By contrast, I hardly had a hair on my head and, if you had stuck a cigar in my mouth, I would have looked like the prime minister, Winston Churchhill.

'Who was the judge, Mum?'

'The Provost of Cowdenbeath, son.'

I found out afterwards that the provost was a friend and political colleague of my grandfather and I suspect to this day that the result of the competition was a Labour Group decision. If it was a political fix, it was Old Labour, and I was the beneficiary. In later life, I was to find myself on the wrong end of some New Labour decisions which were much more devious.

I remember vividly the day that my older brother, Ian, started school. It was only a couple of weeks after my third birthday but I was desperate to go with him. Ian, by contrast, was a reluctant scholar. He had suffered from pneumonia and other health problems during infancy and, as a result, he was a rather clingy bairn.

On the day that Ian started school, Mum, Ian and I set off, with baby Kathleen in the pram. But when Mum attempted to hand Ian over to Miss Mullen, the infants mistress at St Bride's Primary School, Ian was having none of it. He let out a roar which could have been heard all over Cowdenbeath.

Miss Mullen, a genial wee woman with rosy cheeks and half-moon specs, assured my mother that, if we left, Ian would soon settle down. So we went down the street to do some shopping but, on the way home, Mum insisted on going into the school playground and listening at the classroom window to find out if Ian had indeed settled down. But we could still hear him bawling away. When I saw how upset my Mum was, I asked her if I could go to school instead of Ian and I was almost as upset as Ian when it was explained that I would have to wait another two years.

I do not recall any pre-school provision at all at that time. Nowadays, all children in Scotland have an opportunity of pre-school education and, as a result, the first day at primary school is not the traumatic experience it was for my brother Ian. But, in a sense, Miss Mullen was right. Ian did settle in and he became Dux of St Bride's at the age of ten.

My parents, especially my Mum, were very ambitious for us and keen for us to do well at school. I enjoyed primary school and my academic performance was good, or at least that's what the school reports usually said. However, I sometimes found myself at loggerheads with some of the teachers. There were only two male teachers in St Bride's Primary School at that time: Mr Wallace, who was the headteacher, and Mr Gilhooly, who taught the top class, which consisted of a mixture of ten, eleven and twelve year-olds. Mr Gilhooly came from Lochgelly, which was very appropriate because the Lochgelly Special was the world famous leather weapon, manufactured by George W. (another George Dubya) Dick of Lochgelly and used by generations of Scottish schoolteachers to discipline their charges. Mr Gilhooly was a very strict disciplinarian and showed no mercy to recalcitrant pupils. It was corporal punishment with a vengeance and it did not matter whether the recipient was male or female. I even remember a disabled friend of mine being forced to hold out his shaking, withered limb to be thrashed by Mr Gilhooly's belt.

One day, after one of those ritual executions, a group of pupils, including myself, resorted to the use of graffiti, with stolen chalk, to name and shame the executioner.

'Gilhooly is a bully' was the simple poetic message which

appeared at strategic points all the way along Stenhouse Street, the main road leading to the school. Unfortunately, somebody clyped on us and, the following day, the culprits were arraigned before Gilhooly. The punishment was six lashes each but the executioner was not satisfied with belting the living daylights out of us. We were detained after school and ordered to write several hundred lines. Most of us managed to complete the exercise within an hour or so but my friend, Rab Dunne, was a slow writer and he might have been there until midnight before finishing. When Gilhooly disappeared to the staff room for a smoke, the bold Rab decided to take advantage of his absence by leaving with the rest of us.

The next morning, Rab was hauled out in front of the class for yet another public execution but he had obviously had enough. When he was ordered to hold out his hand, he resolutely refused and bolted out the door. The rest of the class were told to get on with our work and an uneasy hush descended.

The silence was shattered 20 minutes later when the classroom was invaded by a dark, helmeted figure in pit boots and working clothes, covered in coal dust from head to foot. It was Rab's father, straight from his shift at No. 7 Pit but, for Gilhooly's victims, it was like the advent of the fifth cavalry at the Saturday afternoon matinee in the local Picture House. We almost stood up and cheered when the dark figure made a bee-line for Gilhooly perched on his high seat. But Gilhooly saw his come-uppance on the way. With all the diplomatic aplomb he could muster, he jumped from his seat and just about fell to his knees.

'Aha, Mr Dunne. How nice to see you. Come this way, please.'

And he persuaded Rab's father to continue the conversation out in the corridor. I do not know what was said or done but Gilhooly knew he had met his match that day and Rab escaped any further punishment. I was very envious of him because my parents took the view that I deserved everything I got.

The coronation of the Queen in 1953 was another occasion which sticks in my mind. To mark the occasion, Fife County Council had decided to present every pupil in Fife with a Bible embossed with the royal insignia and the letters EIIR. At that time, there was a raging dispute in Scotland because many Scots thought that the Queen's title should be Queen Elizabeth the First rather than the Second, because she was the first Queen Elizabeth of Scotland and also the first Queen Elizabeth since the Union of the Crowns.

However, the Labour-controlled council of the Kingdom of Fife sided with the royal establishment and insisted that EIIR should be the inscription.

There was another controversy when the Catholic Church authorities decided that children in Catholic schools should receive a Catholic prayer book rather than a Bible to commemorate the coronation. To this day, I do not understand why. There are significant differences between the Catholic and Protestant Churches, including their interpretations of certain parts of the Bible, but both believe that it is the word of God. The refusal to give Catholic children a Bible reinforced the belief that the Catholic Church did not trust their own laity to have access to it without priests interpreting it for them.

The presentation of the coronation prayer books took place at a school assembly and my grandfather, Frank Canavan JP, was invited to do the honours. I had a great admiration for my grandad, but even then I could not understand how he got involved in such royalist propaganda.

For several weeks prior to the coronation ceremony, the children from all the schools in Cowdenbeath were marched up and down the playgrounds rehearsing for a coronation pageant to be held at Central Park. We were conscripted into a mass choir and ordered to sing songs like 'Rule Britannia' and 'Land of Hope and Glory', but even at that age I had theological objections to mouthing: 'God who made thee mighty make thee mightier yet.' We were instructed to report for the ceremonial parade at Central Park on a Saturday morning. By this time, I was utterly bored with the whole occasion and I could not understand why my mother and my young sister and every other female in our street were intent on cramming themselves into the home of the only family with a TV in order to watch the coronation in Westminster Abbey. I had had enough. Central Park was for football, not for royal pomp and ceremony. I decided to make a stand by boycotting the pageant.

The following Monday, I was upbraided in front of the whole school by Mr Wallace, the headteacher. I was told that I was a disgrace to my school and to my family, especially as my grandfather was a respected Justice of the Peace and had presented the pupils with their coronation prayer books.

So I left St Bride's under a bit of a cloud, and maybe the teachers were glad to see the back of me. After a meeting between my parents and Messrs Wallace and Gilhooly, I was told that I was being kicked upstairs to St Columba's High School. At first I found that difficult to understand, because I was still only ten years old, having completed just six years of primary education. However, I soon warmed to the idea of moving on to fresh challenges and so it was that, in August 1953, I was enrolled at St Columba's High School, at that time situated a few hundred yards up the road from St Bride's.

CHAPTER THREE

Gettin' a grip and haudin' oan

St Columba's High School motto is: 'Tenui nec dimittam.' It's a biblical quote from the Song of Solomon, surely the most sensuous love song ever written. Taken literally, the motto describes two lovers in a clinch. The school's official translation was: 'I have held and I shall not let go' but, in the Cowdenbeath vernacular, a rough translation would be: 'Ah've gotta grip an' Ah'm gonnae haud oan.' Which is not a bad motto for life in general because tenacity can be a useful attribute, especially when you find that things are going against you, and what you're holding onto is something worthwhile.

I was very excited about going to St Columba's but I am now not sure that it was a good idea for me to go to High School so soon. I was perceived by some people as a precocious little brat and, although I coped well with most academic subjects, I was always a year behind my classmates in terms of physical and emotional development. This was first brought home to me at the school's football trials, held at Kirkford Park shortly after the start of my first term.

I was cocky enough to think that I was a pretty good footballer and I was desperate to make the school team. During the trial match, I played my heart out and scored a goal, which I thought would ensure me a place in the team. I felt confident that I had done enough to impress Mr Watson, the Physical Education teacher and team selector, who was standing on the touchline. Then, to my astonishment, I overheard him saying to one of his sidekicks: 'Canavan's not a bad player but he's far too small.' I was blazing and, on Friday morning, I rushed to the school notice board where the teams were posted for the next day's matches. When I saw that I was not even listed as a reserve, I almost burst into tears.

The following morning, my eldest brother, Raymond, who was in sixth year, was due to play for the First Eleven against Buckhaven High School and I went along with him to lend my support. The St Columba's team was a man short and it looked like they would have to play with ten men. I volunteered my services and, because our house was only about 200 yards from the school, I was able to run home for my boots. The senior team jersey stretched almost down to my ankles. I must have looked ridiculous but I felt very pleased with myself. I cannot remember who won but I well remember the following Monday morning when Mr Dalgleish, the Maths teacher, said to our class: 'Stand up, all members of the First Eleven!' I stood alone, my face beaming with a mixture of pride and embarrassment. It was one in the eye for Watson, the PE teacher, and that made me feel good, because I could already detect a sadistic streak in him.

For some pupils, his Physical Education classes must have been sheer torture. Most of them could not afford gym kit and the only changing accommodation was the corridor leading to the gym. Boys had to strip to the waist and, if they did not have gym shoes, they had to go barefoot. Some of the boys had their trousers held up by elastic galluses and Watson took great delight in stretching them back then letting them go like a catapult so that they would rebound with a loud thwack onto the pupils' bare backs. He seemed to think that that was funny, and a reasonable method of encouraging them to bring gym shorts or at least wear a belt instead of galluses.

At St Columba's, corporal punishment was rife. Pupils were regularly belted not just for indiscipline but for poor academic performance, failing to do homework and even for being late for school, despite the fact that some of them had to travel well over 20 miles to get there!

As at most schools, the quality of teachers at St Columba's varied a lot. The headteacher or rector was Mr Hugh Tuckerman, whose nickname was Tuck. Not surprisingly, some of the pupils used their creative skills to come up with some hilarious rhyming slang. I got to know Tuck even before going to St Columba's, mainly because I was about the same age as two of his sons, Michael and Hugh (Junior). Occasionally I would visit their home, which was situated in the only 'posh' part of Cowdenbeath, if that is not an oxymoron.

Apart from the coal bings, most of Cowdenbeath was fairly flat, with the exception of Kirkford Hill and a hill at the north end of the High Street. At the top of the latter hill is the war memorial, on each side of which were the big houses which were occupied in the main by managerial, professional and business people. Those houses were like mansions compared with the miners' rows and council houses in which most of the people lived. Fife County Council owned three of the 'mansions', which were used to house the headteachers of the three local high schools: Beath High, St Columba's and Moss-side. It was very common at that time for headteachers to live in such tied accommodation and, in places like Cowdenbeath, there were not many opportunities for buying a house.

Hugh Tuckerman (Senior) had previously been Principal Teacher of Science at St Columba's and, when he was appointed rector, he and his family moved from Kirkcaldy to their house on the hill in Cowdenbeath. Michael, young Hugh and I struck up a friendship and we did most of the things that boys did together: playing football, climbing Benarty Hill, cycling, fishing, camping and, of course, mischief. Their father was not very popular among some of the pupils and, as I later discovered, some of the staff could not stand him. However, possibly because of my friendship with his sons, I got on reasonably well with him. In my childhood, I thought that the Tuckermans were toffs because they lived on the hill and it was not until many years later, at Old Tuck's funeral, that I discovered he came from good proletarian stock. At the request of the Tuckerman family, I read a lesson at the Requiem Mass. After the service, old Tuck's brother, Robert, who had been an accomplished boxer as well as a blacksmith to trade, told me how Hugh had gained an Honours degree from Glasgow University. Hugh was the youngest child in a working-class family from Alloa. He was disabled with polio from infancy, and in later life he walked with a stick and a specially designed boot on one foot. Because of his disability, he was deemed unsuitable for heavy manual work, unlike his elder brother. It was therefore decided that Hugh should stay on at school but his parents wanted him to have a Catholic education. As there was no Catholic High School in the Alloa area, Hugh travelled every day by train from Alloa to Glasgow and back to attend St Mungo's Academy and then Glasgow University. Because of the lack of state support available at that time, Hugh's siblings all had to chip in to pay for his education out of their wages.

When Hugh's brother told me his family story, it made me realise even more the sacrifices which had to be made by many working-class families to send even one member of the family to university at that time. It also made me wonder how many more potential graduates had virtually no choice but the coalface or the factory floor.

Mr Tuckerman's deputy was Mr Michael Boland, who was also Principal Teacher of English. Mr Boland, nicknamed 'Wee Sanny', was a very strict disciplinarian who would think nothing of belting the living daylights out of you if you forgot the words of a poem. A lot of education at that time was rote learning and Wee Sanny was pretty good at coaching people to pass exams. For English Literature, he would dictate notes about Shakespeare or Chaucer or Macaulay and, when it came to the exam, the pupils were expected simply to regurgitate his notes. I later had pity on the examiners who had the misfortune of marking the Higher English papers from St Columba's. They must have been bored out of their minds by the tedious repetition and the lack of original thought. It was not until years afterwards that I discovered the joys of Shakespeare on stage or film. Shakespeare was never meant to be taught with a book in one hand and a belt in the other.

When it came to essay writing, Wee Sanny was even less inspiring. Rather than encourage creative writing, his teaching technique was more likely to give you a severe dose of verbal constipation. Before you could even start, you were forced to recall a huge list of Sanny's commandments by writing down a series of questions:

Have I used get, got, getting?
Have I begun any sentence with a conjunction?
Have I ended any sentence with a preposition? etc

Even Tennyson would have been belted by Wee Sanny for penning: 'More things are wrought by prayer than this world dreams of.'

The Latin teacher was a dear old lady called Annie Reid, a graduate of St Andrews University. I liked Latin and I think it is a very lyrical language. I had begun learning Latin as an altar boy at the age of seven. However, the Church used the Roman pronunciation of Latin, which was quite different from Annie Reid's pronunciation. For example, Annie would pronounce Cicero like KIKERO, whereas the Roman pronunciation was CHICHERO and another common pronunciation was SISERO. Despite such initial confusion, I enjoyed Latin and I thought that Annie Reid was a good teacher, although rather eccentric.

After my third year, I chose to do both Higher Latin and Higher Science, which was unprecedented at St Columba's because of time-tabling difficulties. As a result, a special one-off time-table was created for me but one consequence was that I had to surrender a double period of games on a Friday afternoon to receive one-to-one tuition in Latin from Annie Reid. Mr Tuckerman, the rector, thought that my playing for the school football team on a Saturday morning was ample compensation for losing a double period of games.

The Principal Teacher of Science was Henry McCusker, who was quite good at teaching Chemistry but not so good at Physics. Henry, however, had other talents. He loved foxtrotting and waltzing around with the girls at the school Christmas parties and might have had a career on *Strictly Come Dancing*.

The head of the Maths department was Rowland Dalgleish, who was an absolute martinet. 'Dally' taught with great rigour and also with vigour, and woe betide anyone who stepped out of line. To his credit, Dally generously gave up a lot of his Saturday mornings to referee school football matches and, along with Paddy Donnelly, who succeeded Watson as PE teacher, he would sometimes take us cross-country running after school. That must have meant some considerable effort on Dally's part, because he was rather plump.

The Modern Languages teacher was Jock ('Pa') Ritchie, an absolute gentleman, a Francophile who loved to embellish his lessons with a Cook's tour of all the Parisian churches and art galleries or, perhaps, a recipe for bouillabaisse. I studied both French and German, which I later found useful when travelling abroad.

The Brits and the Americans are probably the laziest linguists in the world because English is so widely spoken. However, it is rather arrogant of us to expect everybody to speak our language. When I was abroad on parliamentary delegations, I found that people really appreciated it if you made an effort to speak their language, or even a 'neutral' language. One of the most interesting French conversations I ever had was with a politician from Mali, a Francophone country in north-west Africa. Although my interlocutor's first language was not French, he was far more fluent than I. Despite initial difficulties, we managed to communicate with each other, he in his broad African accent and I in my guttural Scottish accent, although a Sorbonne professor would probably not have understood a word we were saying.

I left St Columba's at the age of fifteen, having completed five years' secondary education under the tutelage of some of the worst and some of the best teachers I have ever experienced. They made me Dux of the school and, when the press arrived to cover the event, the rector would not let them take my photograph without school uniform. I had never had a school uniform. Some of my school clothes were passed on from my older brothers and I was still wearing short trousers when I sat my Highers. The press asked for a photograph of me, as School Dux, along with my good friend Janette Conway, who was Proxime Accessit, a Latin title for runner-up. When I turned up in my second-hand shirt with no tie and no blazer, the rector looked at me in dismay and insisted that I wear school uniform for the photograph. I told him politely that I did not have a school uniform and, at one stage, it looked as if the photo-call could be a non-starter until one of my classmates, Rose Boyle, came to the rescue.

I had fancied Rose when we started primary school on the same day, but my love was completely unrequited until that day when she lent me her school blazer, tie and scarf. I shall always be grateful to Rose for her kindness but, when the photographs appeared in the newspapers, my mother was most embarrassed because I was wearing a girl's blazer. When I asked what was the difference, she explained that it had something to do with the buttons, but I could not understand what all the fuss was about.

I was formally 'crowned' as Dux of St Columba's at the school prize-giving ceremony in The Tivoli. I also received a certificate stating that I had enough Highers to enter any faculty of any Scottish university, but even my ambitious mother thought that was probably a bit much for a 15 year-old.

'What would you like to do now?'

'I told you when I was ten that I wanted to be a priest.'

'What?'

'A priest.'

'A priest? A priest? I can never see you being a priest.'

'Why not?'

'You're too wild, too rebellious.'

'Well, that's what I want to do. So please give me a chance.'

In the 1950s there were some Catholic parents who were so keen for at least one of their sons to be a priest that some of them were almost dragooned into the seminary. In my case, it was practically the opposite. My parents were very sceptical, to say the least, but I persuaded them to let me 'try my vocation'.

I was accepted by St Andrew's College, Drygrange, which was the senior seminary serving the Archdiocese of St Andrews and Edinburgh. I think that my acceptance at such an early age was partly due to the fact that the rector of Drygrange was Canon Roger Gallagher, who knew me personally from his previous position as parish priest in Cowdenbeath. As far as I know, I was the youngest student ever accepted by Drygrange but, in retrospect, I do not think that it was a good thing to admit someone of that age.

I received a letter from the seminary informing me of my acceptance and containing a list of clothes, books and other items I had to take with me. To kit me out, my mum took me to the best emporium in Cowdenbeath, which was the Co-operative, locally referred to as The Store. The gear included the first suit I had ever had in my life, black jacket, black trousers, black tie, black socks, black shoes and white shirt. Worse was yet to come. On the prescribed list was a black hat and, when the young lassie in the Co-op stuck it on my head, she nearly burst out laughing at the spectacle. No wonder! When I looked in the mirror, I blushed furiously. I looked like Al Capone at a funeral.

—— ◆ ——

CHAPTER FOUR

A thriving mining community

In general, I enjoyed my time at high school and, although I am now very critical of certain aspects of education at that time, most of the staff tried to give us a good education in the Scottish tradition of a broad-based curriculum. In the upper school, however, pupils tended to specialise in either languages or science but everybody had to do English and Mathematics.

Most of my contemporaries from primary school left at the end of their third year of secondary education. They had virtually no choice because they had 'failed' the Qualifying Examination at the age of 11. Even at that time, I thought there was something wrong with a system which branded pupils as successes or failures at such a tender age and then segregated them on the result of one test. In many cases, segregation meant that children who had gone to the same primary school parted company at the age of 11 or 12. Those who passed the Qualifying Examination went to high school and the rest went to junior secondary school.

St Columba's, however, had a fairly comprehensive intake. All my contemporaries at primary school went on to St Columba's, but the pupils were strictly streamed. Pupils who passed the Qualifying Examination were put into class 1A or 1B, depending on their exam results. Pupils who failed the Qualifying Examination were put into class 1C or 1D or 1E. There was very little, if any, movement of pupils from one stream to another. Only the A and B pupils had the opportunity of studying a foreign language, which was essential in those days for going on to university, and only a small minority of the A and B pupils managed to attain university entrance qualifications.

I remember years later playing football for Edinburgh University against Heriot-Watt University. One of the Heriot-Watt players was a former teammate of mine at St Columba's. He had been in a C class and left school at the age of 15 without a Scottish Leaving Certificate which, at that time, was the normal prerequisite to go on to university. He told me that he had done an engineering apprenticeship with the National Coal Board and then studied at night school for a Higher National Diploma. That enabled him to gain entrance to Heriot-Watt and successfully complete a degree in engineering. I wonder how many more young people were virtually written off at the age of 11 whereas, if they had been given the chance, they could have gone on to higher education.

At that time, less than 5 per cent of school leavers went to university and, although West Fife was a very working-class area, the proportion going on to higher education probably compared well with other parts of Scotland. There was certainly a growing realisation of the importance of education. The population of Cowdenbeath at that time was only about 10,000 but there were three secondary schools: Beath High School, St Columba's High School and Moss-side Secondary, which was a girls' school specialising in business studies, or commercial subjects, as they were called at that time. There was also a college of further education, namely Fife Mining School, located in Broad Street.

Cowdenbeath was a single-industry community built on coal. There was even a colliery right in the town centre and there were another dozen or so pits within a mile radius. Also located in Cowdenbeath were the National Coal Board (NCB) workshops, which served a large part of the Scottish coal industry.

Most young people left school at the age of 15, but there was more variety of job opportunities available to them at that time than there is now in the Cowdenbeath area. Young men could train to work down the pit, or they could do an apprenticeship at the NCB workshops, which produced generations of highly skilled engineers, electricians, fitters, turners, welders and joiners. If they wanted to improve their qualifications, they could go to night school or day-release at Fife Mining School, and a few would go on from there to higher education.

There was no gender equality. The law did not allow women to work down the pit, but there were women employed at the pit-head tables, separating the stones from the coal. I remember seeing some of the 'pit-heid lassies' going home from their work in the late 1940s. They were as black as the ace of spades, covered in coal dust from head to toe. They would tie their headscarves like turbans, their language was unrepeatable and they would walk with a sexy swagger along the street, sometimes breaking out into bawdy songs which would make a sailor blush. My maternal grandmother had been a 'pit-heid lassie', but I could never imagine her using such vocabulary.

There were also busloads of women transported out of Cowdenbeath every working day to the factories and linen mills of Dunfermline. For a woman to do an apprenticeship at that time was virtually unheard of, but I remember one of our neighbours, an unmarried woman, who worked in some kind of engineering trade at the NCB workshops. During the Second World War, many women had to do jobs formerly done by men and some of them continued after the war.

Many of the young women who had attended Moss-side Secondary School found employment as typists, secretaries and administrators in the NCB offices. Other young men and women would be employed by the Cowdenbeath Co-operative Society Limited or other retailers in the area. There was relatively full employment, but wages were pretty meagre. Amongst the Cowdenbeath working class, the coalface miners probably had the highest wages, but they also had the highest risks of accident and disease.

My grandfather's brother, Bernard (Barney) Canavan, was awarded the British Empire Medal for his mine rescue work. As far as I know, that is the only imperial gong in my family, but we were all proud of Uncle Barney, who won his medal for digging his comrades out of the ground after some of the most terrible disasters in the history of Scottish coalmining. He was in the rescue team at Donibristle Colliery in 1901 when the roof collapsed, resulting in eight men being buried or drowned in liquid peat. Twenty-eight years later, Barney was called into action again when an explosion at Valleyfield Colliery killed thirty-nine miners.

Every day, as children, we were reminded of the dangers faced by miners. On our way to and from school, we would pass the mine rescue station in Stenhouse Street. Sometimes we would stop and peer through the windows to goggle at the safety lamps, the helmets, the protective clothing, the oxygen cylinders, the gas masks, the stretchers, the first-aid kits and all the other equipment there at the ready for an emergency. The most intriguing sight, however, was the row of caged canaries which were used to test for the presence of gas. Where and when would the next disaster be? How many lives would be saved by the death of a poor wee bird and how many more would be saved by the courage of the rescue team?

After the nationalisation of the coal industry in 1947, safety standards were greatly improved, but serious accidents were still a fairly regular occurrence, some of them with fatal consequences. I well remember the Lindsay Colliery disaster in the neighbouring village of Kelty, when nine men perished and eleven were injured as the result of a fire. That was in 1958, the year that I left Cowdenbeath to go to Drygrange Seminary.

CHAPTER FIVE

Too wild to be a priest?

A few weeks after my sixteenth birthday, I arrived at Drygrange, a large baronial mansion in a country estate, surrounded by some of the finest landscapes in the Scottish Borders. The River Leader meets the Tweed a few hundred yards from the big house, and the Eildon Hills are only a couple of miles away. Within reasonable walking distance are Scott's View at Bemersyde and the historic abbeys of Melrose, Dryburgh, Kelso and Jedburgh. Compared with the bings of Cowdenbeath, it was like God's own country.

As the students were not allowed to use public transport, we had to walk or cycle whenever we went outside the college grounds. That could be rather punishing in inclement weather but, on the positive side, it helped to develop in me an appreciation of the countryside and a love of walking which have remained with me all my life.

The course of study leading to the priesthood at that time consisted of two years of philosophy followed by four years of theology. There are not many 16 year-olds who get the opportunity to study philosophy and I found it rather strange at first, because it was so different from the subjects I had studied at school. However, thanks to Father Karl Kruger, who was our Professor of Philosophy, I soon got the hang of it and grew to like it.

The core philosophy course taught in the Catholic seminaries was Thomistic, named after Thomas Aquinas, who had based much of his work on that of Aristotle. However, Karl Kruger introduced us to the thinking of a wide range of other philosophers, including Socrates, Plato, Kant, Hegel, Descartes, Kierkegaarde, John Stuart Mill and David Hume. There were also courses in Moral Philosophy, Cosmology, Logic and Metaphysics. I became fascinated by the study of philosophy. It certainly taught me to think critically and, years later, to see through the sophistry and sloppy thinking of many politicians. I am not the sort of guy who instinctively believes everything the teacher or the priest or the politician or the papers tell me, and it was my philosophy course at Drygrange that helped to open my mind.

I did not enjoy the study of theology to the same extent, because I found it too dogmatic. In fact, one of the courses was actually called Dogmatic Theology, and anyone who challenged the orthodox dogma ran the risk of being branded a heretic. It was just as well that the Spanish Inquisition had ended, because I was very often questioning and sometimes unbelieving.

I have never seriously questioned my belief in God or in the basic teachings of Jesus Christ, but some theologians seem to get their breeks in a twist over esoteric debates like how many angels can dance on a pin. Some of the moral theologians seemed to be obsessed with other people's sexual behaviour and I wonder whether that had anything to do with celibacy and the prohibition of women priests. There are some good arguments in favour of celibacy on a voluntary basis, but making it a pre-condition for entry to the priesthood deprives the Church of people who have a lot to offer in terms of priestly ministry. Similarly, I know of many women who would make excellent priests and, if we look at other denominations, the Church of Scotland, for example, the contributions of female ministers has been very positive.

In contrast, the Catholic Church has a poor record on gender equality. The only female residents at Drygrange seminary were a group of about half a dozen nuns, but they were not there to study philosophy or theology. They were there to do the cleaning and the cooking for the students and the staff. They were not allowed to mix with the students even at religious services. They had their own separate chapel and, when they were not praying or working, they were virtually confined to their own separate living quarters. Treating women like mere skivvies should have no place in any educational establishment, especially a seminary. I found out afterwards that some of the nuns at Drygrange were university graduates who were better qualified than some of the so-called professors.

When I started in the seminary, I was rather naïve about sexual matters, although I had attended co-educational schools, whereas most of the other students had attended Blairs College in Aberdeenshire, a minor seminary for boys aged from 12 to 18. At Drygrange, the students would assemble in the chapel every evening for a talk by the rector, Canon Roger Gallagher. I found some of his talks inspiring, but he very frequently went on and on about 'self abuse'. He described it as a grave sin which could undermine your vocation to the priesthood. At first, I did not know what he was on about. I thought that he was perhaps referring to self-flagellation, but I could not understand how that could be a grave sin because I had read stories about some of the saints who had scourged themselves as a form of punishment for their sins. If the rector had made just an occasional reference to 'self abuse', I would probably not have worried too much about it, but he went on and on.

I therefore plucked up the courage to ask for an explanation from one of the older students, who replied with a wry smile: 'In Cowdenbeath, you probably call it wanking.' I then started to wonder what kind of community I had joined when the rector felt obliged to issue such regular dire warnings about the dangers of masturbation, but I soon came to realise that the rector's obsession with the subject was a standing joke amongst the students.

It might have been more apposite for frequent lectures to be given to seminarians on the evils of child abuse rather than self abuse. Although I was unaware of any sexual abuse of students at Drygrange, it did go on at Blairs College and I know of one contemporary of mine at Drygrange who, after he was ordained as a priest, was convicted of child abuse and sent to prison.

The number of cases of priests abusing children has been the biggest scandal to hit the Catholic Church in recent years and God alone knows how many other cases went undetected or unreported because the Church authorities would simply move the culprit on to another parish or another job. The abuse of an innocent child must be one of the gravest sins, but it took the Church nearly 2,000 years to face up to the problem amongst some of its own clergy.

I have no doubt that the vast majority of priests are good people whom I would trust with my own child, but the Church must ensure that lessons have been learned from past misdeeds and that the protection of children is given more importance than the protection of clergy.

One of my happiest recollections of Drygrange was of a visiting professor called Eric Barbour, who came once a week to give us 'elocution' lessons. I suppose that the purpose of the exercise was to turn us all into brilliant preachers to go out and teach the Gospel. Eric had been educated at the Royal Academy of Dramatic Art (RADA) and, after a successful career as a professional actor, he converted to Catholicism and became a priest. He was the absolute epitome of a cultured English gentleman and, when I first met him and listened to his RADA accent, I was worried that he might not understand a word of what I was saying in my broad Fife tongue.

During the summer, he used to take us for alfresco lessons on the former lawn tennis court. He would give each student in turn one minute's notice to deliver a two-minute speech on a particular subject, following which he and the other students would do a critique of the effort. When my turn came, I was just about wetting myself. Afterwards, Eric told me that I should never be ashamed of my Scottish accent. He said that I had a very powerful, resonant voice, but that I should try to put more modulation into my delivery in order to capture and hold the attention of the audience. The Fife accent is not very conducive to modulation, but Eric suggested putting more questions into my speeches rather than just bland statements. That suited my style, because I am a very questioning character and I later found that Eric's advice was very useful, whether it was asking questions or making speeches in parliament, or doing open-air street meetings at Falkirk Steeple. My only problem was that, when I went home to Cowdenbeath on holidays, some of my old school pals thought that I was speaking too posh.

Another happy memory of the seminary was the singing. In the 1950s, the Mass and many other services were still in Latin and much of the liturgical music was Gregorian plainchant. All the students were members of the choir, even those who were tone deaf, and every student had to take a turn at being cantor. It was the cantor's job to lead the singing and very often there was no accompanying organ music. It was therefore pot luck whether we got off to a good start and consequently the quality of performance ranged from the divine to the hilarious.

Every Sunday evening we sang Vespers, which is the part of the Divine Office, or obligatory prayer, said every day by clergy and religious orders. Vespers consisted of psalms, prayers and hymns, sung in Latin, and I usually found it to be a spiritually uplifting experience, especially if the choir was in good form. Unfortunately that was not always the case.

On one particular Sunday afternoon, I had been playing football when I suddenly remembered that one of my jobs for that week was to be thurifer for Vespers. It was the thurifer's job to carry the thurible, which is a metal container in which incense is burned. Before the service started, the thurifer had to light charcoal to put into the thurible and I knew that I was running out of time to get that done. I had to think quickly to avoid the ignominy of being late for Vespers.

I sprinted to my room and, instead of washing and changing, I simply put my cassock and dog collar on top of my football gear, although I did manage to replace my football boots with a pair of shoes. As the pitch had been very wet that day, I realised that my football gear and legs would be very muddy, but I was confident that my cassock, a long black garment stretching from neck to ankles, would cover a multitude of sins.

During the service, the duties of the thurifer included swinging the thurible from a chain to offer incense to all those present. Believe it or not, the procedure is called incensing and, when I turned round to incense the people in the public pews, I saw that there were some visitors. I gave them a few extra puffs of smoke to give them a warm welcome, before turning round to genuflect in front of the altar. I thought that the service went off fairly well, although the choir was not at its best, possibly because the cantor for that week was tone deaf.

Later that evening, when the rector came back to the chapel to give us his nightly talk, he was so incensed that smoke was snorting out his nose. He told us that he had never been so ashamed in all his life. The visitors had apparently been a BBC TV production team who had been looking at the possibility of broadcasting Vespers from our college chapel. We had obviously failed the audition and the rector went absolutely ballistic in his attempt to name and shame those responsible. He tore strips off the choir-master and left the hapless cantor without a name, before turning on me to vent his rage:

'And then to complete the fiasco, we had a thurifer genuflecting in front of the altar to reveal a football sock and about nine inches of filthy, naked leg! Is it any wonder that the BBC won't be coming back?'

That was my TV debut that never was but I have often thought that, if the BBC had done a live broadcast that night, the entertainment value would have eclipsed *Father Ted* and *The Vicar of Dibley*. It was sheer hilarity.

One of the most memorable events at Drygrange was the party to celebrate the appointment of the first Scottish cardinal since the Reformation. Who he? A good question for a pub quiz. Even many practising Catholics would probably think it was Cardinal Gordon

Joseph Gray, who was Archbishop of St Andrews and Edinburgh and became a cardinal in 1969. But, ten years previously, a Scot called William Theodore Heard was appointed a cardinal by Pope John XXIII. Cardinal Heard was completely unknown to most Scottish Catholics. Even some of the seminarians joked: 'Heard? Never heard of him.' He was a brilliant canon lawyer who had worked virtually unseen in the Vatican for over 30 years, emerging in 1958 as the Dean of the Holy Roman Rota, the most senior judicial appointment in the Church. The following year, he was elevated to the position of cardinal and the Church decided to celebrate the occasion with a garden party at Drygrange.

A huge marquee was erected in the grounds and the place was teeming with bishops and clergy from all over Scotland and further afield. The Pope's representative, the papal nuncio, was at the top table along with members of the Scottish hierarchy and the new cardinal, who seemed an amiable old guy with a sharp mind which belied his 75 years.

Some of the students, including myself, were conscripted as wine waiters but we were allowed to sit down with the guests for lunch after serving the wine, provided we got up between courses to ensure that all the glasses were topped up.

Apart from an occasional glass of my grandmother's ginger wine at Christmas, I had never tasted wine before in my life. The students had been told that, as it was a very special occasion, they could drink wine, provided they did so in moderation. Unfortunately, nobody explained whether moderation should be measured by the glass or the bottle.

When I first tasted the wine, I did not think it did much for me at all but, as the meal went on, I began to feel more and more pleasant and I got more and more garrulous. At the end of the meal, the student wine waiters had to collect the empty and partially empty bottles from the table and some of us thought that it would be a terrible waste to pour the contents of the partially empty bottles down the drain. What seemed a reasonable idea at the time turned out to have almost disastrous consequences.

Shortly after the meal, an evening service called Benediction was to be held in the college chapel and the students were all lined up in their cassocks and surplices along the corridor ready to file in solemn procession into the chapel. By this time, the wine was really beginning to take effect. There was a bit of jostling and staggering and some of us thought it would be a good idea to start the first hymn a bit early. We were singing away so lustily that we did not see the snatch squad of senior students coming towards us. There were attempts to resist arrest and, at one point, it looked as if the fracas was going to develop into a full-scale battle. Eventually, however, the wine waiters were overpowered and frog-marched along to the shower room, where we were stripped and forced into the cold water.

Old Cardinal Heard did not have a clue what was going on, which was just as well. Not even the most brilliant canon lawyer in the world could have sorted that one out! But I have often thought that the seminary regime in the 1950s was more like a monastic existence than an adequate preparation of young men to live and work amongst ordinary people in the towns and cities of Scotland.

In 1960, John Barry took over from Roger Gallagher as Rector of Drygrange but, as far as I was concerned, it was out of the frying pan into the fire. Monsignor Barry, who had a doctorate in canon law, produced a rule book which was as legalistic and almost as long as the Book of Leviticus. The rule book prescribed everything that the student should or should not do and imposed a rigid timetable for virtually every minute of every day. There was a time to get up, a time to pray, a time to play, a time to eat, a time to attend lectures, a time to study, a time to shop, a time to speak, a time to be silent, a time for lights out and a time to sleep. As a result, there was very little opportunity to plan your own day or make your own decisions or develop a spirit of independence.

I believe in the need for discipline, but the best discipline is self-discipline rather than discipline imposed by other people. The seminary establishment also taught that each of the rector's rules was the will of God and that any breach of the rules was therefore a sin. I told my spiritual adviser that I could not accept such a spurious form of theocracy. If it were applied to the real world, it could lead to fascism and there have been some cosy relationships between fascist regimes and the Catholic Church. I never could understand why the Catholic Church in Scotland continued sending young men to study for the priesthood in Spain during the Franco regime. Even after senior seminaries like Drygrange were established in Scotland, some seminarians were still sent to the Scots College in Spain.

Others went to the Scots College in Rome. In fact, if I had continued studying for the priesthood, I would have been sent to Rome. By 1960, the college authorities at Drygrange were probably getting fed up with my rebellious conduct, but they may have put it down to youthful exuberance. There was also a personality clash between me and the rector, Monsignor Barry, who came from a posh background and could be very pompous at times. Poshness and pomposity are not synonymous. Father Jock Dalrymple, who was spiritual director at Drygrange, also came from a posh background. His father was a baronet, but Father Jock was anything but pompous. He was a very humble man and I found his asceticism inspiring. By contrast, Monsignor John Barry got up my nose and the feeling was probably mutual. When he told me one day that the archbishop wanted to see me, I suspected that John Barry had reported me for misconduct and that I was going to be formally reprimanded by the archbishop, or maybe even expelled.

On the next occasion that the archbishop visited Drygrange, I was summoned to his room. I felt quite nervous about it all and, when I knocked on his door, his deep, sonorous voice boomed out: 'Come in!' I took a deep breath, opened the door and entered, fearing the worst.

Gordon Joseph Gray was a giant of a man, in more ways than one. A native of Leith, he attended Holy Cross Academy, Edinburgh, where I would later teach. After attending a seminary in England, he studied at St Andrews University and became the first Catholic priest to graduate there since the Reformation. He was appointed Archbishop of St Andrews and Edinburgh in 1951 and, two years later, he founded Drygrange Seminary. He was huge in stature, with a massive head and a large bulbous nose. In 1959, when the very first priests from Drygrange were ordained at St Mary's Cathedral in Edinburgh, I was the train-bearer for the archbishop, who wore a cappa magna, a voluminous purple garment with a long train stretching out some 20 feet or more. I had never seen anything like it before and had to quickly acquire the knack of walking at exactly the same pace as the archbishop, otherwise the train would become too tight or too slack. The fact that the archbishop's legs were twice as long as mine did not make the knack any easier to acquire. As I trotted behind him, I had a terrible vision of tripping over the cappa magna and falling in a heap in the middle of the cathedral aisle. On another occasion, I nearly collided with the archbishop when I was bounding down the professor's staircase at Drygrange. I should not even have been using the staircase, as it was supposed to be for the exclusive use of the staff and, to make things worse, I mistakenly blurted out: 'Sorry, your Arch' instead of 'Sorry, Your Grace'.

All this came flooding through my mind as I entered the room, but the archbishop gave me a welcoming smile and ushered me to a seat. He told me that he was very impressed with my academic progress and he explained that he had a special proposal which he wanted to put to me. He reminded me that, according to canon law, the minimum age for ordination to the priesthood was 24 and that I would be only 21 by the time I finished the course at Drygrange. He therefore thought that it would be a good idea for me to go to the Scots College in Rome, where I would be able to do a degree in theology at the Gregorian University.

I had visited the Scots College in Rome during the summer holidays of the previous year along with my friend Pat Clarke, who was also a student at Drygrange. We hitch-hiked through Europe for three weeks on a budget of £30 each and we stayed for a few days at the Scots College villa on the outskirts of Rome, where the students resided during the summer. It was in general a pleasant experience, and Rome is a fantastic city. The archbishop's proposal certainly had its attractions and I gave it a great deal of thought. However, I came to the conclusion that the seminary regime in Rome would probably be just as authoritarian as that at Drygrange, possibly even more so.

By this time, I had serious doubts about whether I really had a vocation to the priesthood and I recalled my mother's words when I left school that I was too wild, too rebellious to be a priest. I eventually came to the conclusion that Mum was right after all. I confided in my spiritual director, Father Jock Dalrymple, and then I wrote a letter to the archbishop telling him that, after a great deal of reflection, I had decided not to pursue his proposal for me to go to Rome.

I have no bitterness about my time in the seminary and the experience helped to make me what I am. The study of philosophy taught me to think critically and to ask questions, including awkward questions. Eric Barbour's course on public speaking gave me a degree of self-confidence which was invaluable in teaching and in politics. I also made many friends, some of whom I have kept up with in later life, such as Jim Thomson, who became chaplain of St Modan's High School, Stirling, and then chaplain of St Andrews University. Several of my fellow students went on to senior positions in the Catholic Church, including Cardinal Keith O'Brien, Archbishop of St Andrews and Edinburgh, and Vincent Logan, Bishop of Dunkeld.

I have also seen some effort being made by the Church to address the criticisms which I made about the seminary regime in the 1950s. Maybe some day they might even take up my suggestions about women priests and married priests. I sometimes wonder how things would have turned out if I had gone to Rome, but I remain convinced that I came to the correct decision. It was not for me.

CHAPTER SIX

Thrown in at the deep end

Shortly before I retired from full-time politics I was invited to speak to a Modern Studies class at Bannockburn High School. Two of my grandchildren, Sonny and Amy, were pupils at that school, although neither of them was in that particular class. The young teacher treated me like a VIP and maybe he assumed that his pupils, like himself, were political anoraks, some of whom might recognise me. Before introducing me by name he said: 'You may have seen this man on TV. Does anyone know who he is?' A young lad immediately replied: 'Aye, that's Sonny's grandad.'

Children often come up with the unexpected. On another occasion, I gave a talk to some pupils about the Scottish Parliament. After I had finished, I asked if there were any questions and a wee girl raised her hand.

'Please sir, whit did ye dae before ye were an MSP?'

'Before I was an MSP, I was an MP.'

She did not look too impressed.

'Please sir, whit did ye dae before ye were an MP?'

'Before I was an MP, I was a teacher.'

'Please sir, huv ye never hud a real job?'

She was probably trying to wind me up. Despite the many jokes about teachers, I often look back on my time teaching as some of the happiest days of my life, but it was almost by accident that I entered the teaching profession.

After leaving the seminary, I did not have a clue what I wanted to do with the rest of my life. I knew that I did not want to continue studying for the priesthood and that I wanted to keep open my options for the future. I was too late to gain admission to university for that particular academic year and I therefore decided to have what is now commonly referred to as a gap year. I needed time to think.

I got a job as a labourer, which I quite enjoyed, but it was only temporary seasonal work and I soon found myself faced with the threat of unemployment for the first and only time in my life. I felt useless and depressed, I did not have any clear sense of purpose and I had no idea what the future held for me. Then a strange sequence of events unfolded.

A young teacher, Mary McPherson, who lived in our street in Cowdenbeath, became seriously ill. As she required hospitalisation, she had to take a couple of months' sick leave from her job at St Kenneth's Primary School, Crosshill, near Lochore. I was asked if I was interested in taking Mary's class at St Kenneth's while she was in hospital.

At that time, many parts of Scotland, including Fife, were so desperately short of teachers that it was possible for students to get temporary employment as unqualified teachers, especially if they expressed an interest in eventually taking up teaching as a career. I cannot even remember who asked me if I would be interested in taking Mary's class. It might have been the headteacher, Mr Barnes, or it might have been Mary herself. In any event, I agreed to give it a try because it was better than just kicking my heels. It turned out to be one of the best decisions I ever made in my life. I found out that I enjoyed teaching and it gave me a great deal of job satisfaction.

To begin with, however, it was more a challenge than a joy. Mary McPherson was a hard act to follow, albeit for only a couple of months. She was an excellent teacher and, like many of the best primary schoolteachers, she specialised in teaching children with learning difficulties, or remedial education as it was called at that time. Mary's class consisted of nearly thirty pupils, ranging in age from seven to twelve years, and in IQ from seventy minus to about eighty. Many of them had emotional and behavioural difficulties as well as learning difficulties.

At the age of nineteen, I was thrown in at the deep end, as a temporary unqualified teacher with a salary of two guineas (£2.10) per working day. I had had no training whatsoever and the only advice I received was a five-minute pep talk from Mr Barnes before he introduced me to the class and left me to it. In retrospect, I think the pupils initially taught me more than I taught them.

Most of the primary curriculum was taken up with the three Rs, but one day I decided, for a change, to give the class a series of lessons on environmental studies, beginning with their own environment. Crosshill, like many villages in West Fife, was a coal-mining community. It was just along the road from Glencraig Colliery, where many of the children's fathers were employed, and I assumed that most, if not all, of the children would know something about the coal industry. Nevertheless, I thought that I should start from the beginning, giving them an elementary lesson in geology, followed by the story of the discovery of coal, its importance as a fuel and a brief history of the coal industry. It was all accompanied by child-friendly diagrams and blackboard sketches of collieries, seams and pit shafts and I encouraged the pupils to do their own drawings in their jotters. All of the children probably had a coal fire at home, but I explained the importance of coal in the generation of electricity and, at that time, the production of gas for domestic and industrial use. I pointed out that the miners were responsible for supplying the energy needs of the nation and, if it were not for the miners, the wheels of industry would stop turning and the economy would collapse. I thought that my lessons would give them a sense of pride in their community and the importance of the work done by their own family members.

Afterwards, I decided to ascertain how much the children had learned. It was pointless giving them a written test, because some of them had great difficulty in reading and writing. I therefore asked them a series of oral questions, one of which was: 'Where does coal come from?' A girl called Anne put up her hand and innocently said: 'Please sir, the bing.'

The bing consisted of all the stones and low-grade coal which had been rejected at the pit head because it was deemed unsuitable for homes, factories or power stations. It formed a huge heap which, to a child, seemed to be of almost mountainous proportions. The working miners got concessionary coal from the National Coal Board, but it was almost traditional for the wives and children of the unemployed to go to the bing with buckets or sacks or even old prams to rummage through the debris, hunting for pieces of coal to heat their homes, especially in winter. It was rather like the tradition of picking the tatties left in a field after the harvest. It was therefore ironic that the West Fife farmers, who were perceived as Tories, tolerated such a practice, but not the National Coal Board. To this day, I find it almost incredible that the bosses of a nationalised industry, the property of the people, had a policy of prosecuting some of the poorest people in mining communities for the heinous crime of taking scraps of coal which had been discarded as unfit for purpose. The police were instructed to stop and charge the rummagers with theft, and they were treated like common criminals. If they were lucky, they might appear before a sympathetic magistrate like my grandfather, who would admonish them, but most magistrates would impose a fine and, if the 'felons' were unable to pay the fine, they ran the risk of imprisonment.

So when my pupil, Anne, told me that the coal came from the bing, I knew what she meant. Her father was either unemployed or had disappeared. She told me that she and her wee brother, Michael, were regularly sent to the bing to fetch the coal for her mother so that the family would at least have the comfort of a warm fire.

Michael and Anne were in the same class, although Michael was about three years younger than his sister, and there were several other children of pre-school age in the family. Their school attendance was very erratic and, after a while, I noticed that, when Anne was present, Michael was absent and vice versa. I sensed that something was wrong at home, perhaps a sick parent or a younger child who needed care. I took Anne aside after class one day and asked her about her and Michael's pattern of absences.

'Anne, why is it that, when you are here, Michael is absent and, when Michael is here, you are absent? Is there a problem at home?'

At first Anne just bit her lip and refused to respond. I said: 'Please, Anne, tell me if I can help in any way. Why are you here today but Michael is not?'

Anne burst into tears and, after a long period of embarrassing silence, she stammered: 'Please, sir, it's Tuesday and it's my turn for the shoes.'

I looked down at her feet. The 'shoes' were an old pair of leaking welly boots which looked too wee for Anne and probably far too big for Michael. I asked Anne to promise that she would come to school every day if I managed to get her a decent pair of shoes. She nodded through the tears and, when I asked her, she told me her shoe size.

I knew exactly where I would find a decent pair of shoes. My sister, Kathleen, who must have been 16 at the time, had a collection of shoes going back several years. She was not exactly in the same league as Imelda Marcos but, to my pupil, Anne, Kathleen's wardrobe would have seemed like Aladdin's cave. When I explained Anne's predicament, Kathleen had no hesitation in filling a plastic bag with some shoes, which I delivered to Anne the following day. For the rest of my time at St Kenneth's, she never missed another day and even her wee brother Michael put in more regular appearances as sole proprietor of the wellies.

Many years later, David Blunkett, when Secretary of State for Education, came up with the outrageous suggestion that parents should be fined or even imprisoned if their children failed to attend school. He even suggested that such parents should have their state benefits docked. It was a typical Blunkett right-wing reaction to a complex problem. What good would it have done Anne and Michael if their parents had been jailed? Even if their parents were deemed to be responsible for the predicament of the family, why should children be punished for the inadequacies of the parents?

I sometimes wonder what happened to Anne and Michael. They were very unfortunate in their family circumstances but they were very fortunate in having Mary McPherson as their teacher. Sadly that did not last long either. Mary returned to school after her sick leave, but she was later diagnosed as having a terminal illness and she died a young woman.

After my spell at St Kenneth's, I got another post as a temporary supply teacher at Foulford Primary School, Cowdenbeath, where my grandad had been the jannie. Foulford School was situated very close to St Bride's Primary School, which I had attended as a child. As with many neighbouring schools, there was some rivalry between the pupils, which sometimes manifested itself in football matches or snowball fights. I never detected any hard-core sectarianism, although there were misconceptions of a religious nature. For example, when I was a primary one pupil, I was conscious of the fact that the Catholic children went to St Bride's and the Protestant children went to Foulford. I therefore concluded that the word Foulford was synonymous with the word Protestant and that misunderstanding continued until I realised that not all Protestant children in Cowdenbeath went to Foulford, but some went to Broad Street Primary School or Lumphinnans Primary School.

When I started teaching at Foulford, I politely asked the head-teacher what I should do regarding the religious education of the pupils in my class. In Scotland, religious education is the only subject which is specified as mandatory by Act of Parliament. The headteacher, who knew that I was a Catholic, did not seem at all concerned and I therefore concentrated on matters which were common to most Christian denominations rather than getting involved in matters of controversy. That formula seemed to work, and I never received any complaints from parents about proselytising their children.

Nowadays, of course, the situation would be very different because of the diversity of faiths and cultures amongst the people of Scotland, including people with faiths other than Christian and people with no faith at all. Faith schools are often criticised for allegedly indoctrinating children and encouraging sectarianism. Having taught in both denominational and non-denominational schools, I think that, in Scotland, such accusations are without foundation and are an insult to the teaching profession. Most teachers in both types of school make every endeavour to encourage children to respect each other's beliefs. It is perfectly possible for parents or teachers to educate children in a particular faith while at the same time teaching them to know about and to respect the beliefs of other people. Blaming the school system for encouraging sectarianism is passing the buck. Parents must face up to their responsibilities by setting their children a good example.

After Foulford School, I taught for over six months at Benarty Primary School in Ballingry. I also played for the local football team, Ballingry Rovers, and sometimes the spectators would include a group of my pupils, some of them cheering and others jeering whenever I kicked the ball.

By this time, I was enjoying teaching and I felt that I was good at it, judging by the reaction of my pupils and fellow teachers. I began to think seriously about teaching as a career, but I was still not certain. Having packed up one vocational course of study, I did not want to embark on another. I wanted to keep my options open and therefore decided to do a degree course in mathematical science at Edinburgh University, mainly because I thought it would give me a reasonable choice of future career.

I am not sure now whether it was the best choice. I would probably have got more enjoyment out of studying politics, philosophy and economics and it would have better equipped me for my future life. However, I have no great regrets about my decision, although Edinburgh University in the 1960s was a culture shock for me, after three years in Drygrange Seminary.

At Drygrange, the biggest class consisted of about 25 students and the lecture rooms were about the same size as the classrooms at school. When I walked into my first lecture at Edinburgh University's Old Quad, I could hardly believe my eyes. There must have been about 200 students and the lecture room looked like the terracing of a football stadium.

I soon found out that the standard of teaching was abysmal. A typical lecture would consist of an old man writing differential equations on a distant blackboard and muttering inaudibly to a largely bewildered audience. It was a huge challenge to copy down all the blackboard notes before he rubbed them out with a duster to replace them with more incomprehensible scribbles. This went on for about an hour, during which time the writing on the blackboard got more and more illegible. There was no break for questions and no hope of understanding the lesson there and then. My main aim was to copy everything from the blackboard accurately in the hope of being able to digest it later. The latter was impossible without the former. Even one dot instead of two dots above a letter would make the entire differential equation incomprehensible.

The lectures were supplemented with tutorial classes which were supposed to facilitate learning in a smaller group. The tutorials consisted of about 40 students crammed into a small room in Chambers Street, which was more conducive to claustrophobia than learning. Postgraduate students were on hand supposedly to help, but the average undergraduate was lucky to receive five minutes of individual attention.

Nobody seemed to care. There was no record of attendance and nobody bothered whether you turned up for lectures or tutorials or whatever. Even the class examinations at the end of each term were almost irrelevant. All that mattered was to pass the degree examination at the end of the academic year. I soon came to the conclusion that I would probably have been better doing a correspondence course. At least I would have received accurate notes instead of trying slavishly to copy everything down from a distant blackboard.

At one stage, I thought about packing it all in but, having already given up one course of study, I decided to persevere. I was also enjoying the social life as well as the sporting opportunities which the university offered. It was a very liberating experience compared with the monastic life at the seminary. The university union in Teviot Row was a hub of activity and every Saturday night a dance was held in the debating hall upstairs. Many female students attended the Saturday night sessions, but I could never understand why the union would not allow women to become members. It may have been due to the fact that many of the union committee were products of fee-paying schools for boys only, but the result was that the union was like a male chauvinist club. The only time that females were made welcome was for the weekend dances, which some students likened to a cattle market.

Although I enjoyed the social life of university, I felt no inclination to participate in student politics. Most of the students seemed to be on a different political planet from me. For example, I was shocked to meet people who worshipped Winston Churchill. In my childhood I had sat in Slora's cinema in Cowdenbeath, when Churchill would regularly appear on the news bulletins. The verbal abuse was so vitriolic that it sometimes almost developed into a riot which had to be suppressed by torch-wielding usherettes. When he was Home Secretary, Churchill had sanctioned the sending of troops to Wales to quell striking miners and, during a lock-out of Fife miners in 1921, soldiers had been billeted in Cowdenbeath and military guards posted at every pit-head in the area. Embellishment of local folklore led future generations of children to believe that Churchill was a villain who had sent tanks into Cowdenbeath High Street to crush the miners. Yet, a few miles away, on the other side of the River Forth, the same Churchill was hailed as a hero.

Many of the student politicians I met were obviously intent on a parliamentary career but, to me, they seemed out of touch with the real world. Even those in the Labour Club did not seem to have much in common with the working-class people whom they purported to represent, and it appeared to me that many of them were on the make. Those were my initial impressions and, since then, nothing has happened to convince me otherwise. I have also seen countless student left-wing 'revolutionaries' becoming right-wing reactionaries in later life.

When I was MP for West Stirlingshire in the 1970s, the University of Stirling was in my constituency. I remember one particular student revolutionary who was a member of the Communist Party at that time because the Labour Party was not fashionable in student politics, especially for those aspiring to leadership of the students' union. This particular student was leading a protest against the Labour Government because it had refused to increase the student grant by at least the rate of inflation. Inflation at the time was over 20 per cent! After graduating, the erstwhile revolutionary swapped his Communist party card for a Labour Party one because the latter was more suitable for a parliamentary career. He eventually became a member of Tony Blair's government and voted for the introduction of tuition fees and the complete abolition of student grants. John Reid was not the only student politician with such a career path.

During the 1960s, students were much better off financially than they are now. In fact, we were better off than many working people.

When I first started at university, my grant was £300 per annum, which worked out at £10 per week for a 30-week academic year. It was fairly easy to pick up temporary vacational work, especially during the long summer break and, during the Christmas holidays, there were always vacancies for temporary posties delivering the Christmas mail. I had a fair variety of different jobs covering a spectrum of human activities such as working in Campbell, Hope & King's Brewery, being lifeguard at Warrender Swimming Pool, digging graves at Kirk o'Beath Cemetery, pouring pints in Doyle's bar at Tollcross, net-fishing for salmon in the River Tay and selling ice-cream in Sighthill.

The salmon fishing was the most dangerous job I ever had. It was before the Health and Safety Executive was established but, even in those days, I was surprised that such employment conditions were allowed. The Tay Salmon Fisheries Company had the netting rights in the Tay estuary and the north bank of the river between Perth and Dundee was dotted with little bothies, some of which are still there today. The fishing was seasonal and the workforce consisted mostly of students and young men from the Highlands and Islands, although our gaffer was a local man from Newburgh on the Fife side of the river. There were about six in our squad and, because of the tides in the river, we worked five-hour shifts followed by five-hour rest periods right round the clock. Our 'home' was a bothy and we had to cook for ourselves as well as try to grab some sleep during the five-hour rest periods. By the end of the week, we were sometimes so deprived of sleep and so disorientated that we did not know what day of the week it was.

The job itself involved one member of the squad using a small boat to lay the net in the river then the other five, located on the river bank, would haul the net in, using ropes attached to the ends of the net. We took it in turns to lay the net, and physically it was easier than hauling, but it was much more dangerous. The net was folded many times into a bundle, which was placed on a small platform at the back of the boat. The end of the net was attached to a rope which was held by one of the land-based members of the squad. The boat was powered by an outboard motor and, in order to lay the net, the boat had to be steered out into the middle of the river, followed by a wide U-turn back to a point on the bank, downstream from the starting point.

The Tay is a very deep and fast-flowing river with dangerous tidal currents, and laying the net was a very tricky operation, especially in the dark. Nobody even asked if we could swim and I knew for a fact that none of the Western Islanders could swim a stroke. When laying the net, we had to stand at the back of the moving boat with one hand on the tiller and the other hand ready to undo any tangle which appeared in the folded net. One foot in the wrong place would have meant a human being as well as the net being pulled overboard, and the current was sometimes so strong that the corpse would have been swept out into the North Sea within an hour. It was a miracle that there were no fatalities and I wonder how the employers got away with it. I discovered later that one of the principal shareholders in the Tay Salmon Fisheries Company was the Earl of Mansfield, who became a Tory government minister.

If my parents had found out the nature of that job, they would have had nightmares. The basic hourly rate of pay was a pittance, although we would get bonus payments if we had a particularly good catch of salmon. Sometimes, at the end of the week, we felt like millionaires, going home with as much as £12 in our pockets. That was more than my father earned in a week.

Towards the end of his working life, Dad was not physically able to do the long hours of overtime which he had done as a younger man, sometimes in appalling weather conditions. As a result, he suffered a cut in his wages. Because the amount of student grant depended on parental income, I always received the maximum grant. Every year, my father had to complete his part of the student grant application form, giving details of income, and I had to complete the other part. On one occasion, he filled in his part of the form first and that was how I discovered that his total annual income for that year was only £667. I felt embarrassed because my own annual income for that year, taking into account my grant and holiday earnings, was greater than my father's, although I was classified as his dependant. That is a measure of how generous the student grant system was in the 1960s, although it is also a measure of the low wages of many working-class people at that time.

My temporary employment during university holidays gave me an insight into the conditions suffered by many people throughout their working lives. I found most of the jobs were tolerable for a few weeks, but I wondered how on earth people could survive such an experience for 40 or 50 years.

I always looked forward to August, when the school term started. I usually got a job teaching from August until October, when the university term commenced. The job would usually consist of teaching science or mathematics in Edinburgh schools.

The toughest school I ever taught in was Niddrie Marischal Junior Secondary in the Craigmillar area. When I asked one of my colleagues how on earth the school got the name Marischal (pronounced 'marshall') I was told that the teachers needed a degree in martial arts to survive in it. It was no joke. The school's catchment area was one of the roughest and toughest neighbourhoods in Scotland, but that was largely due to social and economic deprivation. The Edinburgh Corporation houses looked so depressing compared with the good quality council housing I had experienced in Cowdenbeath. Unemployment was well above the national average and so was the crime rate, especially violent crime.

One of the teachers, Mr Scott, insisted on giving me a lift in his car after school and he would always wait in the staff room for me, even if I stayed behind to prepare some lessons for the following day. Mr Scott must have been approaching retirement age, but he looked as if he should have been sent out to grass years ago. The poor man was a nervous wreck and I do not know how he ever managed to control a class. I thought it was very kind of him to wait behind for me every day to give me a lift in his car, but I soon found out the real reason. A gang of young thugs used to lie in wait for him at the school gates. Mr Scott was terrified that they would attack him or his car or both, and he felt that he might be safer with me as his bodyguard. I have never had the physique of a bouncer, but I was young and fit and my presence in the front passenger seat of Mr Scott's car seemed to do the trick. After a few days, the thugs disappeared, but I wonder what became of Mr Scott after I finished at Niddrie Marischal. One positive thing about such an experience was that it increased my self-confidence. After surviving a few weeks in that kind of school, I knew that I could survive anything.

My early experience of teaching also made me realise the huge inequalities in educational opportunity which existed at that time, especially in the City of Edinburgh, where about 20 per cent of pupils attended fee-paying schools. Even some of the council schools charged fees and all of the high schools had a selective intake, as did some of the primary schools. The majority of the children failed the selection test for high school and were condemned to three years in a junior secondary school before leaving at the age of 15. The selection test at the age of 11 or 12 was meant to predict success or failure in later life, but the post-test division of children into two different types of school virtually ensured the accuracy of the so-called prediction. The difference between a junior secondary and a high school was like the difference between night and day. A child attending Niddrie Marischal, for example, had very little educational opportunity compared with a child attending the Royal High School or Fettes. In the junior secondaries, some of the teachers were not qualified and even the buildings were grossly inferior.

I also taught in St Anthony's Junior Secondary School annexe adjacent to Easter Road Stadium, home of Hibernian Football Club. The annexe, which was like a warehouse, had been previously occupied by Strang's Football Pools and so both teachers and pupils referred to it colloquially as 'Strang's' to distinguish it from the main school building in Lochend Road. Strang's annexe did not even have windows in the classrooms and, when the atmosphere became too hot or smelly, the teacher had no option but to open the skylights, provided of course that it was not raining. Needless to say, the children who were sent to Strang's were those with learning difficulties, the very ones who most needed something to brighten their lives.

As a young student, I felt that was an appalling indictment of our educational system. I could not understand how Her Majesty's Inspectors had not condemned the building or how Edinburgh Corporation allowed such conditions to continue for as long as it did. It is to the eternal credit of the teachers and children in such schools that many pupils made every endeavour to overcome adverse circumstances and went on to pursue successful careers in many walks of life, including public service, business and sport.

One of the best-organised and most entertaining school football squads I have ever seen was the St Anthony's team which, in the 1967–69 period, swept the boards in schools football, winning every competition open to it, including the Scottish Schools Championship three times in a row. The captain was a wee guy called Paul Hegarty, who became a big star with Dundee United and Scotland before going on to football management. Paul never forgot the encouragement he got from dedicated teachers at St Anthony's.

Another school where I taught as a student was Carrickvale Secondary School, which provided me with one of my most embarrassing experiences. I had two jobs at the time: my day job was teaching and my evening job was selling ice-cream.

By coincidence, the school catchment area and the ice-cream

vending pitch happened to overlap and, one evening, the inevitable happened. One of my ice-cream customers turned out to be one of my pupils, Jeannie, who lived in Sighthill. As soon as she saw me, she blurted out in front of her pals: 'Hi, mister, you're a dead ringer for oor science teacher.' I smiled and joked with her that that must be my brother (who was indeed a science teacher) and I thought I had her convinced. The joke continued for several days and, every evening, Jeannie would run up to the ice-cream van and tell me what my brother had been up to in the science lab.

Then one day, while doing a demonstration experiment in the lab, I accidentally broke a test tube and cut my finger. I took out the first aid kit, hurriedly put an elastoplast round the injured finger and carried on regardless.

That evening, Jeannie came running up to the ice-cream van with her pals. She watched me with hawkish eyes as I spooned out the ice-cream then she loudly declared to all and sundry: 'It is so you, you're oor science teacher richt enough!'

When I tried to protest my innocence of such a ridiculous charge, she pointed to the smoking gun or, rather, the plastered finger. I knew instantly that my cover was blown. From that day onwards every pupil in the school knew that I was moonlighting as an ice-cream man. Most of them thought that it was a huge joke and I sensed that, for some of them, I went up in their estimation. Which all goes to prove that ice cream is more popular than chemistry and physics.

It was mainly my experience of temporary teaching as a student which influenced me to enter the teaching profession. I found out that I enjoyed working with young people even though it was very challenging at times, especially when teaching a mixed-ability class with as many as 50 pupils. I also found that teaching a rather abstract subject like Mathematics was more interesting than studying the subject simply for my own edification. Many pupils find Mathematics quite a difficult subject to grasp, and it is a subject where a good teacher can make a huge difference. A brilliant mathematician is not necessarily a good teacher of Mathematics. In fact, some mathematicians are so brilliant that they could never teach the subject because they could not understand the difficulties experienced by lesser mortals. To be a good teacher, you have to try to look into the mind of the least gifted of pupils and try to understand their thought processes and anticipate the pitfalls which they might encounter in the learning process. Teaching gifted, well-motivated pupils from good home backgrounds is relatively easy. Teaching less able children from deprived home backgrounds is much more challenging.

I found teaching to be a very fulfilling experience. It gave me a great deal of job satisfaction and I am still on good, friendly terms with many of my former pupils, some of whom are now in important positions in fields as diverse as business, law, industry, religion, politics and the media.

One of my pupils at St Modan's High School, Stirling, was Philip Differ, who has produced some of BBC Scotland's best comedy shows, including *Scotch and Wry*, *Watson's Wind-Up* and *Only an Excuse*. I also taught Gordon Brewer, presenter of BBC *Newsnight Scotland*, but Gordon was not in the same class as Philip. Another former pupil of mine at St Modan's was Mary Theresa Kelly, who is now doing an excellent job as headteacher of St Mary's Primary School, Bannockburn, where my son Adam is one of her pupils. When I taught at St Augustine's High School in Edinburgh, one of the leading lights in my form class was Philip Kerr, now Monsignor Kerr, parish priest at St Francis Xavier's in Falkirk and Vicar General of the Archdiocese of St Andrews and Edinburgh.

I also taught Paul Cullen QC, who was Solicitor General for Scotland in John Major's Government. I remember meeting him shortly after his appointment. The occasion was the Secretary of State for Scotland's annual reception for the Moderator of the General Assembly of the Church of Scotland, in Dover House, Whitehall. When I was introduced to the recently appointed Solicitor General, I told him that I never thought that I would live to see the day when a former pupil of mine would be a member of any Tory Government, especially the right wing, discredited corrupt outfit which he had joined. Paul gave me an apologetic look before saluting me military style and responding: 'I am sorry, sir!' We then removed our tongues from our cheeks, dissolved into laughter and decided to switch the subject from politics. Paul later stood as a Tory parliamentary candidate in the west of Scotland, but had had a sufficiently good education to jalouse that there was not much future in that. He is now pursuing a legal career and successfully defended his colleague, Donald Findlay QC, when he was threatened with getting kicked out of the Faculty of Advocates for alleged sectarianism.

Most of my encounters with former pupils have been happy

occasions, often with hilarious recollections of classroom incidents from 30 or 40 years ago. The job satisfaction from teaching is not just something which happens on a day-to-day basis when actually doing the job. It is something which lasts a lifetime and, looking back, I certainly made more friends through teaching than I ever did through politics.

———— ◆ ————

CHAPTER SEVEN

Fun and games

Since childhood, I have always loved sport, especially football.

I remember playing truant from primary school on a Wednesday afternoon in order to watch a thrilling Scottish Cup replay between Cowdenbeath and Morton. The Morton team included Jimmy Cowan, the famous Scotland goalkeeper, and Neil Mochan, who also went on to play for Scotland as well as becoming a Celtic legend.

Cowdenbeath Football Club was in the Second, or B, Division, but their league matches regularly attracted several thousand spectators. It cost seven pence for admission at the boys' gate and, when we did not have the money, that did not stop us seeing the match. In good mining tradition, we tunnelled under the perimeter fence but, when the team was doing badly, there was sometimes a rush to the tunnel before the final whistle. It was like the Great Escape!

I always preferred playing to spectating. Unfortunately, post-war Cowdenbeath was not well endowed with playing fields, but we made our own. We often played on farm fields or any piece of open space we could find and even our official school home ground at Kirkford was a rather makeshift pitch, with a surface consisting of residue from the pit bing and sawdust to mark the touch-lines.

I was so fitba' daft that I often played twice on a Saturday, for the school team in the morning and for the Scouts' team in the afternoon. I was a member of the St Columba's team which won the West Fife Schools League Championship in 1958. Other members of that team were Willie Callaghan, who went on to play senior football for Dunfermline and Scotland and his brother, Tommy, who also started his senior career with Dunfermline before moving to Celtic. Jock Stein was the man who signed Tommy and he was also the man who revolutionised Dunfermline Athletic Football Club.

In the mid-1950s I played at Dunfermline's home ground, East End Park, in the final of the Elder Cup, which was a football competition for all the Scout Groups in Dunfermline District. At that time, the stand at East End Park was like a wooden cow shed, but when Jock Stein became manager he brought almost instant success, which generated additional revenue for a magnificent new stand.

I first saw Jock Stein playing for Celtic in the early 1950s against East Fife, who were in the top league at that time. My brother Raymond had taken me through to Bayview Park, Methil, for the game. Jock hardly broke sweat during the whole match. His reading of the game and his positional sense, as centre half, were so good that he seemed to stroll effortlessly through the game, but I was rather bemused when he sprinted for the changing room as soon as the ref blew the final whistle.

It was almost a decade later that I discovered why. I was playing at Bayview for Ballingry Rovers in a Cup final against a team called Novar Star. Ballingry must have drawn the short straw because we had the visitors' changing room. When I entered the changing room, I could hardly believe my eyes. There were no showers and the only bathing facility for the entire team was a small one-man bath about the same size as what you would see in a council house bathroom. I then realised why Stein had sprinted off the park at the final whistle. The big man, being an ex-miner, was making sure he would be first in the bath!

The Cowdenbeath Co-operative Gala was a great annual sporting event. We used to organise our own teams for the seven-a-side football competition and there was great rivalry between teams from different areas. The village of Hill o'Beath had a particularly good team and their star player was a skinny young genius called Jim Baxter, who later went on to play for Rangers and Scotland. The local folklore was that Slim Jim's career would have lasted much longer if he had not spent so much time in Kirkford Tavern, sometimes even on a Saturday morning before a big match.

In 1958, I was the Gala Sports Champion and also captained the team which won the seven-a-side football. But my fondest memory is of a dramatic final a few years earlier, when my brother Ian was the star of the show.

At that time, if both teams finished with an equal number of goals, they did not have penalty kick deciders. The rule was that the team with the most corners won the match. So corners were almost as precious as goals.

With about 90 seconds to go, we were drawing one–one when I rather rashly gave away the only corner of the match. Six heads immediately went down. We were just about in tears because we thought we'd blown it. But not Ian. He demanded the ball as soon as it was back in play and what followed was the most breathtaking bravura I have ever witnessed.

He must have run with the ball about three-quarters of the length of the park, which was an uphill struggle all the way, because Cowdenbeath public park had a gradient that looked almost as steep as the pit bing. Like a whippet sprung from its trap, Ian raced past every player in the opposition team before dribbling the ball round the goalkeeper and into the net. The referee blew the final whistle. It was all over. It was Ian's finest hour. A roar of applause erupted and even the ranks of Hill o'Beath could scarce forbear to cheer.

My interest in sport continued at university. Edinburgh University in the 1960s was renowned for its sporting prowess, with some students representing their country at the highest level in sports such as athletics, rugby and hockey.

Football was my favourite sport, but there was one freezing winter in the early '60s when the weather conditions were so severe that it was virtually impossible to play football for several weeks. I therefore took up cross-country running to keep myself fit and I was selected to represent the university, running in the colours of the Hares and Hounds, the university's cross-country team.

There was one occasion when we travelled to Dundee to take part in a cross-country relay event. We entered two teams, with eight runners in each team, and I was selected for the second team. One of the best long-distance runners in Scotland, Fergus Murray, was selected for the first team, but there was some doubt as to whether he would be able to make it as he was returning from the Tokyo Olympics, where he had competed in the 10,000 metres.

About 15 minutes before the start of the race, there was no sign of Fergus and the club captain told me that I was to be promoted to the first team in his place. Five minutes later, Fergus turned up in his running gear all ready to start, but the captain told him he was too late. I immediately offered to step down but the captain would have none of it. Fergus was too late and that was that. So, for the first and only time in my life, I actually displaced an Olympic athlete. Fergus was allowed to run in the race as a 'wild card' individual runner and he was streets ahead of us to such an extent that he ran the entire race himself and still beat all the relay teams!

I was not fit to lace Fergus' shoes but I continued to enjoy long-distance running even in later life. When I was in my 40s, I did the race from Fort William to the top of Ben Nevis and back in just over two hours. I have run about 15 marathons, most of them in London, although my personal best was on a dreich day in Glasgow in 1985, when I managed to finish in two hours and fifty-eight minutes. About the same time, Chris Brasher, an Olympic gold medallist, asked me to set up an all-party group of MPs to help him with some organisational problems relating to the London Marathon. Chris was co-founder of the London Marathon, and the Race Director. He was determined to make it the best event of its kind in the world, but he was encountering some difficulties with the various authorities along the route. For example, he had several different local authorities as well as four different police or quasi police forces to deal with: the Metropolitan Police, the City of London Police, the Royal Parks Police and the Yeoman of the Guard. At that time, there was no mayor of London to cut through all the bureaucracy and Chris Brasher was getting very frustrated. I therefore suggested that I lead an all-party delegation of MPs to see the appropriate ministers. Chris came with us and put forward a well-argued case. The ministers were convinced and the London Marathon became a successful event of huge international status. As a reward for our efforts, Chris Brasher promised the MPs on the all-party marathon group that we would have a guaranteed entry to the London Marathon for as long as the event lasted, or for as long as our legs could make it.

Some MPs used to compete regularly, including Dick Douglas, Dougie Henderson, Matthew Parris and myself. Jeffrey Archer showed some interest in our all-party marathon group but I do not recall him actually competing. Jonathan Aitken took part a couple of times and, on one occasion, the media requested a photo opportunity a few days before the race. Jonathan very kindly suggested that we could change into our running gear at his flat.

I thought that Jonathan was genuinely interested in sport, because we had played together in the House of Commons Football team which had beaten Germany in an inter-parliamentary contest. At that time, Margaret Thatcher's daughter, Carol, had her eye on Jonathan and she came along to the match to cheer him on. Margaret was said to have been very angry when Jonathan ditched Carol and maybe that was the reason why she would not have him in her ministerial team. However, he seemed a useful member of our marathon team.

Jonathan, who is an Old Etonian and a grand-nephew of Lord Beaverbrook, had a very luxurious pad in Lord North Street, just a few minutes' walk from the Palace of Westminster. When I rang the doorbell I was greeted by a butler, who told me that the master would be with me shortly. While I was waiting in the drawing room, the butler brought me some freshly crushed orange juice in a crystal glass on a silver tray. Apart from Jonathan and me, nobody else turned up for the photo-call but Jonathan had good media contacts and we received excellent coverage, with several of the national newspapers carrying pictures of us posing together and running around nearby College Green.

A few years later, Jonathan Aitken again hit the headlines in different circumstances. John Major made him a cabinet minister, but it did not last long. Aitken was jailed for perjury and declared bankrupt after an infamous court case against the *Guardian* which had exposed his involvement in an arms deal scam.

There were also some memorable social events to promote the London Marathon, including press conferences and receptions. On one of those occasions, we were on a boat on the Thames when I overhead a famous former marathon runner called Jim Alder regaling some journalists and politicians with tales of some of the great English marathon runners of yesteryear, especially himself. When the name Jim Peters cropped up, I asked Jim Alder if he had ever come across a Scotsman called Joe McGhee. Alder replied to the effect that Joe McGhee was just a plodder and not in the same league as Jim Peters and himself.

When I reminded him that Joe McGhee had beaten Peters to win gold in the 1954 Empire and Commonwealth Games, Alder claimed that it was a fluke. By this time I was so enraged that I retorted: 'Your man fell flat on his face but wee Joe finished the course and won the gold.' That was rather unkind to Jim Peters, but I felt I had to puncture Jim Alder's pomposity and defend Joe McGhee's honour.

Although I did not share Joe's athletic prowess, we had some things in common. We were both Scots, we had both taught at St Modan's High School, Stirling, and we had both run for Falkirk Victoria Harriers, although not at the same time. Joe was also the big hero of one of my greatest sporting memories.

It was the day before my twelfth birthday. I was on holiday at St Andrews in August 1954 when the Commonwealth (and Empire!) Games were taking place in Vancouver. We had no TV and were very dependent on radio and the press for news of what was happening, but the events of that day are still etched in my memory as if I had been there.

Roger Bannister had just won gold for England in the mile. The cheering for his victory had hardly died down when Jim Peters of England staggered into the stadium on the last stage of the marathon. He was on his last legs but still well in front with only a lap of the stadium to go. There was a sudden lull in the applause when Peters collapsed. For a full two minutes, he lay still and, although police and medics gathered around him, they knew that physically assisting him would mean his disqualification.

Peters managed to rise unsteadily to his feet, tried to carry on, but almost immediately his legs gave way. Yet again he struggled to his feet, but he reeled from side to side of the track and went down again. Fifteen minutes after he had entered the stadium, he had covered only 150 yards. At last he crossed what he thought was the finishing line and was carried exhausted from the track. He did not realise that he still had 200 yards to go. The line he had crossed was the finishing line for the mile event. Jim Peters was down and out.

Shortly afterwards, a little known Scot called Joe McGhee ran into the stadium. He held off a strong challenge from two South Africans to win the marathon in two hours thirty-nine minutes and thirty-six seconds. Not the fastest marathon in the world, but surely one of the most dramatic in the history of the event.

McGhee never got the credit that he deserved. Like now, many of the sports commentators were biased towards England. Peters was acclaimed as a national hero and there were even demands for the Queen to strike a special medal in his honour.

Joe McGhee scarcely rated a mention despite the fact that he won the race. On the day, he judged the hot, humid conditions better than anyone else. He paced himself accordingly and he finished the course. It was a gold for Scotland. What a day to remember, and I took great delight in reminding Jim Alder about it 30 years later.

Some of my happiest sporting memories are of playing football for Edinburgh University and Spartans in the East of Scotland League. Spartans are now a very well-organised outfit who regularly qualify to play in the Scottish Cup and are strong candidates for admission to the Scottish Football League, but the Spartan experience of the 1960s was rather different. Sometimes we were struggling to get a full team to turn up on a Saturday afternoon and, when we managed that, the next struggle was finding a full set of jerseys of the same colour. Although we played senior football, it was professionalism in reverse. Instead of being paid to play, we paid to play and, like Edinburgh University, we were very proud of our amateur status.

I was the only member of the university team who made any money out of playing and that was because my financial circumstances forced me to volunteer to provide the team laundry service. I would collect a shilling from each of the players for washing the jerseys, which I did myself at a coin-operated launderette. The washing machine and the drying machine took half-a-crown each, leaving me with a profit of six shillings per week. The players considered that to be good value because I saved them the bother of washing their own jerseys.

Amateur football can be very enjoyable, but also unpredictable. I shall never forget the occasion when Edinburgh University was drawn away from home against a team called Dedridge in the Scottish Amateur Cup. We fancied our chances not just of beating Dedridge, but of possibly going on to Cup final glory at Hampden. Although we were amateurs, we played senior football in the East of Scotland League. Hibs and Hearts had reserve teams in that League and there were other clubs with professional or semi-professional players. Earlier that year, Edinburgh University had beaten an Oxford–Cambridge Select and about half of the Edinburgh players, including myself, were members of the Scotland team which won the British Universities championship.

We had never heard of Dedridge and our bus driver had to do a tour of West Lothian to find the place. When we eventually got there, we discovered that there was no changing accommodation or showers and so we had to change on the team bus, which turned out to be a blessing in disguise. The surface of the pitch consisted of a black ashy substance, probably a by-product of the local mining industry. I was not too fazed by that because I had played on a similar surface at Kirkford, in Cowdenbeath, but most of my pampered university colleagues had never seen anything like it.

The surface was probably worth at least two goals of a start to Dedridge and the home supporters were worth another two. The whole village must have turned up for the match and the spectators stood on the touchline to roar their team on with a ferocity which was intimidating. The referee may have started the match as a neutral but, after about ten minutes, his instinct for self-preservation took over. For the rest of the match, the ref was a homer and we knew that we had a battle on our hands, 11 men against 12.

About halfway through the second half, one of the Dedridge players was sprinting up the wing towards our goal and I rushed over to slide-tackle him. I thought it was a perfectly legitimate challenge, but there was a collision and both of us ended up in a tangled heap on the other side of the touchline. What happened next was a nightmare. A crowd of angry spectators gathered round us and a woman started hitting me repeatedly with her umbrella. But it was the expletives hurled from her mouth which were unforgettable.

'Ya poof!' she snarled. 'Yir nuthin but a fuckin dirty English poof!' I was disinclined to get into an argument with her about my ethnicity or sexuality, but the incident gave me a stunning insight into a proletarian perception of university students in the 1960s.

The match almost ended in a riot and, as soon as the ref blew the final whistle, the students sprinted to the team bus and escaped back to Edinburgh with our dreams of Hampden glory shattered yet again.

However, we went on to win the Queens Park Shield, which was awarded to the Scottish universities' champions. There were only seven universities in the competition at that time: Aberdeen, Glasgow, Strathclyde, Edinburgh, Heriot-Watt, St Andrews and Dundee. We played each other twice, home and away, and the League winners received the Queens Park Shield, a massive and magnificent trophy donated by Queens Park Football Club. Our final match of the season was an away game against Glasgow and we had to win it to get the coveted shield. It was always a tough match between the Weegies and the Edinbuggers but, on that occasion, we came out on top and afterwards we went to Glasgow University Union to celebrate our success.

The celebrations continued until the beer bar closed at 10 p.m., but we were informed that there was a late bar at a social function organised by Glasgow University Rugby Club. The social function was upstairs in the debating chamber but, when we enquired about admission tickets, we got a blunt refusal.

We were very incensed about this poor sportsmanship and lack of hospitality on the part of the Glasgow students and we devised a plan to rush the door. We faced an uphill struggle because the bouncers were all hefty rugby players, standing at the top of the stairs with massive superiority in terms of height and weight. Nevertheless, we were all fired up with our earlier conquest and we decided to pursue our plan.

The result was an absolute stramash. Although some of us were successful in gaining entry, others were pushed down the stairs in what looked like a lopsided rugby scrum. Then the unforgiveable happened. One of the Glasgow University Union officials called the police. This was almost unheard of. The university unions in those days were like gentlemen's clubs and there were reciprocal membership rights for visiting students from other universities. There was an unwritten rule that the police were never invited onto the union premises unless, of course, there was a grave risk of someone being killed or badly injured.

Calling the police simply confirmed our view that Glasgow University Union officials were behaving in a very unsportsmanlike manner. Half of the victorious Edinburgh University football team were locked up in the police cells overnight and appeared at Glasgow Sheriff Court in the morning. I was fortunate enough to escape on that occasion, but the accused were found guilty of breach of the peace and fined.

I do not know which Glasgow University Union official had called the police, but the president of the union at that time was Menzies Campbell, captain of the UK Olympic team, who later became MP for North-East Fife and leader of the Liberal Democrats. Many years afterwards, I told Ming about that event at Glasgow University Union. A strange look came over his face, but he never admitted to any personal involvement.

The Queens Park Shield was not the only national trophy that almost got me into trouble. In 1987, I invited my good friend Alex Smith to do the official opening of my constituency office in Denny. Alex hailed from Cowie, a Stirlingshire mining village, and, after a successful career as a professional footballer, he took up football management. He was one of the longest-serving football managers in the history of Scottish football, with spells at Stenhousemuir, Stirling Albion, St Mirren, Aberdeen, Dundee United, Ross County and Clyde. He was also involved in coaching the Scottish youth international squad before joining Falkirk FC's management team.

When he came to open my office, Alex had just led St Mirren to a famous Scottish Cup Final victory against Dundee United and I asked him to bring the Scottish Cup with him. Alex was happy to oblige and he arrived at my office with the Scottish Cup bedecked in St Mirren colours. Unfortunately, Alex had to leave shortly after giving his speech, because he wanted to take in a football match to check out some potential new signing. When I asked him about the Cup, he said that he would leave it in my good hands.

As the night went on, the Cup was filled with every conceivable kind of liquor and many of the guests had their photographs taken consuming a dram or whatever. It must have been after midnight when the transport arrived to take us home and I can remember trying to din into my befuddled brain that it was my personal responsibility to ensure that the Scottish Cup was put in a safe place because Alex had entrusted it to me.

Unfortunately, on the morning after the night before, I could not remember where the safe place was. I hunted all over the house, but could not find it. I then phoned around some of the people who had attended the opening ceremony and subsequent party. Still no luck.

By this time, I was beginning to panic. In terms of silverware, the value of the Scottish Cup is probably not huge, but it is the oldest national trophy of its type in the world. It is literally priceless and all I could imagine was the apoplectic expression on the face of Jim Farry, Chief Executive of the SFA.

'What do you mean, Dennis, you've lost the Scottish Cup?'

There would be a national if not an international outcry with banner headlines:

'Idiotic MP loses Scottish Cup after office orgy.'

'My Cup's full and running over, but where is it?'

After countless more fruitless phone calls, I decided to search the house again. I even looked in the attic, the garage and the tumble-drier before a final frantic phone call revealed that the Crown Jewels of Scottish football were hidden under my brother's bed. I had given the Cup to Raymond for safe-keeping because I would trust my big brother with my very life. He had taken it home with him and decided to keep it close by him all through the night. I heaved a huge sigh of relief when it was safely returned to Alex Smith. If only Jim Farry knew!

Jim Farry was perceived by many to be some kind of fascist dictator who ruled Scottish football with an iron fist. Facially he reminded me of the old Spanish postage stamps with General Franco's image. But I always found him to be a reasonable man in the days when I would meet him regularly in my post as Convener of the All Party Scottish Sports Group in the House of Commons. When Hampden Park was in a state of terminal decline, Jim and his SFA colleagues were lobbying MPs to get public funding for the construction of a new national stadium at Hampden. I was very supportive of the Hampden project but my enthusiasm was not shared by all my parliamentary colleagues, some of whom thought there were other suitable venues for international matches.

When one of the MPs suggested that Scotland should play at Ibrox, Jim Farry, to his credit, replied that there was no way that Scotland would ever play at Ibrox as long as Rangers continued their sectarian employment policy.

Jim's comment at that meeting reminded me of another meeting I had attended, shortly after I was first elected to parliament in 1974. Maurice Miller, Labour MP for East Kilbride, told me that John Lawrence wanted to see me. John Lawrence was a millionaire who owned one of the biggest building companies in Scotland and he was also chairman of Rangers Football Club. I wondered why Maurice was being used as a conduit to set up such a meeting and I assumed that he was on some kind of a retainer to act as an adviser to John Lawrence's building company. As there was no Register of Members' Interests at that time, there was no way of officially checking this, but I had heard that many MPs on both sides of the House were on the payroll of various companies as non-executive directors or advisers. As I did not approve of such links, I was hesitant about accepting the invitation but Maurice explained that Lawrence was a constituent of mine and the purpose of the meeting was to brief me on a proposed housing development which Lawrence's building company was planning in the Strathblane area of my constituency.

As I have always been prepared to meet constituents, I agreed to the request. Maurice suggested meeting over lunch at Lawrence's Strathblane Country Club, but I did not want to lay myself open to accusations of being wined and dined by a millionaire on his home turf. I therefore suggested a more modest neutral venue at the King Robert Hotel, Bannockburn. The meeting was attended by John Lawrence, one of his company directors and Maurice Miller.

My first impression of John Lawrence was that he was an amiable old gentleman and, after exchanging pleasantries over lunch, he outlined his proposed development at Strathblane. I thanked him for explaining his proposal to me, but reminded him that it would be Stirling District Council that would decide on the planning application, and that I was no longer a member of the council. Nevertheless, I was grateful to him for briefing me on an important development in my constituency.

After the lunch, the conversation turned to other things. Maurice had probably told John Lawrence of my interest in football and it was not surprising that Rangers Football Club cropped up in our discussion. At that time, Rangers had a practice of not signing any Catholic players and I decided to take the opportunity of politely questioning the chairman about his club's sectarian employment policy. John Lawrence said to me: 'Mr Canavan, it is not true that Rangers do not employ Roman Catholics. We employ a Catholic woman as a cleaner at Ibrox Stadium and I can assure you that she is the best cleaner that we have ever had.'

It was on the tip of my tongue to say: 'Is that all we're good for?' but I saw Lawrence's company director wince in embarrassment at his chairman's remarks and Maurice Miller quickly switched the conversation to another topic.

The saddest aspect of this story is that John Lawrence, one of the most powerful people in Scottish business and Scottish football, did not even realise that he had said anything which might cause offence. It would take another 15 years before Rangers eventually signed a high-profile Catholic. Graeme Souness broke the mould (and a few Celtic hearts) in 1989 when he signed Mo Johnston, and since then Rangers have had many Catholic players. That is progress but the problem is still with us. Football is not the root cause of sectarianism, but unfortunately football often acts as a focus for the bigots.

Getting agreement on what constitutes sectarian conduct can sometimes be difficult. In general, people should be perfectly entitled to express love of their religious or cultural heritage as long as they do not express hatred of other people's religious or cultural heritage. However, when it comes down to particular incidents, there is not always universal agreement. Overseas visitors have been known to shake their heads in disbelief on being told that, in twenty-first-century Scotland, a footballer making the sign of the cross was accused by opposing fans of inflammatory behaviour. The Scotsman newspaper even published a photograph of the 'offensive' gesture on the front page of its sport section. When I asked the Crown Office for clarification, Elish Angiolini, the Solicitor General, made it absolutely clear that making the sign of the cross is not a criminal offence, but why should such clarification be required?

If a teenage footballer in England with, say, Jamaican grandparents was subjected to verbal abuse for choosing to play for his ancestral homeland rather than for England, the media would rightly condemn such verbal abuse as racist.

Try reading the above sentence again, replacing England with Scotland and Jamaican with Irish. Now think of Aiden McGeady and ask yourself: *Are racism and sectarianism alive and kicking in Scotland today?*

When I had the above letter published in the *Herald* newspaper, my office was inundated with letters and emails trying to justify the verbal abuse which young McGeady suffered when he announced that he wanted to pursue his international career with Ireland rather than Scotland. Personally I would have preferred McGeady to play for Scotland, but the bigots could not respect his choice and some of the media pundits and callers to BBC radio phone-in programmes claimed that the verbal abuse was 'fair dos'.

More recently, I have heard the same people trying to justify the singing of a chant: 'The famine is over. Why don't you go home?' The famine referred to in the chant is the Irish famine of the 1840s in which a million people died. No decent Rangers supporter should sing that song and no decent Celtic supporter should glorify IRA terrorism or sing: 'Go home, ya Huns, go home'. For many people, the term 'Hun' is synonymous with 'Nazi', and some of the so-called 'Hun supporters' are the children and grandchildren of people who gave their lives fighting against the Nazis.

It is dangerous nonsense to try to dismiss such offensive chanting as mere banter. People have been killed in Scotland just because they happened to be wearing the 'wrong' football colours and, if we are serious about stopping it, we must stop using the language of hate.

I made that point very forcibly when, as Convener of the Cross-party Sports Group in the Scottish Parliament, I organised and chaired a meeting at Holyrood to discuss a campaign to kick racism and sectarianism out of football. The Chief Executives of Rangers and Celtic were present and I got the impression that both clubs were intent on making serious efforts to solve the problem. However, we still have a long way to go and too many people in Scottish football turned a blind eye to the problem until UEFA started taking action against clubs for the misconduct of their supporters.

Despite all the problems, it would be wrong to tar all Old Firm supporters with the same brush. I can count both Rangers and Celtic fans amongst my most fervent supporters over the years. My late son, Paul, was a passionate Celtic fan. He used to drag me along to see his beloved 'Hoops' before he was old enough to go on his own, but I found the atmosphere at Old Firm games intolerable. The last Old Firm match I attended was over 20 years ago at Ibrox, when Frank McAvennie, Chris Woods and Terry Butcher were all sent off and Woods and Butcher subsequently got criminal convictions for behaviour likely to cause a breach of the peace.

I now prefer the more peaceful atmosphere of Falkirk Stadium, but that reminds me of another story about the skulduggery of the Scottish football authorities.

In 2003, Falkirk won the Scottish Football League First Division Championship, but were denied promotion to the Scottish Premier League (SPL). I therefore lodged a motion of protest which became the subject of a parliamentary debate.

The SPL at that time insisted that any member club must have a stadium with a capacity to seat at least 10,000 spectators, despite the fact that the attendance at many games was less than half that figure. Falkirk was still using Brockville Park, which did not meet the SPL criteria, but plans were underway to build a new stadium and, as an interim measure, the club had an agreement to share Airdrie's Excelsior Stadium with Airdrie United. Some of the member clubs in the SPL, however, especially those facing the possibility of relegation, had a vested interest in keeping Falkirk out.

During the course of the parliamentary debate, I accused the SPL of bringing Scottish football into disrepute by operating a cartel and ignoring the basic principle of fair competition whereby promotion should be decided on merit.

I also referred to an element of double standards, in that Celtic had been allowed to share Hampden with Queens Park for a season while Celtic Park was being reconstructed, but now Falkirk were being denied an opportunity to ground-share.

Perhaps the political pressure and bad publicity eventually helped to persuade the SPL to relax the criteria by dropping the minimum stadium capacity to 6,000 and allowing clubs to ground-share. It was too late to help Falkirk, but Inverness Caley Thistle was the first club to benefit when they won the First Division championship the following season. The SPL admitted Inverness and allowed the club to ground-share with Aberdeen until the stadium at Inverness met the SPL criteria.

Falkirk had to wait until 2005 before winning promotion to the SPL, and the club now plays at the new Falkirk Stadium. I was very supportive of the new stadium project and I could not understand why some Labour councillors were opposed to it. I foresaw it as being not just a home for Falkirk Football Club but also an asset for the wider community. I now enjoy watching top-grade football at the stadium and I also enjoy watching my son Adam and other youngsters at the coaching sessions organised by 'Falkirk in the Community' at the training ground adjacent to the stadium.

Some of those youngsters may turn out to be the stars of the future but, more importantly, all of them enjoy the experience, and that's what sport is all about.

CHAPTER EIGHT

Starting off in politics and ending up in jail

In some respects, I feel that I was virtually born and brought up in the Labour Party, but I did not become really active in Labour politics until the 1960s, when I was a member of the Executive Committee of Edinburgh Central Constituency Labour Party. Because of my interest and experience in education, I was invited by Edinburgh City Labour Party to join a working group with responsibility for drawing up a policy for the introduction of comprehensive education into the city's secondary school system.

In the early 1960s, Edinburgh had the most divisive and elitist educational system in Scotland. About one in five secondary pupils attended private fee-paying schools and even some of the state schools, such as the Royal High School, charged fees. Within the local education authority sector, a system of selection operated and, in some cases, the selection began at the age of five!

I remember arguing vociferously against such nonsense in the staff-room of a selective school in Edinburgh which had a primary as well as a secondary department. The Principal Teacher of Physics strongly defended the selective system on the grounds that any infants mistress worth her salt could pick out the bright children at the age of five by asking them a few simple questions. When I asked him for an example of such 'simple questions', he said: 'What colour is the box where Mummy posts the letters?' When I suggested that a child suffering from colour-blindness might give the wrong answer, but nevertheless have the potential to be a rocket scientist, my physicist friend remained unconvinced. So much talent must have been rejected at the age of five and the fortunate few who passed that entry test were virtually guaranteed a place in the secondary department of the school, whereas other applicants had to undergo another selection system at the age of eleven. The majority of pupils in the state sector were deemed to have failed the selection system. They attended junior secondary schools and left at the age of 15 with no formal educational qualifications.

Harold Wilson's Labour Government was determined to replace such an unfair, divisive system with a system that would guarantee equality of educational opportunity for all children. However, the Tory councillors in Edinburgh strongly resisted such a change, which some of them denounced as pure Marxism. It was rather ironic that the Tory councillors described themselves on the ballot paper as 'Progressive' because, in terms of educational philosophy, they were Neanderthal. However, they managed to cling on to power at the City Chambers, sometimes through a remarkable combination of political guile and populism. They even managed to cash in on Celtic Football Club's historic European Cup Victory in 1967 by persuading the Celtic goalkeeper, Ronnie Simpson, to stand as a 'Progressive' candidate at the council elections.

The Labour Party in Edinburgh seemed doomed to eternal opposition but, in the 1960s, there was a belief amongst young party activists, including myself, that the tide would turn and that the Labour Party's policy on education would be the key to success. Other party activists of that era included Robin Cook (who later became Foreign Secretary), George Foulkes (now Lord Foulkes), Bob Cuddihy (who became a presenter for Scottish Television), Dr Henry Drucker (then a young lecturer in politics at Edinburgh University) and Archy Kirkwood. I remember Archy claiming that Harold Wilson lost the 1970 general election because the Labour Government was not left wing enough. Archy later moved right to join the Liberal Party and now sits in the House of Lords as Baron Kirkwood of Kirkhope!

George Foulkes, Bob Cuddihy and I were members of the working group on education along with Councillor Charlie Stuart, who later became the first Labour Education Convener on Edinburgh Corporation. It was our job to produce detailed policy papers to ensure the introduction of comprehensive education when Labour won power.

Although we were unanimous on the abolition of fee-paying and selection, we were not always agreed on the detail of the replacement system. George Foulkes favoured neighbourhood comprehensive schools, whereby all the children in a particular area would attend the same school, with no parental choice. I argued strongly that a successful comprehensive school would require a comprehensive intake of pupils with a reasonable mix of different abilities and socio-economic backgrounds. A neighbourhood comprehensive would only succeed in a comprehensive neighbourhood. Such neighbourhoods existed in many of the smaller towns in Scotland, but unfortunately, in an urban area like Edinburgh, there were many deprived neighbourhoods which did not have a comprehensive mix.

I therefore proposed that, wherever possible, the catchment area of any particular school should consist of a mix of different neighbourhoods and that there should be an element of parental choice, taking into account curricular specialisation as well as religious and philosophical convictions. My proposal was not popular with Labour colleagues at the time and some of them were rather miffed when I had one of my papers on the subject published in the *Times Educational Supplement*. It took another few decades before the Labour Party eventually had to face up to the reality that the wishes of parents had to be considered in the vital matter of their children's education.

Despite disagreements on some matters of detail, the plans eventually produced by Edinburgh City Labour Party's education working group led to revolutionary changes in the city's education system. In the early 1970s, Labour won control of the Corporation and Jack Kane became Lord Provost, the only Labour councillor to hold that position in the history of the old Edinburgh Corporation. Under Jack Kane's radical leadership, the council enthusiastically embraced comprehensive reform and George Foulkes continued that work when he became Convener of Education for Lothian, following regionalisation in 1974. As I had predicted, some of the neighbourhood comprehensives unfortunately turned out to be so-called 'sink schools' but, for the most part, generations of Edinburgh's children have experienced a huge improvement in educational opportunity as a result of the efforts of Labour's working group in the 1960s.

Bringing about political change in Edinburgh's City Chambers was not an easy matter. The Tories, or 'Progressives', had had a grip on power for years and, following Winnie Ewing's triumph at the Hamilton by-election in 1967, the SNP began to make inroads into Labour's heartlands throughout Scotland. As a result, there were fierce political contests, some of them involving sitting Labour councillors with previously safe seats who suddenly found themselves under serious threat for the first time in their political lives.

Baillie James McInally was the Labour councillor for the St Giles ward. Jimmy came from sound working-class stock but he had a guid conceit o' himsel' and he loved the baillie's street-lamp attached to the outside wall of his tenement house in Fountainbridge. He also loved sitting on the magistrate's bench, dispensing his version of justice to the various unfortunates and miscreants who appeared before him. I sometimes thought that Jimmy would relish the return of capital punishment because it might give him the power of life and death over his fellow citizens.

During one of his campaigns for re-election, it became obvious that Jimmy was in trouble and we realised that we had to pull out all the stops to keep his seat for Labour. I took a transit van along to the lodging houses in the Grassmarket area and ran a shuttle service to the polling station. The Grassmarket in the 1960s was a poverty-stricken dump, populated largely by down-and-outs and alcoholics. Some of them were 'here today and gone tomorrow' but, when I checked the voters' roll, I discovered that there were several hundred on the register with addresses in the various lodging houses, some of which had grandiose names like the Castle Trades Hotel.

When I ventured into the common lounge of the Castle Trades, it was like entering a den of iniquity. The atmosphere reeked of alcohol, body odour and stale tobacco and I found the rough, unwashed inhabitants rather unnerving at first sight. However, I had the advantage of being the only person in the place who was stone cold sober. I stood up in front of them and gave a brief speech about the importance of voting Labour in the election. I then proceeded to read out the names from the voters' roll like a teacher checking pupils' attendance at school. I asked all those present to line up. When I had enough 'volunteers' to fill the transit van, I took them to the polling station at Tollcross School, where the candidate, Baillie James McInally, was standing at the school gate wearing a red rosette.

The good baillie was initially delighted when he saw the van-load of voters whom I had enlisted for the cause but, when I told him where they had come from, he promptly disappeared. He afterwards explained that many of them had no doubt been arraigned before him in the court on the morning after the night before and, if they recognised him, they would probably lynch him rather than vote for him.

But not all the Edinburgh baillies were of the same mould as James McInally, as my brother Ian and I were to find out later.

I still miss Ian a lot. He died in 2006, a few days after reaching his sixty-sixth birthday. He had cancer of the pancreas, which caused him great pain, but Ian dealt very courageously with his final illness, especially considering he had had to cope with another illness throughout his life.

In his early 20s, Ian was diagnosed as suffering from schizophrenia, but he had probably suffered from it for years before it was diagnosed. God alone knows the mental turmoil he experienced and the resultant anguish for our parents. Ian's aggressive and anti-social behaviour made Mum and Dad terrified at times and, after Dad died in 1974, Mum continued looking after Ian like a child until she was in her 80s. It is very easy to feel sorry for someone who is physically ill, but sometimes it is much more difficult in the case of someone who is mentally ill. There is still a stigma and a lot of misunderstanding about mental illness and, for some people, it is the great unmentionable. My mother was frequently reduced to tears in her efforts to understand and help Ian, and at times she did not know where to turn for help. As for Ian, he must have thought he was being shunted from pillar to post. General practitioners, psychiatrists, nurses, therapists, social workers, clinics, hospitals, police, court, prison. Poor Ian experienced the lot. They put him on medication for most of his life and, as he got older, he seemed to calm down a bit, but there was no cure. Sometimes he would appear to be fairly normal, but you never knew when he would take a bad turn.

I shall never forget one Saturday night in the late 1960s when Ian paid me a visit. I was staying in Edinburgh at the time and we went out to Robertson's pub in Rose Street. Closing time then was 10 o'clock but, in Ian's local in Cowdenbeath, it was a fairly flexible 10 o'clock and it was not unusual for the bar staff to be still pouring pints at half past ten or beyond.

In Rose Street, however, it was a different story. They rang a bell at ten minutes to ten and shouted: 'Last orders!' They then rang another bell at 10 o'clock and shouted: 'Time up!' Exactly ten minutes later, they opened the doors, lifted the glasses and threw the punters out onto the street.

On that particular evening, when the second bell rang, Ian asked me if I would like one for the road. I tried to explain to him that it was too late, but he would not listen and he headed for the bar. I shrugged my shoulders and went to the toilet.

When I returned, I noticed a kerfuffle at the far end of the bar and, when I went to investigate, I saw a huge barman sitting on Ian and another one seemed about to kick his head in. I went to the rescue, but the next thing I remember was Ian and me being huckled out the door by two burly policemen. They frog-marched us along the street into a Tardis-style police box and locked the door after them. I thought at first that they were going to beat us up, but that fear soon gave way to a greater one of extreme claustrophobia. Imagine being locked in a windowless phone box with three other people and you do not know when you are going to get out. It was a great feeling of relief when we heard the siren of an approaching police vehicle. We were bundled into the back of a Black Maria and taken to a cell at Parliament Square, just off the Royal Mile.

'Cell' is too kind a description of the accommodation. It was more like a medieval dungeon. The 'furniture' consisted of a wooden bunker on the stone floor which was presumably where we were supposed to sleep. There was not even a blanket and there was a stench of urine permeating the entire place. In that atmosphere it was virtually impossible to sleep and all we could do was wait patiently until the morning.

About 7 a.m., there was a knock on the cell door and the police gave us a meagre breakfast of bread and tea. They then threw the book at us by charging us with assaulting the bar staff, assaulting the police, resisting arrest and breach of the peace. I could not believe it, but I was reluctant to argue with them there and then in case they added more allegations to the charge sheet.

About 9 a.m. on Sunday we were told that we would appear in court on the Monday morning, but that we could be released on bail of £10 each. The police had emptied the contents of our pockets before locking us up and, when all the money was counted, it was not even enough to release one of us on bail. When told that we could make one phone call, I phoned Elnor, my wife, to explain our predicament. She did not have enough money to secure our release, but I persuaded her to visit a relative to borrow the required sum. As a result, we were left waiting for several hours with the thought of another night in the dungeon looming over us. Eventually, about mid-afternoon, Elnor arrived with the bail money and the police let us go. When we walked out onto the cobblestones of Parliament Square, I felt a huge sense of freedom, but I suspected worse was to follow.

I got in touch with a former university friend, John (Banjo) Rodgers, who was a practising solicitor in Edinburgh. When the case was called in court on the Monday morning, Banjo appeared on behalf of Ian and me and tendered a plea of not guilty to all the charges. A date was then set for a further hearing and this gave Banjo the opportunity of studying the statements made by the police and the bar staff at Robertson's. The evidence for the prosecution was pretty damning and, of course, in the case of any bar-room brawl, the court was more likely to believe the evidence of the bar staff and the police. In my discussions with Banjo, I insisted that I was completely innocent and that Ian appeared to be the victim rather than the perpetrator of an assault. I also explained Ian's mental health problem. Nevertheless, the tactical advice we received was to try to get the charges reduced and to consider pleading guilty to a lesser charge.

Banjo was pretty successful with his efforts at plea bargaining. The procurator fiscal agreed to drop all the assault charges and the charge of resisting arrest, provided we both pled guilty to the lesser charge of breach of the peace. After a great deal of deliberation and with considerable reluctance, Ian and I agreed to the recommended course of action and Banjo agreed to put in a plea of mitigation. Our best hope was to get off with a fine, the exact amount depending on which magistrate was on the bench.

As I was teaching on the day of the second court hearing, I did not want to ask for a day off in case I lost my job. I did not think it would be a good idea for Ian to attend court on his own and so Banjo agreed to appear on our behalf, but explained that the court did have the power to order the accused to appear personally at a later date. As soon as I got home from school I phoned Banjo, who told me that he was absolutely flabbergasted when the magistrate announced that he would let us off with an admonition. I could not believe our good luck and I asked who was the magistrate responsible for dispensing justice with such mercy. When Banjo told me it was Owen Hand, the penny dropped. Owen was a Labour councillor on the old Edinburgh Corporation. The ward he represented was Holyrood, which was part of Edinburgh Central Constituency, and I was a member of the Constituency Labour Party Executive. In fact, Owen was election agent for Tom Oswald MP and I was a member of his campaign team. When Owen next set eyes on me, I blushed ashamedly and apologised profusely. He ticked me off, asked kindly about my brother and told us to be more careful in future.

To this day, I consider myself to have been very fortunate. If Owen Hand had been New Labour, he would probably have jailed me and had me expelled for bringing the party into disrepute!

Years afterwards, I was told, as a potential Labour candidate, that I should inform the party hierarchy of any skeletons in my cupboard, but I do not regret keeping stumm about my criminal record. The Labour Party's dirty tricks department would no doubt have used it as ammunition in their efforts to discredit me.

———— ◆ ————

CHAPTER NINE

Labour's choice

There were two general elections in 1974. The first was held in February during a nationwide miners' strike. At that time, the UK economy was very dependent on coal and when the miners went on strike there was an energy crisis, with frequent power cuts. The Tory prime minister, Ted Heath, responded by declaring a three-day working week, supposedly to save energy, but the result was a fiasco. The nation was plunged into darkness and, to compound his error, Heath decided to call a general election on the question: 'Who governs Britain? The government or the miners?'

I was residing in Bannockburn, having taken up a post as head of the Mathematics department at St Modan's High School, Stirling, in 1970. I was the secretary of West Stirlingshire Constituency Labour Party and also election agent for Willie Baxter, the Labour MP for West Stirlingshire.

The general election resulted in a hung parliament, with no party having an overall majority of seats in the House of Commons. However, Labour won the biggest number of seats and, in that sense, we thought we had won and that the Queen would call Harold Wilson, leader of the Labour Party, to form a government. Initially, however, the Queen did no such thing. She gave Ted Heath the opportunity to cobble together some kind of coalition deal with Jeremy Thorpe, leader of the Liberal Party. As a result, there was a delay of several days when Harold Wilson had to wait in the wings and many Labour Party members and supporters feared that we had been robbed of victory.

During this hiatus, the bold William Baxter, newly re-elected Labour MP for West Stirlingshire, suddenly appeared on TV. This came as a great surprise to most of us in the local party because Willie did not exactly have a very high media profile. Indeed, he was often conspicuous by his silence as well as his absence.

During the course of the TV interview, Willie pompously opined that the crisis facing the country was so grave that no single party should take the reins of government and that the country should be governed by a council of state consisting of representatives of all the major parties. When asked by the interviewer who should chair such a council of state, Willie replied: 'Somebody neutral, like Prince Philip.'

That was Willie's political deathknell.

Immediately all hell was let loose. As secretary of the Constituency Labour Party, I was inundated with calls for Baxter's resignation. On Sunday, walking home from church with my four young children, I was accosted by Lawrence Ritchie, an old retired miner.

'Are you Canavan?'

'Aye.'

'Are you the Labour election agent?'

'Aye.'

'I've voted Labour a' ma life and noo yer man Baxter is telling us that we should be ruled by Philip the Greek. What are ye gaun tae dae aboot that, then?'

I mumbled something about a fat chance of Philip the Duke being the next prime minister but my ex-miner comrade was not impressed.

That altercation was indicative of a public mood which led to a chain of events culminating in William Baxter eventually announcing that he would not stand for re-election to parliament.

Baxter had been MP for the constituency for 15 years. He was a millionaire with big business interests, including construction and farming. He was also into land speculation, and many traditional Labour voters were shocked when a tabloid newspaper published a story that Baxter had made a huge profit out of buying land at agricultural prices then selling to Cumbernauld Development Corporation at an inflated price. There was a suggestion of inside knowledge about what land the Corporation would require for development.

Willie Baxter had convinced a fair number of local party members, especially Labour councillors, that West Stirlingshire was a Tory–Labour marginal and that he managed to win it because, with his entrepreneurial and agricultural experience, he appealed to both the business and farming communities. The perceived wisdom was that a left-wing candidate would simply alienate such voters and lose the seat. Willie also had some of the Labour councillors literally on his pay-roll, including the chairman of the Constituency Labour Party, ex-provost Pat McCann of Kilsyth, who was employed as a safety officer by Baxter's building firm. Pat's loyalty to his master was unquestionable, but the same could not be said about his loyalty to the party. When I was nominated to succeed Baxter, McCann told a fellow councillor: 'Canavan might become the Labour candidate but I'll make sure that he never rests his arse in parliament.' As I would soon find out, McCann did his level best to ensure the fulfilment of his own prophecy.

Soon after he dropped his clanger about Prince Philip, Willie Baxter must have realised that he had committed political suicide. In the eyes of most Labour voters in the constituency, he was completely discredited and even the Labour establishment at Westminster disowned him because he had spoken out publicly against the formation of a Labour government. Strangely enough, he still had more than a few toadies in the Constituency Labour Party who felt that he should carry on. Councillor Pat McCann was so unwilling to allow any criticism of Baxter that he was ousted from the chairmanship of the Constituency Labour Party at the 1974 AGM and replaced by Albert Monkman, a very well-respected headteacher. Jimmy Parker, councillor for Bonnybridge, thought that Baxter had done well to hang onto the seat and felt it rather ironic that, in the neighbouring constituency of Clackmannan and East Stirlingshire, the sitting Labour MP, Dick Douglas, had lost his seat to the SNP but was nevertheless re-selected as Labour candidate.

However, the overwhelming majority of West Stirlingshire Constituency Labour Party members wanted Baxter to go, and in the end he couldn't ignore them any longer. Baxter announced his resignation in May 1974 and, in June, the Constituency Labour Party invited nominations for the selection of a parliamentary candidate to succeed him. According to the Labour Party rules, nominations were confined to Labour Party branches within the constituency, and branches of affiliated organisations, mainly trade unions.

I was nominated by all the Labour Party branches in the Bannockburn area, as well as several trade union branches. By the closing date, nine nominations had been received, including Donald Dewar, Archie Lafferty, Norman McEwan, Pat Craven and myself.

Donald Dewar was a Glasgow lawyer who had been elected as Labour MP for Aberdeen South in 1966. When he lost his seat in 1970, he made it clear that he did not want to fight to win it back. He was after a safer Labour seat and, whenever a suitable vacancy cropped up, Donald was always there, looking for a nomination. He was therefore perceived as a carpet-bagger by some Labour Party activists, especially those on the left. However, Donald was the favourite son of the Labour Party establishment and, if Labour Party headquarters had had the power and influence which they now have, Donald would have been parachuted into West Stirlingshire as the Labour candidate and that would have been that.

Pat Craven was the Militant Tendency candidate. *Militant* was a Trotskyite newspaper with a readership confined to the ultra-left. Most Trotskyite factions would not touch the Labour Party with a barge pole but Militant supporters were encouraged to join the Labour Party in order to capture Constituency Labour Parties with the intention of eventually taking over the entire Labour Party. This tactic was referred to as entryism, and Militant supporters operated like a party within a party, with their own group meetings and strict discipline. They had full-time organisers strategically located throughout Britain and Pat Craven was one of them. Militant's main message was a simple recipe for simple minds: nationalise the 300 monopolies, put the workers in control and we would all live happily ever after in a socialist utopia.

Norman McEwan and Archie Lafferty were both good friends of mine. Norman had his own legal business in Stirling and he also served as member of both Stirling Town Council and Stirling County Council. As a lawyer and as a councillor, he was champion of the underdog and he was not afraid to take up unpopular causes. He was a man of unbending principle and tenacious in his pursuit of justice. I later joined forces with him in the campaign to abolish corporal punishment in schools.

Archie Lafferty was Provost of Denny, where he had served on the town council for many years. He also taught Maths at St Modan's High School, Stirling, where I was his boss. Archie was a former pupil of St Modan's and spent his entire teaching career there. He was a superb teacher and the pupils loved him. He and his wife, Margaret, had been delegates to West Stirlingshire Constituency Labour Party for many years and Archie, like me, had been the parliamentary election agent. Despite the fact that we were rivals for the candidature, we had an understanding that, when it came to the ballot, whoever was eliminated first would recommend to his supporters that they switch their votes to the other candidate.

During the lead-up to the selection conference for choosing the Labour candidate, it was brought to my attention that an insidious whispering campaign was being conducted against me. The gist of the allegation was that I had been arrested for taking part in a pro-IRA demonstration. The rumour spread like wildfire and my closest supporters informed me that some leading Labour councillors, including Pat McCann of Kilsyth and Charlie Brown of Fallin, were involved in spreading it.

Proving the source of the rumours was difficult but, when a report reached me that a local publican was telling the whole pub about my alleged terrorist activities, I decided to meet him head-on. Tommy Monaghan, Henry Dawson and I went to the pub in question, the Halfway House, near Millhall, on the road between Stirling and Fallin. None of us was known personally to the publican who, on first impressions, seemed very hospitable and loquacious. We ordered a round of drinks and Tommy picked up a copy of the local paper, the *Stirling Observer*, which was lying on the bar. The paper contained a story about the Bannockburn branch of the Labour Party nominating me for the parliamentary candidature. Referring to the newspaper report, Tommy said: 'I see that the Bannockburn branch of the Labour Party is nominating some guy called Canavan for the MP's job.'

The man behind the bar rose to the bait immediately, announcing to all and sundry that I had been arrested in Glasgow for taking part in an IRA march and that, because I had been detained by the police, I was unable to attend my teaching job. When Henry asked the publican how he knew all this, he mentioned councillors Charlie Brown and Pat McCann.

After leaving the pub, Henry, Tommy and I discussed our next move. The publican was obviously just the message boy, albeit a very pliant one, but we concluded that action must be taken to stop Brown and McCann. I phoned up the publican and told him that I had heard him defaming me in front of two witnesses and that he would be receiving a letter from my lawyer. That soon shut him up, and the councillors also received warning letters from my lawyer.

A few weeks later, I received the following letter from James Meldrum, Director of Education for Stirling County:

:PHONE No. 3111

IES S. MELDRUM,
M.A., M.Ed., F.C.I.S.
Director of Education

County Council of the County of Stirling

IF TELEPHONING OR
CALLING ASK FOR
Mr. Meldrum.
Extension 503.

Please Quote. Staffing.

Your Ref.............

Room 217,
COUNTY OFFICES,
VIEWFORTH,
STIRLING, FK8 2ET.

August 30, 1974.

Mr. Dennis A. Canavan,
12 Margaret Road,
Bannockburn.

Dear Mr. Canavan,

A serious situation concerning your personal position has come to light and I wish to do everything I can to redress an injustice which apparently has been done to you.

Some considerable time ago (it may have been as much as 2 years ago) I made a statement to the effect that you had been involved in a political rally in Glasgow and had fallen foul of the police resulting in your being detained and being unable to return to duty on the Monday morning. The occasion of the statement was a meeting of the small Staffing Sub-Committee of the Education Committee when your name appeared on a list of applicants for a promoted post. I had accepted in all good faith a statement which in turn had been made to me.

I was horrified recently on being asked for verification of the story by ex-Provost McCann of Kilsyth to discover that your name had been confused with that of another teacher in the County and that though the incident had, in fact, taken place you were not the person involved.

The fact that no harm has apparently resulted since you later received promotion and have only recently been adopted as a parliamentary candidate is providential but at the same time it does not take away from the seriousness of the mis-representation to your reputation.

The original statement was made in confidence to a small group of Members (which no doubt explains why it has never been given wider currency) and it is my intention to make a statement to these Members giving them the true situation. The few members of my staff who had known of the story have I am glad to say, maintained completely the confidentiality of their knowledge but I have, of course, seen them all individually.

I regret exceedingly what has happened and want to apologise most sincerely for it. Is there any further step you would wish me to take? I go on holiday

2.

Mr. D.A. Canavan.   August 30, 1974.

this evening but would be very happy to meet you to discuss the matter
further after I return on Tuesday, 24th September.

Meantime may I wish you every success in your affairs politically,
educationally and privately.

Yours sincerely,

Director of Education.

When I first read the above, I could hardly believe it. I suspect
that, when Pat McCann received the letter from my lawyer, he
contacted the Director of Education for proof of my alleged criminal
activity, only to be told that a mistake had been made. The mistake
would probably never have come to light if my lawyer had not sent
the letter following the visit to the Halfway House. Not one of the
Labour councillors involved in spreading the rumour had the good
grace to apologise or even to discuss the matter with me.

The Director of Education's assertion that 'the original statement
was made in confidence to a small group of members (which no
doubt explains why it has never been given wider currency)' is only
partially correct. At least one of the members involved had deliberately used the information to stop me becoming a Labour candidate and the spread of false allegations was not confined to Labour
Party members. The Director of Education's letter was written after
I had been selected as parliamentary candidate but, although the
Director describes that as 'providential', it was not the end of the
story. The damage had been done and, during the subsequent
general election campaign, my political opponents seized on the
same rumours which had been started by Labour councillors. That

was when I first discovered that, in politics, your worst enemies are sometimes within your own party, and that was something which I was to experience again and again in later years.

As the Director of Education's letter referred to a false statement about me being made at a meeting of the small Staffing Sub-Committee of the Education Committee, I went to see Councillor Michael Kelly, Convener of the Education Committee, for an explanation. Rather than telephone him, I decided to doorstep him at his home in the Raploch, Stirling. When he came to the door, he was so pleased to see me that he did not even invite me over the threshold. He denied all knowledge of the matter, but I was incredulous because Michael knew everything that went on in Stirling County Council's Education Department, especially on matters regarding applications for promoted posts. Michael belonged to an era when councillors played an over-active part in the appointment and promotion of council employees and he was one of the worst examples of someone who was responsible for giving jobs to people on the grounds of their political or religious affiliations. He later received a papal knighthood for his services!

Despite the dirty tricks operating against me, I was very hopeful of winning the Labour nomination for West Stirlingshire. The selection conference was due to be held on Sunday, 18 August, and during the preceding months Henry Dawson and I travelled the length and breadth of the constituency many times, drumming up support from Labour Party branches and trade unions. In 1974, the Labour Party's selection system was not based on 'one member, one vote' as it is now. If it had been, it would have favoured me because John 'Bunt' Somerville, a retired miner, was such a successful recruiting sergeant that there were probably more members in the Bannockburn-Whins of Milton area than the rest of the constituency put together.

Each branch of the Labour Party was entitled to send delegates to the Selection Conference, and the number of delegates depended on the branch membership. Similarly, every affiliated trade union branch was entitled to send delegates, but the delegates had to be fully paid-up members of the Labour Party resident within the constituency.

When Henry and I went round the various Labour Party branches, we quickly came to the conclusion that it was a two-horse race between Donald Dewar and myself. In broad terms, Donald was favoured by the right and I by the left, but the division was geographical as well as ideological. The village of Banknock was like a turning-point, with nearly everyone west of that point supporting Donald and nearly everyone north-east of that point supporting me. Henry and I knew that, on a count of Labour Party branch delegates, it would be pretty close and we therefore decided to concentrate on the trade union delegations. In that respect Henry's assistance was invaluable. From his previous experience working in the coal industry, he had many old friends in the mining communities, and he also had good trade union contacts in many other workplaces such as the United Glass factory in Bridge of Allan, the University of Stirling, the NHS hospitals, the local authorities, the paper mills in Denny and the foundries in Bonnybridge. He had, of course, to ensure that their affiliation fees were fully paid up and that they had appointed delegates before the 'freezing' date decided by Labour Party headquarters.

The Selection Conference was held on Sunday, 18 August 1974, in Banknock Community Centre and it was overseen by the late Jimmy Allison, who was then Assistant Scottish Organiser for the Labour Party. The party had a strict rule that a delegate could enter the hall only after production of the appropriate credentials, namely a party membership card and certificate of delegation signed by the branch secretary. Furthermore, no delegate was allowed to enter the hall after the first candidate had begun speaking. That was a very sensible rule because it meant that all the candidates had to be heard before the delegates cast their votes. Nowadays, the delegates do not even need to turn up to cast their votes. Any delegate for any reason can apply for a postal vote, with the result that many selections are cut and dried before the Selection Conference takes place. The candidates are therefore denied an equal opportunity of addressing the delegates and answering their questions. Widespread postal voting is also open to abuse because there is no guarantee that the person putting the cross on the ballot box is the same person to whom the ballot paper was addressed.

The attendance at the West Stirlingshire Selection Conference in 1974 was about 100, despite the fact that only delegates could attend. I have heard of recent Labour Party selection conferences with only a fraction of that attendance, despite the fact that all constituency party members are now entitled to attend. That does not say much for New Labour's stated intention of building an inclusive party of mass membership. If you were to discount all Labour MPs, MEPs, MSPs, councillors, employees and trade union officials along with spouses and employees of the aforesaid, there would not be many party members left.

The West Stirlingshire Selection Conference in 1974 may not have been a perfect model of democracy, but it did consist of a fair number of working people from different areas and different workplaces within the constituency, who were there as representatives from their Labour Party branches or affiliated trade unions. Each of the candidates had the opportunity to address the meeting for ten minutes, followed by ten minutes of questions. We drew lots to decide the order of speaking, and I was pleased when my name came up first because I was nervous and I wanted the whole thing over and done with as quickly as possible.

I had put a fair amount of preparation into my speech and, when I was delivering it, I could tell from my eye contact with the audience that some of them were definite supporters, others were definite opponents and a good number were keeping their cards close to their chests. I spoke about the relevance of socialism to the National Health Service and the creation of more opportunities in education and employment. But it was my reference to the Battle of Bannockburn which brought the most positive response from the audience. Denouncing the anglophobia which was prevalent in the SNP at that time, I pointed out the irrelevance in the twentieth century of trying to rekindle the hostilities of the fourteenth century. 'The battle we should be fighting now is not between the Scots and the English but between the haves and the have-nots. The challenge facing socialists is to eradicate injustice by ensuring equal opportunities for everyone, irrespective of nationality.'

As I expected, I was asked what I thought about proposals for a Scottish Parliament, or a Scottish Assembly as it was then called, in Labour Party circles. I knew that the Labour Party was deeply divided on the issue and that that division was reflected in the audience. Some of the delegates, including some of my supporters, had previously told me that they thought the whole idea of a Scottish Assembly was simply pandering to the SNP. I disagreed, but I knew that I risked losing some support if I expressed my disagreement in a hostile manner. However, there was no way I could sit on the fence and, anticipating the question, I had already decided how I was going to answer it. I pointed out that, if we had had a Scottish Assembly during the time of the 1970–74 Tory government, then the people of Scotland would not have had to suffer Tory policies in areas such as Education, Health and Housing, policies which the people of Scotland had rejected at the ballot box. A Scottish Assembly or Parliament would be able to implement socialist policies in many fields and, of course, it would be more democratic because it would make the government of Scotland closer and more accountable to the people of Scotland. My argument was facilitated by the fact that, only months prior to the Selection Conference, a Tory government had been foisting unwanted policies onto the people of Scotland, such as forcing local councils to increase the rents of council house tenants. The delegates' memories were still fresh.

The question of nuclear disarmament also arose and I expressed my unequivocal opposition to nuclear weapons and other weapons of mass destruction. I gave what I thought were competent answers to a few more questions before the chairman ruled that my time was up and I retired to the anteroom where the other candidates were waiting. Donald Dewar was fidgeting around with a nervous look about him. He knew that it was a two-horse race and the applause at the end of my speech told him that I had got off to a good start.

According to the rules, the successful candidate had to win an overall majority of the votes cast. If that was not achieved in the first ballot, the candidate with the lowest number of votes was eliminated and another ballot held. That was repeated until a candidate achieved an overall majority. Henry and I had done the arithmetic in advance and reckoned that we'd just win on the first ballot. I was slightly concerned when I heard that another ballot was necessary but, in the event, I won it comfortably on the second ballot. I felt elated, but I knew that I had a much bigger fight ahead of me. I remembered Pat McCann's words: 'Canavan might win the Labour nomination, but I'll make sure he never rests his arse in parliament.'

--- ◆ ---

CHAPTER TEN

A close contest

At the next meeting of the Constituency Labour Party, Henry Dawson was appointed as my election agent. Henry was, and still is, an amazing character. I had been introduced to him by his father, the late Jock Dawson, a retired miner who lived in Whins of Milton. Henry left school at the age of 15 to go to work down the pit. His potential was recognised by the National Union of Mineworkers, who sent him on a course at Ruskin College, Oxford. He later left the pit to work in the construction industry, where his man-management skills quickly brought him promotion as a 'gaffer'.

I persuaded Henry to join the Labour Party and he soon became secretary of his local branch. I had seen him in action during the local government election campaign in 1974. He seemed to have a limitless supply of energy and enthusiasm, combined with leadership qualities that inspired other people. When Henry was canvassing, he did not walk. He ran from door to door. When Henry was putting up election posters, he did not need a ladder. He could shin up a lamp-post in five seconds. I remember one occasion when some of our political opponents erected, without planning permission, a huge hoarding advertising their candidate. We were advised that the massive structure was unlawful and, when the local authority failed to take any action to enforce its removal, Henry tore it down with his bare hands.

Henry's energy was matched by his enthusiasm and loyalty. During the course of my lifetime, I have met less than a handful of people whom I would trust enough to say: 'That person would walk to the ends of the earth for me.' Henry Dawson is one of them.

Shortly after Henry agreed to be my agent, our first job was to go round every Labour Party branch in the constituency trying to form the nucleus of an election team in each area. That was no mean feat because of the time constraints and the divisions within the party over the parliamentary selection process. Less than a month after I was selected as a candidate, Harold Wilson called a general election for 10 October. As it was the second general election of that year, the Constituency Labour Party had virtually no money in the election account.

By contrast, SNP members were on a high. They had won a record seven seats at Westminster earlier that year and were openly boasting that they would more than double that number in October. They had slashed the Labour majority in West Stirlingshire to less than 5,000 in February and had made it one of their target seats for the autumn election.

The SNP had a very good candidate, Janette Jones. She was from a Kilsyth working-class background and won a seat from Labour on Kilsyth town council. She had run a very active campaign against Willie Baxter in the February 1974 general election and had beaten the Tories into third place. In May 1974, at the first elections to Strathclyde Regional Council, she beat Labour to become the first regional councillor to represent Kilsyth and the neighbouring villages of Banton, Croy and Queenzieburn. She therefore had a big electoral base and seemed more than capable of using it as a springboard for victory at the autumn general election.

Janette worked very hard in what was virtually a non-stop SNP campaign from the spring through to the autumn. She was not deeply political, but she had a gift of communicating with people of different backgrounds. Many working-class people found it far easier to identify with her than with a millionaire like Willie Baxter, who had become increasingly indolent, arrogant and aloof from the people he was supposed to represent.

While Janette Jones was campaigning throughout the entire summer of 1974, the Labour Party in West Stirlingshire was virtually silent. After announcing his resignation, Baxter was even more conspicuous by his silence and was no doubt preoccupied in preparing his flitting to some off-shore tax haven. The party activists were involved in campaigning for their favoured candidate to replace Baxter. The result was that a divided, disorganised, penniless Constituency Labour Party with a new, inexperienced candidate was up against a buoyant, well-organised SNP with plenty of resources and a good candidate. Many of the political pundits wrote us off and, although I did not suspect it at the time, I now think that Labour Party headquarters did likewise. West Stirlingshire should have been identified as a key seat and money and resources should have been poured into it. Instead, Henry Dawson and I were left to organise a campaign with very little assistance or advice from party headquarters.

To make matters worse, the Tories and the SNP latched on to the malicious rumours which had been started by Labour councillors to try to discredit me, and there was a nasty sectarianism to it all. Cases were reported to us of Opposition canvassers who were trying to scare off Catholic voters by claiming I was a communist and Protestant voters by claiming that I was a member of the IRA. After I received the letter of apology from the Director of Education, Henry sent a copy to every Labour Party branch so that our canvassers could rebut the false accusations. When members of the Fallin branch found out that Councillor Charlie Brown was one of those responsible for initially starting the rumours, they threatened to expel him, but were eventually persuaded that such drastic action could be counter-productive, especially during the heat of a general election campaign. Councillor Brown made full use of his reprieve by trying to make amends. He and his son must have climbed every lamp-post in the area because, within a few days of the start of our campaign, the entire village of Fallin was bedecked with 'Vote Canavan' posters.

Fallin has a very special place in my memory. Polmaise Colliery, situated in the village, was the last pit in Stirlingshire, and Fallin was one of the last pit villages in Scotland. There were fewer than 1,000 households in Fallin but every family had a connection, past or present, with the pit.

Polmaise Colliery had been sunk in the early part of the twentieth century and many of the miners and their families migrated from the Lanarkshire coalfield to work in the new pit. They brought with them the coal-mining skills and experience which they had gained in the West of Scotland and some of them also brought with them the sectarian tribalism associated with some of the Lanarkshire mining communities. The Orange Lodge was strong in Fallin and the village was very proud of its flute band, which would perform not only on the Orange walks but also at community events and trade union events like demonstrations during the miners' strikes.

In the west of Scotland, many of the Orange community had been traditional Tory voters and the Tory candidates described themselves as Conservative and Unionist, referring to the inclusion of Northern Ireland as well as Scotland within the United Kingdom. By contrast, most of the Orange community in Fallin were traditional Labour voters, mainly because of the influence of the National

Union of Mineworkers. However, in 1974, for the first time in their lives, they were being asked to vote for a parliamentary candidate who was a Catholic. For many it seemed a step too far, especially with rumours flying around about my alleged IRA activities.

To be fair, I must say that I never heard any openly sectarian comments in Fallin, but I have a vivid recollection of one of my first visits to the Miners' Welfare Club in the neighbouring village of Plean. I was going round the tables wearing my Labour Party rosette and having an informal chat with some of the locals, most of whom were very friendly and supportive. At one table, however, I was told in no uncertain terms to 'fuck off' and, when I politely asked why, I was told that there was no way in which any of that company would ever vote Labour because the Labour Party was controlled by a crowd of 'Fenian bastards'. To emphasise the point, the company spokesperson said 'You just have to look at their Fenian names: "Callaghan, Healey and Canavan".' I do not know what Jim Callaghan and Denis Healey would have thought of their names being taken in vain by such a perceptive political commentator, but I concluded that my gifts of persuasion were so limited that I'd better move on to the next table.

My good friend Terry McMeel, who was district councillor for Fallin and also NUM delegate for Polmaise Colliery, was all too aware of the sectarian mutterings against me and he came up with a brilliant idea to convince the miners that I was just 'one of them'. Terry took me underground and we crawled together along every inch of the coalface at Polmaise to speak to the miners as they worked. That meant reporting to the pit head at five o'clock in the morning then coming back to repeat the entire exercise for the back shift and then the night shift. It was an unforgettable experience. I had never been down a pit before in my life, but I had heard much about what it was like from friends who were miners. Going down the shaft in the 'cage' was much as expected, rather like a rough ride in an elevator. Walking from the pit bottom to the coalface was not too bad, although it was a bit longer than expected and I had to watch my step to avoid tripping over the rough ground and the railtracks. However, I was not prepared for the claustrophobic, noisy conditions at the coalface.

The coal seam at Polmaise was only about two feet high and I soon realised why some of the best Scottish miners were men who were short in stature but with a very muscular physique. A tall man would have found it very difficult, if not impossible, to work in such cramped conditions. The noise was so deafening that I could hardly make out a word that anybody was saying. When someone spoke to me, I smiled back, hoping that my facial expression did not look like some inane grin. All around me were blackened faces cursing and swearing and shouting orders at each other, but what I found most unexpected and most frightening was the creaking and groaning caused by the roof moving above me and the continuous fall of coal and rock from overhead. At first, I thought that the roof was in danger of imminent collapse and I was not entirely consoled when I observed some of the men around me laughing and joking. I thought to myself: 'Is this some kind of gallows humour or are these guys just mad?'

I realised later that they were probably laughing at my discomfiture, but Terry told me that those underground visits were a huge success in terms of improving my reputation amongst the miners. I certainly was amazed by the number of people who later said that they had met me 'doon the pit' and they seemed to be well impressed.

We also had open-air pithead meetings, organised by John McCormack, chairman of the Polmaise branch of the NUM and a great supporter of mine. I would speak for a few minutes and the miners were given the chance to ask me questions. I knew from their response that they were on my side and that was largely due to the hard work of John McCormack and Terry McMeel rather than any effort of mine.

Fallin was not the only place where I initially encountered some problems because of my religion. At the time when my name was being suggested as a potential parliamentary candidate, Tom Meenagh, a very respected deputy headteacher and an active member of the Kilsyth branch of the Labour Party, expressed the view that West Stirlingshire was not ready for a Catholic MP. I had a huge admiration for Tom, who was a thoughtful socialist and certainly not sectarian. However, he sincerely thought that if the Constituency Party put up a candidate who was a Catholic, then Labour would lose the seat because too many voters were too sectarian in their attitudes. That was Tom's judgement, not his wish. He was a fair man and, although he did not vote for me at the Selection Conference, he and his wife, Janette, worked like Trojans for me during the general election campaign.

West Stirlingshire was a huge constituency, stretching all the way from the outskirts of Falkirk to the outskirts of Glasgow and taking in the Carse of Stirling, the Campsies and the east bank of Loch Lomond as far northwards as Inversnaid. Thirty years ago, a parliamentary candidate, especially a new one, was expected to hold a public meeting in every town and village during the course of a general election campaign. As there were over thirty distinct communities in the constituency, and election meetings were not usually held at weekends, that meant two public meetings on most weekdays over a three-week campaign. Using my previous experience as an election agent, our plan was to begin the campaign in the smaller, remote communities with the hope of gradually building up attendance and momentum culminating in an eve of poll rally in one of the larger industrial towns where we could count on a capacity crowd as a final morale booster.

And so it came to pass that my first-ever public meeting as a parliamentary candidate was held in Kippen Primary School, with my agent, Henry Dawson, in the chair and a magnificent total of three people in the audience.

Two of the people, a man and a woman, were dressed like toffs. The third was an old woman who looked rural working class. I thought that the toffs might be spies from the local branch of the Tory Party, but the old woman looked like a potential Labour voter. I therefore decided to devote most of my speech to policies which I thought might appeal to her, such as Labour's plans to increase the retirement pension, invest more in the National Health Service and improve public transport in rural areas. After about 15 minutes, I sat down and Henry asked if there were any questions or comments.

I was absolutely gobsmacked when the old lady immediately launched into a tirade about why she would never vote Labour because Harold Wilson was a traitor who had sold the working class down the river and I had a brass neck coming to Kippen to ask for her vote.

I was completely taken aback. What a start to my first ever parliamentary campaign! I managed to mutter some reply to the effect that we had had only six months of a Labour government, that it was a minority government and that, if Harold Wilson were returned as prime minister with a working majority, then he would be able to do more to help the working class. I finished with a pledge that, if I were elected as MP, I would make myself available to help all my constituents, but I could tell from the old woman's face that she was not impressed.

A further call for questions from the audience was met with a stony silence. Henry therefore explained that it was time to move on to our next meeting in Buchlyvie and we were heading for the door when the two toffs approached. The man greeted me: 'Hello, Mr Canavan. I would like to congratulate you on your performance tonight. I thought you did jolly well, especially for a new candidate.'

I looked at him askance, suspecting that he was being sarcastic, but I could see that he was absolutely serious as he continued:

'I cannot vote for you, but my wife here assures me that she will certainly be voting for you.'

I thanked the woman very much for her support before turning back to her husband.

'But may I ask why you cannot vote for me?'

'Well, as you are no doubt aware, there are three categories of people who cannot vote in a general election: prisoners, lunatics and peers of the realm. As you can see, I am not incarcerated and I can assure you that I am perfectly sane.'

'Ah, so you must be in the House of Lords.'

'Yes, I am Lord Wilson of Langside, aka Harry Wilson, not to be confused with Harold Wilson. I was actually Solicitor-General for Scotland in Harold Wilson's last government.'

I must confess that I had never heard of Lord Wilson of Langside, but I was certainly grateful for his support and even more so for Lady Wilson's vote. The whole experience taught me a valuable lesson: never pre-judge your audience.

On our way along to Buchlyvie, Henry marked our first public meeting as a partial success: One for, one against and one noble abstention.

In terms of attendance at our public meetings, things could only get better after Kippen. We had good attendances in places as disparate as Cowie and Killearn and I could sense that our campaign was gathering momentum.

One of the most entertaining events I ever attended was an election meeting in Strathblane, which had the reputation of being a Tory stronghold. The village hall was packed out and I could sense from their body language that much of the audience had come to heckle or maybe even lynch me. By good fortune my supporting speaker was Reverend Murdo Ewen Macdonald, a very well respected Church of Scotland Minister, who was Professor of Theology at Glasgow University. Murdo began by reminding the audience that he preached occasionally at one of the local kirks when the parish minister was on holiday. He then launched into an evangelical sermon about the merits of Christian Socialism. He virtually told them that voting Tory was a sin because the Tories stood for a greedy, grasping, selfish rat race. He then turned on the Liberals, whom he described as middle of the road, wishy-washy, lukewarm.

'And need I remind you of what the Bible says about the luke-warm? *So then because thou art lukewarm and neither cold nor hot, I will spew thee out of my mouth.*'

Having demolished the Tories and the Liberals, he then dismissed the SNP as an irrelevance and finished with an exhortation: 'In the name of God, I urge you to love your neighbour and vote Labour.'

The lynch mob was silenced and my only worry was: how on earth do I follow that?

Henry Dawson saw the advantage of inviting supporting speakers to our public meetings and he contacted Labour Party headquarters to arrange more big names who would draw the crowds.

In the early 1970s, Tony Benn and Michael Foot were the heroes of the Labour left but, to the Tories, they were a couple of *bêtes noires*. Many of the farms and estates in West Stirlingshire displayed skull-and-crossbones notices with the warning: 'Beware! Foot and Benn Disease'. Michael Foot, who was Secretary of State for Employment, joined Harry Ewing and me on the platform at Falkirk Town Hall and Tony Benn, who was Secretary of State for Industry, spoke at a campaign meeting in Bonnybridge.

It was standing-room only when Benn and I arrived at Bonny-bridge Community Centre and the audience included some who had to come to jeer rather than cheer. But Benn soon had them eating out of his hand and the only slight difficulty came at question time, when someone asked him about the compensation which Tory MP Willie Whitelaw had received when the coal industry was nationalised. Tony would not be aware that the Whitelaw family had owned land and collieries in the Kilsyth-Kirkintilloch area. For a second, he looked rather perplexed, but an old Labour and trade union diehard, Hughie Miller from Kilsyth, quickly came to the rescue. Hughie grabbed the microphone from Tony's hand and just about brought the house down with a mini-speech about rapacious Tory land-owners. The only riposte from the Opposition was a snide little letter in the local paper a few days later, claiming that the Labour candidate was so incapable of speaking on his own behalf that the Labour Party had to import an 'English cabinet minister' to speak for him.

I found out later that it could be a risky business importing

'English cabinet ministers' up to Scotland, because they did not all have the political acumen of Tony Benn or Michael Foot. On one occasion, Dr David Owen shared a platform with me in Kilsyth Burgh Hall. Owen was Secretaryof State for Foreign and Common-wealth Affairs at the time. It was shortly after Airey Neave MP was assassinated and, because of the subsequent security alert, David Owen was accompanied by an armed bodyguard from the Metro-politan Police. During the course of a very lively meeting, I thought for one dreadful moment that the bodyguard was going to draw his gun just because one of the audience launched a hostile attack on me. The attack was only verbal and I managed to signal that to the bodyguard just in time. Afterwards we retired to the Kilsyth Rangers Club to chat up some of the punters. Everything was going fairly well until the naïve Dr Owen asked: 'What was the Keltik score today then?'

Kilsyth was also the scene of some interesting altercations in October 1974, on the Saturday before Polling Day, when a busload of Labour Party Young Socialists invaded the town. Nobody could fault them for a lack of enthusiasm, but some of them had a lack of political nous. The Labour Party Young Socialists at that time were dominated by the Militant Tendency, and many of their members were convinced that the only way in which the working-class struggle could be won was by a Marxist revolution which would bring about a socialist transformation of society. In 1974, in the aftermath of the successful miners' strike, many of the Young Socialists thought that the Revolution was just round the corner. The workers in Kilsyth and other industrial communities were desperate to shake off their shackles and the Militant Tendency would lead the way.

Soon after the busload of Young Socialists was let loose in Kilsyth, reports started filtering back to our campaign headquarters about some interesting doorstep dialogues. When being canvassed by a young revolutionary, one old lady said: 'I've voted Labour all my life, son, but I've heard that this Labour candidate is awfy left wing. In fact, I've heard them say that he's a Marxist.'

'Well, what's wrong with that?' was the response. After that, Henry Dawson ensured that the Young Socialists were always accompanied by an experienced local party member whose job was to ensure that the local people were not scared off by the revolutionaries.

I had a similar experience after a public meeting in Lennoxtown.

The meeting was very well attended and I was surprised to see my former teaching colleague, Margaret Sullivan, sitting in the front row. Before her retirement, Margaret had taught Maths at St Modan's High School, where she was known to generations of pupils as Maggie Tarzan. When I was her boss, we did not always to see eye to eye and it is probably no exaggeration to say that I had precipitated her retirement. When I saw Margaret sitting in the audience, I feared the worst. I thought that she might be there to wreak revenge on me and, when it came to question time, I was expecting her to explode into a castigatory rant, as she had done to so many recalcitrant pupils in her classroom. However, she sat in dignified silence throughout the entire meeting before approaching me afterwards.

'Well, Mr Canavan, I have always voted Labour and I'll definitely be voting for you.'

That remark just about bowled me over and would have had a similar effect on many of her former pupils, who perceived her as a female version of Attila the Hun. But Margaret was not finished.

'I just wanted to say to you, Mr Canavan, that some people think that the Labour Party is now too left wing. Now, I am sure that Michael Foot and Tony Benn are good people and, of course, the New Testament says that Christ's disciples all lived together and owned everything in common and the monks and nuns still do that. Well, it's like a form of communism in a way. But anyway, I thought that I should let you know what some people are saying about being too left wing and all that.'

That was Margaret's way of telling me not to alienate some of the voters by being too extreme. I thanked her for her support and we then had a chat about old times at St Modan's. She seemed happier and more relaxed than she ever had when teaching.

On the eve of poll, we had two rallies, one in Kilsyth followed by one in Bannockburn. In terms of atmosphere, there was a huge contrast between the two. The Kilsyth branch of the Labour Party had never wanted me to be the candidate. Many of them had been strong supporters of my predecessor, Willie Baxter, who had them all convinced that a left-wing candidate would lose the seat. When Baxter eventually resigned, the Kilsyth branch supported Donald Dewar for the candidature and, even after I won it, some of them refused to accept me as the candidate and were conspicuous by their absence throughout our campaign. When Provost Tom Barrie was asked to endorse me in an election leaflet, he refused, but ex-Provost

Hugh Ross came to the rescue with a very strong statement of support. I was later told that some Kilsyth Labour councillors even voted SNP in the general election in an effort to stop Canavan at all costs.

The first eve-of-poll rally was held in the Masonic Hall, Kilsyth. My heart sank when I saw that the hall was half empty. There were very few posters and I could sense an air of nervousness and tension amongst the audience. Even some of my most fervent supporters looked apprehensive. I tried my best to lift their spirits with an up-beat speech claiming that victory was within our grasp, but I knew that the canvass returns were mixed and that everything would depend on getting our voters out the following day. I endeavoured to put on an optimistic, brave face but I came away from Kilsyth feeling despondent.

When I arrived at Bannockburn Miners' Welfare Club for the final eve of poll rally, it was like landing on another planet. The building was bedecked with posters and bunting and, as soon as I entered the hall, the huge crowd gave me a standing ovation which lasted several minutes. I felt a lump in my throat and it took me a wee while to compose myself before starting my speech. When I told them that victory was within our grasp, they believed me without a shadow of a doubt. I could see old retired miners like Jock Dawson and Bunt Somerville cheering me on and it made me very humble that so many solid working-class people were putting such faith in me. I forgot all about the negative aspects of a long, exhausting campaign and concentrated on raising morale and inspiring our campaign workers to play their part in delivering a famous Labour victory in West Stirlingshire and the return of a majority Labour government at Westminster.

I woke up early on polling day, realising that it would be one of the most important days in my life. So much was at stake. If I won I would be hailed by many as a hero but, if I lost, there would be a long queue of denouncers shouting from the rooftops: 'We told you so!'

I had decided to do a tour of the polling stations throughout the constituency with a loudspeaker mounted on the car roof. My council house in Bannockburn was used as the election headquarters because we could not afford to rent premises. Henry Dawson was to concentrate on organising the campaign workers, while I would concentrate on urging the punters to vote by holding a series of street meetings in every town and village.

It was a gruelling schedule, but nevertheless enjoyable. Children would run up to the car with great excitement as soon as they heard the taped music on the loudspeaker. We would give them bright red Labour lapel stickers to remind their parents about the election and I would then take the microphone to make a short speech. People would gather round to listen and afterwards I would shake hands with them and have a chat, before moving on to the next village. Before we were halfway through the tour, I was so hoarse that I was beginning to regret not having taken the advice of pre-recording my message on tape. However, I felt that it was very important for me, as a new candidate, to be seen and heard personally by as many people as possible.

In 1974, the counting of the votes for the West Stirlingshire Constituency was held at the Albert Hall in Stirling and the returning officer was the local sheriff, William Henderson. There was an atmosphere of excitement and tension when Henry and I arrived at the hall and we both realised from our canvass returns that the result was going to be very close indeed. The SNP were so confident of winning that they had booked the nearby Golden Lion Hotel for a victory celebration. By contrast, we had been so busy working for a victory that we had had no time or money or energy to organise any celebration.

It was not possible to get an accurate count of the vote in each ward or electoral area, but an experienced counting agent could get a good idea when the ballot box for a particular area was opened and the ballot papers were being unfolded by the counting officers.

I shall never forget the opening of the Cowie ballot box. It was a joy to behold. It must have been about 98 per cent for Labour and 2 per cent for the SNP. When a solitary Tory vote was unveiled, Henry Mulraney, the Cowie councillor, observed: 'Ah ken who that is.' And he probably did.

Unfortunately for me, Cowie was virtually unique. Most of the ballot boxes revealed that Labour and the SNP were running neck and neck, and it was very difficult to tell who was ahead.

About halfway through the count, I saw Janette Jones, the SNP candidate, and her entourage rushing over to a particular table where a ballot box was just being opened. Out of curiosity I followed them and saw from the label on the box that it was from Fallin. As the counting officer opened the box, I could see great gleams of antici-pation in the eyes of the SNP team, but their faces fell five minutes later, as the ballot papers were unfolded. Fallin's box was not quite as good for us as Cowie's but it was not far behind, maybe about

90 per cent Labour. I breathed a huge sigh of relief because there had been rumours about some of our opponents 'playing the Orange card' in Fallin and I felt so grateful to miners' union stalwarts like John McCormack and Terry McMeel who had worked so hard to deliver the Labour vote. It was a few hours later that I fully realised how crucial that vote was.

As the count proceeded, Henry Dawson was running from table to table in his own energetic style, asking our counting agents for their latest estimates and then totalling them up. When I asked Henry how things were going, he had me believing that we were about 1,000 votes in front. Maybe arithmetic was not the strongest subject for some of our counting agents or maybe Henry just wanted to keep my spirits up, but I did not realise how close it actually was until Sheriff Henderson called all the candidates and agents together to adjudicate on the spoiled or doubtful ballot papers. After they had been dealt with, I was ahead by only 365 votes.

The SNP candidate and agent demanded a recount and I did not object because, if I had been in their shoes, I would have done the same. After all, the result could have been reversed if a couple of bundles of 100 ballot papers had been inadvertently placed in the wrong tray. The sheriff decided that the entire count should be restarted from scratch. By this time, it was well after midnight. Party workers must have been on the verge of complete exhaustion, but the adrenalin somehow kept them going.

After what seemed an eternity, the recount was at last completed and the sheriff called the agents and candidates up to the stage to announce the result. When I got to the stage, I still did not know the result of the recount but mercifully the sheriff let us see it written on a piece of paper, before publicly declaring it. When he reached the words '. . . and I therefore declare Dennis Andrew Canavan to be the duly elected Member of Parliament for the constituency of West Stirlingshire', I thought the roar of the crowd was going to lift the roof off the Albert Hall. It certainly lifted me. The recount had actually increased my majority to 367.

After the official declaration, the sheriff explained that, because there was a large crowd waiting outside the Albert Hall, he was going to repeat the declaration of the result outside from the steps of the hall. It was a silly mistake on his part, but I was so elated that I did not object.

When I saw some of my supporters waving to me in the main body of the hall, I instinctively ran off the side of the stage to hug them and was almost flattened by a massive thump on the head. Whoever designed the stage at the Albert Hall must have been a midget. The clearance between the floor of the stage and the base of the side balconies is only about five feet. As a result, anyone using the stairs at the corner of the stage risks being decapitated by the balcony. That is what almost happened to me. If it had, I would probably have been the most short-lived MP in history, and heaven alone knows what would have happened at the subsequent by-election. However, I was not going to let a mere knock on the head stop me and I managed to pull myself together before going out with my wife, Elnor, to join the sheriff and the other candidates on the steps outside.

As soon as I emerged, I was greeted by the most vitriolic barrage of abuse I have ever experienced. The re-announcement of the result was completely pointless because the people outside the hall had been listening to all the results on transistor radios. There was a crowd of several hundred, but the noise was such that it seemed to me like a baying mob of several thousand. They hurled everything at me, including curses, insults, coins and spittle. Poor Elnor, who was standing beside me, got the worst of it because the spitters were so enraged that they were frequently off-target.

'Traitor!'

'Fuck off, you Fenian scum!'

'Get back to Russia, you communist bastard.'

Those were some of the milder greetings which I received. It was a non-stop onslaught and the sheriff, to my amazement, carried on regardless, reading out the election result for the second time, while the police stood by and did nothing.

My head was still nipping from my collision with the balcony and I felt very dizzy. I just wanted to go home for a rest, but I was determined not to give in to such intimidation. After the sheriff had finished, I went to the microphone and thanked him and his staff for counting the votes accurately. I then thanked my supporters for helping to ensure a magnificent Labour victory and I promised that I would continue campaigning for the socialist policies on which I had fought and won the election.

Mention of the word 'socialist' seemed to get some of my opponents salivating like mad dogs and I thought we'd better head for home before I was accused of inciting a riot. On the way to the car, I was waylaid by some media people demanding interviews. That was followed by some hearty back-slapping, hugging and celebratory drinks with my campaign team, so that dawn was breaking by the time I got to bed.

On the Sunday following the election, Henry organised a car cavalcade which toured the entire constituency. We had a loudspeaker with music and we stopped at each town or village, so that I could get out of the car and publicly thank the people. In general, we got a great response but, when we stopped in Kilsyth, one SNP zealot threatened to report us to the police for breaching the peace on the Sabbath!

In the immediate aftermath of the campaign, there was still a lot of work to be done, including bills to be paid. Whenever the issue of funding for political parties is raised, I cast my mind back to that first election in October 1974. I had been selected as Labour candidate only a few weeks before the prime minister, Harold Wilson, declared a general election. West Stirlingshire Constituency Labour Party was skint because virtually all the funds had been spent during the previous election campaign held in February of the same year. The amount of money expected from Labour Party headquarters amounted to only a few hundred pounds. Unlike many Labour candidates, I was not sponsored by a trade union because my union, the Educational Institute of Scotland, is not affiliated to any political party.

Even before the campaign started, we identified the Scottish National Party as our main rival. Opinion polls indicated that their support was rising and they had targeted West Stirlingshire, pouring what seemed to be unlimited resources into the constituency.

Henry and I had realised that, if we were to have any chance of winning, we had to spend more money than we had. By the end of the campaign, we had run up over £1,000 of debt, a lot of money in those days. A few days after the election, Henry and I went to see the manager of the Bannockburn branch of the Royal Bank of Scotland, where the Constituency Labour Party account was held. We explained our predicament and politely asked for an overdraft facility to cover the election expenses which, by law, had to be paid by a few weeks after the election.

The bank manager was aghast. He told us in no uncertain terms that we had had no right to incur such a huge debt without his prior permission. He made Henry and me feel like a couple of irresponsible profligates and, by the time he finished lecturing us, I was absolutely fuming. I told him that, if we had not spent the money, I would not have been elected to parliament and I gave him a personal pledge that every penny of the debt would be paid off by the end of that year. The bank manager reluctantly agreed to a temporary overdraft facility and, when Henry and I reported back to the Constituency Labour Party, what followed was the most enjoyable series of fundraising events I have ever experienced.

Every Labour Party branch in the constituency was given a target sum of money to raise and, in most cases, this was done by organising a social occasion like a dance or ceilidh, with the takings from the bar and the admission receipts going to the election fund. I would usually donate a bottle of House of Commons whisky so that people could throw 50 pence coins at it and the nearest to the bottle would win it. I used to joke that we only needed 2,000 fifty-pence pieces to clear our debts.

Of course, Henry and I were always invited to those social events along with our wives and I was expected to say a few words during the interval or at the end of the evening. It was like one long victory parade from October to December, singing and dancing our way through places like Fallin, Cowie, Bannockburn, Denny, Bonny-bridge, Banknock, Kilsyth, Milton of Campsie, Lennoxtown and Torrance. Sometimes our social calendars were so congested that we had several events on the same weekend. The mood on those occasions was one of great jubilation. Spirits were high and we usually finished the evening off with a boisterous rendering of 'The Red Flag'.

On one occasion, a band from Cumbernauld was playing at a Labour Party function in Banknock. Cumbernauld at that time was an SNP stronghold and the SNP's favourite song at the time was 'The Flower of Scotland'. Indeed, some Labour Party members wrongly considered it to be the SNP official anthem. At the end of the last dance, the band from Cumbernauld suddenly struck up the opening notes of 'The Flower of Scotland' and the vocalist started belting out the lyrics. Henry had been waltzing around amorously with his wife, Bridene, but when he heard the change of tune, he suddenly jumped from the dance floor onto the stage, grabbed the microphone from the unfortunate singer and, with a few choice words, sent him homeward to think again.

Henry then handed me the mike to lead the company in a spirited rendition of 'The Red Flag' before we dispersed peacefully after a good night's entertainment.

The net result of all those fundraising social events was that we managed to raise enough money to clear our bank overdraft well before Christmas. Henry and I went along to the bank to tell the skinflint manager that we were paying off all our debts. We also had great pleasure in telling him that henceforth the Constituency Labour Party account would be transferred to the Co-operative Bank.

Such fundraising activities would be completely alien to New Labour. Many of their fundraising events are held in posh hotels with rich business people in tuxedos, paying over £100 per plate to hear party leaders and cabinet ministers waxing eloquent on the merits of capitalism. With such dependence on big business donations, it is not surprising that New Labour's economic agenda is so right wing and many people on low incomes feel excluded.

When New Labour started organising their fundraising banquets, Labour MPs were invited, and indeed expected, to attend. I always refused because I thought that they were rather obscene, especially at a time when many of my constituents were suffering dire poverty. I used to think of the party members and supporters who attended that fundraising bash in Banknock all those years ago and wonder how many of them could possibly afford £100 and a dinner suit to attend a New Labour junket.

I am convinced that New Labour has lost touch with many working-class people as a result of its over-dependence on big business. What is the point of being bank-rolled by millionaires if you lose touch with your own grass roots? When I think back on the Labour Party social functions which we used to have, they were not simply fundraising events. They were great community events, attended not just by Labour Party members, but also by supporters and potential supporters. They made local communities aware of the Labour Party and they were great opportunities for the constituency MP or local councillor to give a short speech and mingle informally with all those present. Politicians seem to have lost that kind of connection with ordinary people and, as a result, there is now a class division between the ruling class, comprising politicians and big business, and the under-class, comprising the rest of the population. Nowadays, disillusionment with politicians is so rife that less than 50 per cent of voters turn out to vote in many elections. At my first election, the turn-out was over 80 per cent and it used to be said that, if it ever fell below 70 per cent, the candidate or the agent or both would be sacked!

Part II

—— ◆ ——

Life at Westminster

CHAPTER ELEVEN

◆

A seat in parliament

On the night before I was due to take my seat in the House of Commons, I was invited by some of my campaign team to have a farewell drink with them in Bannockburn Miners Welfare Club before catching the sleeper to London. When I went into the club, it was packed with people who kept slapping me on the back and buying me more drink. The hospitality was so overwhelming that I was glad to escape but, when I arrived at the station, I discovered that there was more in store. A crowd of party members and supporters were there to greet me. I was lifted shoulder high and carried to the platform. When the train pulled into the station, they burst into song and a bewildered sleeping car attendant opened the door to be met with the lyrics of 'The Red Flag' and 'For he's a jolly good fellow'.

After a great deal of hugging and kissing, I was bundled into the sleeping car and the train pulled off with more singing and cheering. I felt like a world champion, although I was almost on my knees. I slumped into my little bunk with the expectation of waking up the following morning in London.

I fell asleep as soon as my head hit the pillow and, when I awoke, I could feel the train slowing down. Thinking that we might have arrived in London, I got up to look out the window. I could hardly believe my eyes when I saw a station sign bearing the name 'Larbert'. I had been asleep for all of nine minutes.

That was when I discovered that a British Rail sleeper was, for me, a misnomer. There were adverts at that time proclaiming the benefits of going to sleep at your local station and waking up in central London the following morning, refreshed and ready for a day's work. But for me it never worked. I could quite easily fall asleep to the steady rhythm of the wheels rolling along the rails but, when the train stopped or slowed down, I would invariably waken up. By the time I reached London, I was even more knackered than when I started.

From that day onwards, I tried to avoid travelling by sleeper, even though I was initially apprehensive about flying, never having been in a plane before starting my job at Westminster. Travelling by plane, however, was not always practicable. The last flight from London to Scotland was about 8 p.m. and very often there would be votes in the House of Commons at 10 p.m. on a Thursday. If I had an early constituency engagement on a Friday morning, I would sometimes get the late-night sleeper from Euston to Glasgow. Even that would present difficulties if there was a series of late votes in the Commons.

The difficulties were sometimes solved by the influential Tom McMillan, Labour MP for Glasgow Central. Tom was sponsored by the National Union of Railwaymen, which had more power in those days than the Minister for Transport. If there was ever any danger of Scottish MPs missing the sleeper because of votes in the House of Commons, Tom would get on the hotline to his trade union brothers at Euston and tell them to hold the train until we arrived. It was not unusual to see some pompous pinstriped businessmen leaning out the carriage windows, looking at their watches and complaining about the train leaving late. Little did they know about the power and influence of Brother McMillan. If they had, there would have been a spate of irate letters to *The Times* and the *Glasgow Herald*!

On my first arrival at the House of Commons to take my seat, I was well impressed by the policeman at the gate, who greeted me by my name. I found out afterwards that the police took great pride in studying photographs of new members so that they could recognise them on arrival. However, I remember Diane Abbott, who was the first black female MP, telling me that, on her first arrival, the policeman on duty ushered her to the servants' quarters because he assumed that she was a cleaner. I suspect that the formidable Diane soon put him in his place!

The members' entrance at the House of Commons leads into the members' cloakroom. Each member had a nameplate with a coat hanger and a pink ribbon. When I asked the attendant what was the purpose of the ribbon, he explained that it was for hanging up my sword. That set me wondering what kind of weird workplace I was entering.

During all my years in the House of Commons, the only guy I ever saw with a sword was the Serjeant at Arms but, if you were to believe all the Westminster stories, there must have been a time when members were allowed to take their swords into the Chamber.

There are two lines marked on the floor separating the government front bench from the Opposition front bench. The distance between the two lines is supposed to be two sword lengths, presumably to stop one lot fencing with the other lot during a heated exchange. If someone inadvertently put a foot or even part of a foot over the line while delivering a speech, it was not unusual for some prat on the other side to shout out: 'Toe the line! Toe the line!' Such puerile nonsense might be the done thing in an English public school, but I could not help but wonder what place it had in a modern parliamentary democracy.

My wonder grew when the House assembled in the Chamber for the first time after the general election. The first item on the agenda was the election of the Speaker. In October 1974 it was a bit of a non-event because there was only one nominee, Selwyn Lloyd. After the second election in 1974, Labour had a majority of only four and there was therefore a reluctance to nominate a Labour MP for the Speaker's position. That would have reduced the government majority even further because the Speaker is expected to be independent and give up party membership.

Selwyn Lloyd was therefore the sole nominee but the House of Commons still had to go through the ritual of reappointing him to the job. Part of the ritual consists of dragging the Speaker-elect from his seat into the Speaker's Chair. The reason is that the person nominated is not supposed to want the job because, in days gone by, when there was a power struggle between Parliament and the Crown, the king might demand the Speaker's head on a plate.

In recent years, however, the Speaker presents no threat to the monarch and the person nominated as Speaker is usually desperate to get the job. George Thomas, son of a Welsh miner, must have worn out several of his dad's kneepads crawling to the Westminster establishment before eventually becoming Speaker in 1976. Over 20 years later, Michael Martin, a Glasgow sheet metal worker, used all his Glesca guile, his trade union negotiating skills and his political networking to land the job, despite having to face more opposing candidates than any other nominee in recent times. But all of them have to go through the pantomime of pretending not to want the job and being hauled 'unwillingly' into the Speaker's Chair.

I doubt very much whether Selwyn Lloyd was desperate to be re-elected as Speaker in 1974. He looked a frail old man. He had already been Speaker since 1971 and, before that, he had held some of the great offices of State, including Foreign Secretary and Chancellor of the Exchequer. He obviously did not need the money and he was getting on in years. Indeed, when his two sponsors were dragging him from his seat, he looked as if he might fall to pieces. Nevertheless, I always found him to be a fair man.

Speaker Selwyn Lloyd shook hands with and congratulated all members individually immediately after they were sworn in. Shortly afterwards, I wrote to him saying that I would like to make my maiden speech at the earliest opportunity.

The earliest opportunity came up the following week but, first of all, we had to endure more pantomime in the form of the state opening of parliament. Part of the ceremony involved a retired military officer titled Black Rod being dispatched from the House of Lords to the House of Commons to summon members to hear the Queen's Speech. Black Rod, so-called because he carries a black stick, is dressed in black knickerbockers, black silk stockings and black patent leather shoes with silver buckles. A little game is then enacted with the Commons pretending to keep him out by slamming the door in his face. Black Rod then knocks on the door three times with his stick and the Commons doorkeeper eventually opens the door to let him in.

The Speaker then leads a procession of members from the Commons to the Lords to hear the Queen reading out a speech on behalf of the government. I trooped along with the rest of them more out of curiosity than anything else. It is the one and only time in my life that I have ever seen the Queen because I found the extravaganza of the state opening to be so off-putting that, in subsequent years, I declined Black Rod's summons.

The Queen sat on a throne surrounded by other members of the royal family and, when I saw the Duke of Edinburgh, I could not help thinking of Willie Baxter's ludicrous suggestion that the country be governed by a Council of State chaired by Prince Philip. All the other seats in the Chamber were occupied by members of the House of Lords bedecked in ermine robes. Members of the House of Commons are not allowed to sit in the House of Lords but are expected to stand at the bar of the House, near the entrance, listening respectfully to Her Majesty repeatedly using the words 'my government' when referring to the legislative programme of the government elected by the people. Much of it is of course mere symbolism, but it symbolises privilege and patronage rather than equality and democracy.

After the pomp and ceremony, we adjourned for lunch and, in the afternoon, the debate on the Queen's Speech began. On the second day of the debate, Selwyn Lloyd called me over to the Speaker's Chair to inform me that he would call me to take part in the debate and I was pleasantly surprised to be informed that he would call me immediately after Jeremy Thorpe, leader of the Liberal Party.

The Foreign Secretary, Jim Callaghan, was to lead off the debate, followed by Jim Prior, Shadow Foreign Secretary, then Sir Geoffrey de Freitas, a senior Labour MP, then Jeremy Thorpe, then me. I did not appreciate it at the time, but Selwyn Lloyd was doing me a great favour because all the previous speakers were Privy Councillors; back-benchers, especially newcomers, were not normally called until much later in the debate.

Before being elected to parliament, I had never visited the House of Commons and I was completely naïve about parliamentary protocol and tradition. For example, I was unaware that the dispatch boxes were traditionally reserved for ministers and shadow ministers. I assumed that the dispatch box was the equivalent of the rostrum at a party conference and, when I perched myself on the government front bench waiting for my turn to speak, one of the whips had to explain to me that new members normally have to serve an apprenticeship on the back benches before being considered for promotion to the front bench! I therefore made a diplomatic retreat before commencing my speech from a more humble location.

During the course of my speech, I expressed strong support for a Scottish Parliament. The Queen's Speech had contained a proposal to set up a Scottish legislative assembly, but I preferred the word 'parliament' in order to give it more status.

Many Labour MPs as well as the Tories were absolutely opposed to the government's policy on devolution and I knew that my use of the term 'Scottish Parliament' would be provocative, to say the least. Nevertheless, I felt that I had to say what I thought and I also used the occasion to take a swipe at the undemocratic House of Lords.

I did not confine my speech to constitutional matters. I expressed the hope that the National Enterprise Board and the Scottish Development Agency would help to bring about a regeneration of the economy and a reduction in unemployment. I supported more public ownership of natural assets like oil and land for the benefit of the people and I concluded by referring to the importance of the environment and the conservation of our natural heritage.

On re-reading the speech now, some of it sounds like revolutionary socialism compared with the anodyne agenda of New

Labour. So it was with some surprise that I heard a subsequent speaker, an old Tory called Richard Wood, congratulating me 'with complete sincerity', stating that he admired many things about my speech, including my 'ability to be uncontroversial'. He then hastily added: '. . . or perhaps I should say reasonably uncontroversial'.

I was glad to get my maiden speech under my belt and I looked forward to making many more contributions to parliamentary debates, even though I found it difficult to adapt to some of the quainter parliamentary traditions.

In the House of Commons, it is customary for MPs to address other MPs as 'Honourable Members' even if they do not merit such a description. Privy Councillors are addressed as 'Right Honourable', QCs as 'Honourable and Learned' and former officers in the armed forces as 'Honourable and Gallant'.

When I first heard all that tosh in the course of a parliamentary debate, it reminded me of the first meetings of Stirling District Council. The very first meeting was almost entirely taken up with a prolonged discussion about the adoption of standing orders. *Inter alia*, we unanimously agreed that, during council meetings, we should address each other as 'Councillor'.

At the next meeting of the council, Provost Laura McCaig, the Tory councillor for the Balmaha area, proposed that we make an exception in the case of her Tory colleague, Councillor Freddie Graham, who should be addressed as 'Major General Graham'. Even Freddie, a very amiable one-nation Tory and a very distinguished veteran of the Argyll and Sutherland Highlanders, looked embarrassed at being singled out in such a way. As Labour Group Leader, I reminded the provost that we had already unanimously agreed on the style of address and that, if we made an exception in one case, it might create a precedent whereby Councillor McMeel would be addressed as 'Miner McMeel' and I would be addressed as 'Teacher Canavan'.

The provost then realised that she was in danger of opening a can of worms and wisely decided not to pursue the matter. A small victory for egalitarianism in the Council Chamber but, as I was to discover later, egalitarianism in the Commons Chamber is interpreted in such a way that all members are equal, but some are more equal than others.

During my first week at Westminster, I wrote a letter to all my campaign workers thanking them personally and telling them that one of the occupational hazards of MPs going to Westminster was a tendency to forget the people who had sent them there. I asked them to give me a shout if I ever displayed that tendency. Some of them showed me that letter 30 years later, but not one of them ever felt the need to give me a shout.

I always did my best to maintain maximum contact with the people I represented, despite the fact that it was not always easy, especially in the early days. The parliamentary allowances in the 1970s were not nearly enough to fund a constituency office and, as a result, my house was my office. Most of my constituents at that time did not have a phone and people with problems would often come literally knocking at my door in 'emergencies', real or imaginary. I now realise that it was a gross invasion of family privacy and very unfair on my wife and four young children. MPs take a conscious decision to go into public life, but their children are often thrust into the goldfish bowl with no choice.

Some MPs go to the other extreme by shielding themselves to such an extent that they are almost inaccessible to the people. Some of them escape to exclusive residential areas and arrange new ex-directory phone numbers. I always felt that going ex-directory would make it more difficult for constituents to contact me, especially in the days before I had a constituency office. I have had the same home phone number in the directory for nearly 40 years and I suspect that there are not many parliamentarians who can say that. It was a nuisance at times, but I always thought it absolutely vital to keep in touch with the people.

CHAPTER TWELVE

Fighting for the right to work

During the 1970s and 1980s, a lot of parliamentary attention was devoted to economic issues and the impact on jobs. With the decline of many heavy industries such as coal, shipbuilding and steel, it was a period of painful transition for the British economy and, for several years, the total number of unemployed people exceeded three million. There was a suspicion that unemployment was being used as an economic weapon and many workers lived in constant fear of losing their jobs. When jobs were threatened, people expected the local MP to take up the cudgels on their behalf.

My first experience of all this was the threatened closure of the chipboard factory at Cowie, shortly after I was elected to parliament. Stirling County Council, under the leadership of Councillor A.K. Davidson, had encouraged the location of the factory in the mining village of Cowie in order to compensate for some of the pit closures in the area. Unfortunately, the initial financial structure of the company was very unstable and the factory was still in its infancy when the owners announced that it had gone into receivership, which threatened the jobs of several hundred workers.

The employees decided to fight for their jobs and, at one stage, they organised a sit-in at the factory. I arranged to meet representatives of the management and trade union to discuss all options for keeping the factory going. The Secretary of State for Scotland at the time was Willie Ross and the Minister of State with responsibility for industry was Gregor Mackenzie, the MP for Rutherglen. I tabled a motion in the House of Commons calling for government intervention to rescue the situation and, after a vigorous campaign, I received a positive response from both Willie Ross and Gregor Mackenzie. Government assistance was made available for a new company to take over production and the chipboard factory was saved. The workforce was obviously delighted and, since then, the factory has apparently flourished.

Over the years, I have been involved in similar campaigns to save jobs in various workplaces: Carrongrove Paper Mill in Denny, McCowan's confectionery factory in Stenhousemuir, Alexander's bus construction works at Camelon and the Ministry of Defence (MOD) Depot at Bandeath on the south bank of the Forth. In the case of Bandeath, I soon realised that it would be very difficult to argue that the depot was an essential element of the national defence strategy. During the Second World War, it had been an Admiralty ammunition depot but, 30 years later, it was being used mainly for storage. When the MOD announced its closure in the mid 1970s, I persuaded Central Regional Council to purchase it and convert it into an industrial estate, where there are more people employed now than there were just prior to its closure by the MOD. It was a small example of beating swords into ploughshares. I have always believed that more should be done to divert unnecessary military expenditure into useful employment.

In the case of Alexander's (now Alexander Dennis), the company, originally a family firm, suffered greatly after being taken over by the Mayflower Group, which became embroiled in a financial scandal before going into administration in 2004. I introduced a parliamentary debate in which I praised the highly skilled work-force, who make the best double-deckers in the world and export to many countries, including China and the USA.

The Alexander Dennis campaign had a very successful outcome, but I learned early on that you can't win them all. As well as having a bus construction industry, Camelon used to be the home of the Scottish Bus Group (SBG) Engineering Workshops. The work-shops at one time employed several hundred people, many of them skilled engineers with responsibility for maintaining the SBG fleet of buses. In 1987, the SBG announced the proposed closure of the workshops and I realised that this would be a devastating blow for the workers and their families, and would have a very damaging effect on the local economy. After visiting the workshops and discussing the matter with the employees and their trade union representatives, I promised that I would do everything in my power to stop the closure.

I remembered that, a few years previously, Prime Minister Margaret Thatcher had stated during Question Time that she would always be willing to meet with any MP who had a threatened closure in his or her constituency. It was an off-the-cuff remark in response to a parliamentary question from a Tory MP who had an employment problem in his patch. However, it stuck in my mind and I decided to write to her, reminding her of her commitment and asking for a meeting to discuss the proposed closure of the SBG workshops. I was not confident that my request for a meeting would meet with a positive response because we had crossed swords several times previously at Prime Minister's Questions. For example, when her son Mark had lost his way in the Sahara Desert during a car rally, I suggested that the next time Mark ventured abroad he should do us all a favour and take his mummy with him. The House had exploded with laughter at that one, but the lady was not amused. However, to her credit, she agreed to my request for a meeting, which was scheduled to take place after Question Time in her room at the House of Commons, behind the Speaker's Chair.

When I arrived at the appointed time, I saw Lord James Douglas-Hamilton MP sitting outside the prime minister's door like a wee lap dug waiting for permission to enter his mistress's room. I asked Lord James why he was there and he explained that he was also going to be attending my meeting with the prime minister because he was Under-Secretary of State for Scotland, with responsibility for transport.

I said to him: 'I hope that we're going to be on the same side, James, because there are a lot of jobs at stake in my constituency. It's my job to fight for the jobs of my constituents and it's your job, as a Scottish Office minister, to fight for the jobs of Scottish workers, especially those who are making a valuable contribution to the Scottish transport system.'

James coughed nervously and said: 'Dennis, you and I have a lot in common.'

'What?' I replied, trying to fathom out what on earth he meant. Lord James was the son of the 14th Duke of Hamilton, premier peer of Scotland and hereditary Keeper of the Palace of Holyroodhouse. Not much commonality there.

'Dennis, don't you remember? You and I were elected to parliament on the same day.'

'Yes, of course, James, how could I possibly forget? So that's all the more reason why we should be on the same side. Let's get in there and tell the prime minister that she must stop the closure and save the workers' jobs.'

Just at that point, some flunkey appeared on the scene to tell us that the prime minister was ready to receive us. After we entered the room, she asked us to have a seat and I thanked her for agreeing to meet me. I then outlined the local employment situation, pointing out that the unemployment rate in Falkirk was well above the national average and would be even higher if the closure went ahead. I described the various skills of the workforce and the valuable service which they provided. I also reminded her that her government had a particular responsibility because the Scottish Bus Group was part of the Scottish Transport Group, which was publicly owned. I therefore asked her to reconsider the closure proposal for economic as well as social reasons.

Towards the end of my introductory remarks, the flunkey reappeared with a tea tray. He put the tray on a little table and was about to start serving up the tea when the prime minister grabbed the teapot out of his hand and started pouring its contents into three cups. She then poured milk into one of the cups and handed it to me. I said: 'Prime Minister, I don't take milk.'

'Take it!' she ordered, 'It's good for you.'

This was the same woman who earned the nickname 'Thatcher the milk snatcher' because, when she had ministerial responsibility for education in Ted Heath's Cabinet, she had stopped free milk for school children. I was minded to say something like: 'You robbed needy children of their milk and now you're trying to force it down my neck.' However, I knew that that would mean the SBG workshops definitely down the swanny. So I bit my tongue and swallowed the milky tea.

The prime minister then replied to my earlier remarks. She began by saying: 'Mr Canavan, I can understand your concern about the high level of unemployment in Falkirk', pronouncing the 'a' in Falkirk like the 'a' in Thatcher. It was on the tip of my tongue to correct her, but she was such a megalomaniac that she probably thought that she had the power to change the pronunciation of Scottish places names just like that. By this time, she was in full flow. It was like a lesson in O-Level Economics delivered in such a condescending manner that I found it difficult to sit there listening to such pap.

'You see, Mr Canavan, it's no use keeping people in a job unless they are making something which other people want to buy. Do you not understand that?'

'Yes, I understand that perfectly well, but the people employed in the workshops use their skills to ensure a reliable and safe transport system for other people. They are contributing to an important public service which is essential to the Scottish economy.'

After a while, I realised that it was futile trying to interrupt her. Her mind was made up.

I came out of the meeting feeling angry about Thatcher's attitude and even angrier with Lord James, who had not opened his cheeper. He had sat in silence throughout the entire meeting and the only sign of life from him was his obsequious nodding whenever his mistress spoke.

As soon as we got outside in the corridor, I was about to get torn into James, but he took the wind out of my sails.

'Dennis, I must say that you put up a very strong case to the prime minister on behalf of your constituents.'

'Well, why did you not back me up?'

'Dennis, I think you said all that could have been said. There was nothing left for me to say.'

I do not know whether James was simply trying to flatter me into submission, but I think he knew that I was fighting a lost cause. The decision had already been taken to close the workshops and it was driven by Thatcher's obsession with privatisation. The real reason for the closure was to slim down the Scottish Bus Group workforce in order to make the Group a more attractive proposition for potential bidders from the private sector.

The campaigns to stop closures and save jobs were not always in industrial situations. In the late 1970s, the Labour Government proposed the closure of several colleges of education, including Callendar Park College in Falkirk and Craiglockhart College in Edinburgh. The latter, founded in 1919, had a well-established tradition of training women to teach in Catholic schools. The former had had a relatively short existence, having been founded in 1964 in an effort to solve the acute shortage of teachers at that time. A decade later, the demographic situation had fundamentally changed. School rolls were falling and newly qualified teachers were finding it difficult to find jobs. The government therefore came up with a proposal to close down or merge some of the colleges of education as being surplus to requirements.

As a local MP, I was very closely involved with the campaign to save Callendar Park College, but I received far more letters and representations objecting to the proposed closure of Craiglockhart. There was obviously a well orchestrated campaign being conducted by the Catholic Church and some of the comments were completely over the top. I attended one rally in the Assembly Rooms in George

Street, Edinburgh, where some of the speakers seemed to believe that the proposed closure was part of a Marxist conspiracy to destroy the Catholic Church.

As a matter of principle, I voted in the House of Commons against all the college closures, but I did not think that the paranoid attitude of some Catholics would win them many friends. I suggested that all the colleges should diversify and questioned whether the role of Craiglockhart, for example, should be confined to enrolling female students from Catholic schools and turning them into teachers to be employed in Catholic schools. I proposed that all the colleges should develop a wide variety of courses, both vocational and non-vocational, and they should be encouraged to seek links with the Scottish universities, as part of a radical re-organisation of Scottish Higher Education. I have always thought that there is great educational value in the coming together of students from different disciplines and aspiring to enter different professions. When I wrote an article to that effect in the *Scottish Catholic Observer*, I received an irate letter from a Catholic priest, a former colleague of mine at the seminary, accusing me of undermining Catholic education. Yet much of what I was proposing was similar to the thinking of Cardinal Newman in his seminal work, *The Idea of a University*, written over a century before!

Some of my suggestions on the reform of higher education have now been taken on board, but the only college which made any meaningful response to my call for diversification at that time was Callendar Park. The Forth Valley College of Nursing and Midwifery moved into part of the Callendar Park College premises, but unfortunately it was under a different administration and it was almost like two separate colleges under one roof.

Nevertheless, the campaign to save Scotland's ten colleges of education was at least temporarily successful. Following pressure from the Tories as well as a rebellion on the part of some Labour MPs, including myself, Bruce Millan, Secretary of State for Scotland, did a U-turn and the colleges remained open, but not for long.

Shortly after the Tories came to power in 1979, they also did a U-turn and closed four of the colleges, including Craiglockhart and Callendar Park. There was not a whimper of protest from the Catholic establishment which had been so vociferous in its opposition to Labour's closure plans just shortly before.

When the Tory government's threat to the colleges first appeared, my parliamentary colleague, Harry Ewing, and I arranged to meet with Alex Fletcher, the Tory Education Minister at the Scottish Office, to seek assurances regarding the future of Callendar Park. Alex Fletcher promised us that the government would issue a consultation document before any final decision was taken. No such document was ever produced and, when the closures were announced, I condemned Alex Fletcher in the House of Commons for breaking his word, pointing out that many people in Scotland would now consider the Minister to be a liar. The Speaker, George Thomas, reprimanded me for using unparliamentary language, but he could not kick me out because of the indirect nature of my accusation. I still feel that my action was justified in order to expose the hypocrisy and duplicity of the Tory government.

Another educational battle concerned the future of Stirling University. In the 1970s, Stirling was the youngest of eight Scottish universities, having been founded in 1967, following the publication of Lord Robbins' report on the expansion of higher education. Initially Stirling had a lot going for it. The first chancellor was Lord Robbins himself and the first principal was Professor Tom Cottrell, a visionary scientist who wanted the university to serve the local community as well as gaining an international reputation for teaching and research.

Unfortunately, the fledgling institution suffered a serious setback during a royal visit in 1972. Some students organised a high-profile protest against the visit, but the demonstrations got completely out of hand. The conduct of the protestors, fuelled by strong drink, received massive publicity. Many national newspapers published a photograph of a drunken student, offering Her Majesty a swig out of his bottle! Students at that time were viewed by many to be an over-privileged minority of wasters and, for some of the local worthies who had campaigned hard for the new university to be located in Stirling, the behaviour of the students was completely outrageous.

The conduct of some of the protestors was inexcusable, but the reaction of some of the local politicians was ridiculous. My predecessor, William Baxter, Labour MP for West Stirlingshire, demanded that the culprits be publicly horse-whipped and then expelled. There were even calls for the entire university to be closed down there and then.

Despite the embarrassing episode, the university managed to recover and succeeded in attracting thousands of students from all over the UK as well as from overseas. Then along came the Thatcher regime, with its massive cuts in higher education. At one stage, the very existence of some universities seemed to be under threat and Stirling was very vulnerable because it was one of the newest kids on the block and many members of the establishment still harboured memories of the royal visit fiasco.

As the local MP for the university, I was invited to several on-campus meetings and rallies organised by the Association of University Teachers and the National Union of Students. I also received a very valuable briefing from the principal, the legendary Professor Ken Alexander, who told me about Stirling's excellent track record, especially in extending access to higher education.

As a result, I introduced a debate in the House of Commons and also sought a meeting with Sir Keith Joseph, the Secretary of State for Education and Science. Keith Joseph had the reputation of being a right-wing monetarist and Margaret Thatcher's mentor. I was rather apprehensive about what attitude he, as a former Oxford don, would take towards a relatively new institution like Stirling University. He received me very courteously and listened attentively to what I had to say. My only cause for discomfort was a very visible vein in his forehead which kept on throbbing throughout the entire meeting. I was not sure whether it was a sign of abnormally high blood pressure or an abnormally high level of cerebral activity.

Despite the distraction, I concentrated on the job in hand and described in detail the University of Stirling's excellent achievements in teaching and research, using the information given to me by Ken Alexander. When I finished, Keith Joseph thanked me politely, congratulated me on presenting a very good case and told me that he would take on board my representations during the course of his review of higher education. He gave no immediate commitment and I did not expect one, but I am convinced to this day that Keith Joseph used his considerable influence in Cabinet to shield the University of Stirling and many other academic institutions from the worst excesses of Thatcherism.

What a pity that there was nobody with the same political clout to make Thatcher see reason in her treatment of the mining industry. The destruction of deep coalmining must be one of the most tragic tales in British industrial history.

There used to be at least a dozen coalmines within a couple of miles of my birthplace in Cowdenbeath and, immediately after the Second World War, the British economy was still very dependent on coal to supply the energy needs of the nation. In the mid 1950s there were around three quarters of a million miners in Britain but, during the 1960s, there was a large number of pit closures. By the time I entered parliament in 1974, Polmaise Colliery was the only pit left in the whole of Stirlingshire.

Shortly after I was elected, the National Coal Board (NCB) announced the proposed closure of Polmaise, which employed about 700 miners, nearly all of them constituents of mine. I raised the matter immediately on the floor of the House of Commons with Alex Eadie MP, the Under-Secretary of State for Energy. The closure of any pit required ministerial approval and I was hopeful of being able to persuade the government to reverse the closure proposal, because there were still plenty of workable coal reserves at Polmaise.

The National Union of Mineworkers (NUM) was very strong and there was a very active branch at Polmaise, led by the redoubtable John McCormack. The president of the Scottish NUM was Mick McGahey, a member of the Communist Party, who had the reputation of being a militant extremist but was in fact a very shrewd negotiator and politician. If Mick McGahey rather than Arthur Scargill had been the UK president of the NUM during the 1984–85 strike, I am convinced that there would have been a better outcome for the miners.

On the Saturday morning after the NCB announced the proposed closure of Polmaise, the NUM organised a mass meeting of the workforce at Fallin Miners' Welfare Club, attended by Mick McGahey, Jimmy Cowan (Scottish Director of the NCB) and myself. John McCormack's speech at that meeting was a virtuoso performance. He said that the NUM must use every means at its disposal to save the pit because closure would have a devastating effect on the local community. John was a hard act to follow but, when it came to my turn to speak, I endorsed everything that John said and I pledged my support in the miners' fight to save their jobs.

John McCormack then asked if there were any questions from those present. There was a prolonged silence before one guy raised his hand and asked how much redundancy payment the workforce would get if the closure went ahead. I thought that John McCormack was going to jump down his throat. John told him in no uncertain terms that there would be no talk of closure and no talk of redundancy payments. There was no way his members were going to be 'bought off'. Jimmy Cowan sat listening on the platform. He did not say anything, but I think he got the message. He knew he had a fight on his hands unless he entered into serious negotiations with the union to keep the pit open.

A few days later, I phoned the NCB's Scottish headquarters in Edinburgh and asked to speak to Mr Cowan. After some delay, I heard a gravelly voice at the other end of the phone: 'Hello, Dennis, Mick McGahey here. What can I dae for ye?'

I was not sure whether the workers had taken over the NCB headquarters or had simply tapped Jimmy Cowan's phone line but, to cut a long story short, the pit closure was stopped and Polmaise Colliery lived to fight another day.

The NCB never revealed why it proposed the closure of Polmaise Colliery in the first place but the pit supposedly had a bit of a reputation for absenteeism and there were other tales, some of them apocryphal, which may have reached the ears of the high heid yins at NCB headquarters. I even heard stories about miners having their ribs broken during a Saturday night brawl, then being taken down the pit and a boulder placed on top of them so that they could claim compensation for industrial injury!

Another story referred to Fallin's unique style of industrial democracy. Even Mick McGahey was perplexed by the fact that whenever the NUM had a ballot, especially a strike ballot, the result at Polmaise Colliery was always unanimous in favour of the union. When Mick went out to Fallin to investigate the balloting procedure, he was shown a ballot box labelled 'Aye' in the union office at the pit head. When he questioned this, he was told of the existence of another ballot box, labelled 'No', with the justification that the system was based on the voting procedure at Westminster where MPs voted in either the 'Aye' lobby or the 'No' lobby.

'If it's guid enough for MPs, it's guid enough for us,' Mick was told.

When Mick then asked the whereabouts of the 'No' box, he was informed: 'At the tap o' the bloody bing!'

Following reversal of the closure proposal at Polmaise in the mid '70s, there was a marked improvement in the pit's performance on things like attendance and productivity. But when Margaret Thatcher appointed Ian McGregor to chair the NCB, the writing was on the wall. McGregor had the reputation of being an anti-trade union hatchet man from his days at British Steel and it was evident that Thatcher brought him in to destroy the British coal industry.

In early 1984, the NCB came out with another proposal to close Polmaise Colliery, despite the pit's good productivity record and the existence of abundant workable coal reserves. The workforce threatened to strike and Harry Ewing MP, Martin O'Neill MP and I arranged a meeting with McGregor at the NCB headquarters in London. McGregor listened politely to what we had to say about the viability of the pit but he did not give an inch. When the Polmaise workforce went on strike, it turned out to be the last throw of the dice.

At national level, there was a growing dispute between the NCB and the NUM about pit closures and the threat to the coal industry. The president of the NUM was Arthur Scargill, who arrogantly but naïvely thought that a national miners' strike could topple the Tory government. On the other hand, Margaret Thatcher was hell-bent on destroying the NUM, even if it meant destroying the entire coal industry in the process. Both Scargill and Thatcher were absolutely intransigent and the result was one of the most bitter and prolonged strikes in the history of the trade union movement. For the miners at Polmaise, it was more prolonged than for anyone else. A lot has been written about the history of the 1984–85 strike and many accounts claim that Cortonwood Colliery in Yorkshire was the pit which led the strike when it was threatened with closure but the fact remains that Polmaise was the first colliery in Britain to go on strike in the lead-up to the national strike.

During the strike, I visited many mining communities and addressed meetings at many venues throughout the country, including Fallin, Cowie, Stirling, Kilsyth, Kirkintilloch, Cowdenbeath and Polkemmet. I found the suffering experienced by many miners' families to be absolutely appalling. Thatcher tried to starve them into submission, and every weapon of the British state was used to try to defeat them, including the police, the criminal justice system and even the withdrawal of social security benefits. Yet the miners and their wives and families displayed a degree of courage and dignity which I found uplifting.

The support which the miners received from Labour MPs was rather patchy. I was a member of the campaign group of Labour MPs who agreed to a weekly levy to give financial assistance to the strikers and their families. We also pledged our utmost solidarity and arranged for MPs to speak at meetings, rallies and picket lines up and down the country. But there was an obvious personality clash between Neil Kinnock, the Labour leader, and Arthur Scargill, the miners' leader. Neil's wife, Glenys, was at pains to tell me that Neil supported the miners, but there were not many miners who believed it. Perhaps Kinnock saw Scargill as a rival, or perhaps King Arthur was considered an obstacle to Neil and Glenys getting their curtains up in No. 10. Whatever the reason, the result was that the miners did not get the support which they deserved because of the enmity between Kinnock and Scargill.

Some other Labour MPs slavishly adopted Kinnock's attitude. At a meeting of the Scottish Group of Labour MPs, I raised a complaint about the police and the procurator fiscal resorting to an abuse of the common law offence of 'breach of the peace' to arrest and charge miners who were simply sitting peacefully in a bus which had been stopped by the police on the A80 between Banknock and Glasgow. The police had assumed that they were travelling to a picket line and therefore arrested them for 'conduct likely to lead to a breach of the peace'. I suggested that the Scottish Group of Labour MPs should protest to the Crown Office and that an announcement be made that a future Labour government would take legislative action, if necessary, to stop such an abuse of the common law of Scotland. Donald Dewar, Shadow Secretary of State for Scotland, spluttered something about the inappropriateness of changing the law as the result of an industrial dispute, yet the Tories did precisely that on a regular basis.

Some of the conduct on the picket lines was so confrontational and so vicious that even the Queen was reputed to be alarmed about the violent scenes appearing almost daily on the TV news. It was at times like a civil war. There was, for example, a pitched battle at Orgreave coking plant in Yorkshire, where an army of mounted police in full riot gear was seen chasing miners who were actually trying to run away from the confrontation. There was one particularly bloody incident when a fleeing miner was attacked repeatedly by a mounted policeman wielding a huge baton.

At Question Time in the House of Commons, I complained about 'hooligans in uniform using truncheons and horses' hooves to beat the miners into submission'. There were roars of protest from the government benches. One Scottish Tory MP, Gerry Malone, said that miners arrested while picketing deserved to be treated as common criminals, 'because that is what they are'. Despite complaints from other MPs about pre-judging cases which were 'sub judice', the Speaker, Bernard Weatherill, let Malone away with it.

I have never claimed that all the miners were angels. Some terrible things happened during that strike when people were under huge stress and tempers got frayed.

Over 20 years after the strike, I gave the following speech in the Scottish Parliament during a debate on the appointment of Elish Angiolini as the first woman in Scotland's history to hold the post of Lord Advocate:

> During the process of canonisation it is customary to have a devil's advocate whose job is to find out something bad about the candidate. I would like to apply for the job of devil's advocate to the Lord Advocate.
>
> I first came across Elish Angiolini more than 20 years ago at Airdrie Sheriff Court. It was during the miners' strike and a very good friend of mine who had been involved in, well, let us just say an altercation on a picket line, was hauled before the sheriff. Elish McPhilomy, as she was at the time, was the prosecutor. She was razor sharp in her prosecution – so razor sharp that I was convinced that my good friend was going to end up in Barlinnie. To cut a long story short, she was successful in her prosecution but did not demand the death penalty or even a custodial sentence and the sheriff let my good friend off with a modest fine. The moral of the story is that justice should always be tempered with mercy – not a bad motto for a Lord Advocate. In that spirit, I congratulate Elish on her nomination and wish her every success in the future.

Elish took my speech in good humour and I gave her a kiss of congratulation when her appointment as Lord Advocate was approved.

The good friend to whom I referred was one of my most stalwart supporters, Tommy Canavan. Tommy will never forget the strike and, although we can have a good laugh now about some of the things that happened, it was a very painful experience for miners and their families at the time. The strike lasted over a year and the aftermath was the death of an erstwhile great industry and a massive increase in unemployment.

Nevertheless, I shall always remember the positive aspects of that experience, particularly the courage and comradeship of workers involved in a desperate struggle to save their industry. Margaret Thatcher may have succeeded in killing the mining industry, but she could never succeed in killing the spirit and solidarity of the mining communities. Much of it still remains to the present day.

CHAPTER THIRTEEN

Ban the belt

On the use of corporal punishment, my old schools, St Columba's and St Bride's, were probably no better and no worse than most schools in Scotland at that time. The tales which came out of Beath High School, just across the road from St Columba's, were very similar, but it is interesting to recall Beath High School's significant contribution in the campaign to abolish the belt.

In 1976, I introduced a bill in the House of Commons to abolish the use of corporal punishment in schools. As a young teacher, I had hated using the belt, even as a last resort, and it was not an effective deterrent. In the case of the most frequent belters, the same miscreants kept coming back for more and, for some of the pupils, it was a badge of honour. As I became more experienced, I managed to keep discipline in my own classroom without using corporal punishment and I encouraged colleagues in my department to do likewise. When introducing my bill, I pointed out that corporal punishment had already been banned in most civilised countries throughout the world, it had been banned in our armed forces and it had been banned in our state penal system for many years. It was also a bad example to set young people when adults were seen to be using violence in an effort to solve a problem. Violence breeds violence. So I thought that my bill had a reasonable chance of making progress, or at least encouraging a rational debate on the issue, but the reaction shook me.

I was unaware of an earlier memo from the Scottish Education Department, dated 19 November 1973, predicting that any attempt to abolish corporal punishment would provoke 'violent' opposition from the teachers' unions. At the time, I would probably have dismissed such a prediction as absurd but it turned out to be not very wide of the mark. Opponents described my bill as a recipe for anarchy and I was virtually disowned by my own trade union, the Educational Institute of Scotland (EIS), which disappointed me because I still had a lot of friends in the EIS and I had a huge admiration for John Pollock, the General Secretary, who would have made an excellent MP.

About that time, my good friend and parliamentary colleague Margaret Ewing and I were invited to address an EIS conference in Edinburgh. Margaret and I had taught together at St Modan's High School, Stirling. In fact, I had been her boss for part of that period but, to her credit, she never held that against me. She and I were elected to parliament for neighbouring constituencies on the same day in 1974. She was the SNP spokesperson for education and I was Convener of the Education Committee of the Scottish Group of Labour MPs. Margaret was one of the co-sponsors of my bill to abolish corporal punishment and we were given a hard time by the EIS members, who sadly kept on repeating the same old line that teachers were *in loco parentis* (taking the place of the parent) and therefore entitled to belt the children in their charge just as parents could physically punish their children.

At least the EIS members were fairly polite in their opposition, but my main antagonist in the House of Commons was Patrick Cormack (now Sir Patrick Cormack), the Tory MP for Staffordshire South, who claimed to have been a teacher but would probably not have lasted five minutes in a Scottish comprehensive school. Cormack, a Billy Bunter lookalike, obviously thought that the whole educational system would collapse if teachers stopped thrashing children and, as an avowed Christian, he probably thought that his view was theologically justified. 'If one spares the rod one spoils the child', he sanctimoniously told the House of Commons.

Cormack reminded me of my experience as a temporary teacher at Queen Anne Secondary School in Dunfermline just over a decade before the parliamentary debate on my bill. I was still a student at the time and I was based in the annexe at Pittencrieff Street, where all the children with learning difficulties were isolated from the rest of the school community. Their only link with the main school was the weekly visit from the headteacher, Jimmy Carmichael, Master of Arts and Fellow of the Educational Institute of Scotland. His weekly visit took the form of a religious assembly followed by a mass session of corporal punishment of the week's most serious offenders, whose crimes were judged to be so heinous that they had to be belted by the headmaster in front of the whole assembly. The irony was that most of those children came from poor, deprived backgrounds and the most 'educated' person they were ever likely to meet in their lives was this pantomime baddy in a black gown descending on their school once a week and attempting to thump them into submission with a big leather belt. On some occasions, the headmaster was obviously too busy to wait until the end of the assembly and the miscreants would be ordered out of the assembly room before the grand finale to receive their punishment. On such occasions, it was not unusual for the Lord's Prayer or the final hymn to be punctuated by wailing and gnashing of teeth.

Perhaps Sir Patrick Cormack MP still believes that God is on the side of the belters and caners. My recollection of him in 1974 was that he was a buffoon and, during the course of the parliamentary debate, he was reduced to an object of ridicule. I felt that I had won the debate but, to my astonishment, I lost the vote. Even some of my Labour colleagues voted against me or abstained, including Tam Dalyell and Robin Cook. I was told afterwards that Tam, an old Etonian, and Robin, a former pupil of Edinburgh's Royal High School, had had a tough time trying to maintain discipline during their brief spells teaching at Bo'ness Academy. Tam then escaped from the classroom to become Director of Studies on the school ship *Dunera* and Robin escaped to become a tutor for the Workers' Educational Association.

Despite the defeat of my bill in the House of Commons, the campaign to abolish corporal punishment continued – which brings me back to the Cowdenbeath connection. A pupil of Beath High School, Jeffrey Cosans, had committed the 'offence' of taking a short-cut home from school by climbing over Beath Cemetery wall, situated near the school. There was never any suggestion that the boy had damaged the wall or shown any disrespect towards the occupants of the cemetery. Nevertheless, the school authorities demanded that the boy should be belted, but he refused to accept the punishment. His mother supported him, but neither the school nor Fife Regional Council, as Education Authority, would back down. The pupil was suspended *sine die* from school and the stand-off between the boy and the Education Authority became a *cause célèbre* which entered the annals of Scottish legal history.

A friend of mine, Norman McEwan, a Stirling lawyer, had been very supportive of my private member's bill. Norman was a Labour councillor and also chaired the Scottish Council for Civil Liberties. He was a passionate campaigner for human rights and he firmly believed that corporal punishment of children was a violation of their human rights. As a lawyer, he was of the opinion that the UK government, being a signatory to the European Convention on

Human Rights, was in breach of the Convention, which specifically bans any treatment or punishment which is inhuman or degrading. Norman took up the case of the Beath High School pupil and, with typical tenacity, he fought it all the way to the European Court of Human Rights in Strasbourg. He was told that the European Court would not even consider the case unless it could be shown that all domestic avenues of redress had already been exhausted. Norman was able to point out that the Scottish courts had already found against the pupil and his mother and that the UK parliament had voted down my bill to abolish corporal punishment. As the matter had already been pursued unsuccessfully through the UK parliament and the judiciary, Norman was able to persuade the European Court to consider the case.

The Court eventually came out with the historic decision that the UK government was in breach of the European Convention on Human Rights, and the UK government was obliged to order the abolition of corporal punishment in all state schools throughout the UK.

I found it rather ironic that my bill failed when Labour was in power and it was a Tory government that eventually abolished corporal punishment. I have since heard some former Strathclyde councillors trying to re-write history by taking the credit, but the man who deserves it is the late Norman McEwan. I was very proud when, years later, his son Norrie and my son Dennis became very good friends and formed a great partnership in my campaign team for election to the Scottish Parliament.

CHAPTER FOURTEEN

———— ◆ ————

Cold war

When I was elected to parliament, I was aged 32 and had never been in an aeroplane in my life. But I had done a fair amount of foreign travel when I was a student, hitch-hiking through many European countries.

In the early 1960s my brother, Ian, was stationed in Germany at RAF Gütersloh, fairly close to what was then called the Iron Curtain, the boundary between Western Europe, which was NATO territory, and Eastern Europe, under Warsaw Pact control. During my university holidays, I hitchhiked to Germany and got a temporary job at a bottling plant in Gütersloh. I had spent what little money I had getting there and, of course, I would not be paid any wages until the end of my first week's work. When I explained my predicament to Ian, he said that I could stay with him and his mates in the RAF base. I wondered about that because there was an armed guard at the gate and a perimeter barbed-wire fence. However, the only alternative was to sleep rough. So in the evenings I would arrange to meet Ian and his mates at a bar in Gütersloh and we walked back to the base in a group, with me in the middle. Not once did the sentry stop us to check our identification.

On one occasion, I missed the rendezvous in the pub and I arrived alone after midnight at the RAF base. At that time of night, security was stricter and I did not want to chance my luck with the armed sentry on duty at the gate. I therefore followed the high perimeter fence until I was out of sight. There was a sign: 'Achtung! Hunde!' indicating that the perimeter of the camp was patrolled by dogs. I did not fancy being torn to shreds by an alsatian but the thought of a warm bunk bed waiting for me gave me the courage to climb the fence, despite the fact that it was over two metres high and topped with barbed wire. On my first attempt, I was disturbed by a barking dog and a flashing light but fortunately I was not within biting distance and, after hiding for a while in a ditch, I managed eventually to scale the fence. So much for British security during the Cold War.

By good luck, somebody in Ian's barrack-room was on leave and I was able to use the empty bunk. In the morning, I had a hearty breakfast in the NAAFI canteen before going off to work.

After about a fortnight, I was getting restless again and felt like moving on. I wanted to visit Berlin and see the infamous wall which had been recently built to stop people moving from East Berlin to West Berlin, although the East German authorities came up with some cock-and-bull story that it was to stop espionage. I had also heard from my old Modern Languages teacher, Mr Ritchie, that pre-war Berlin had been a beautiful city and I wanted to see what, if any, of that beauty remained.

When I explained my intention to Ian and his RAF mates, they were incredulous. They pointed out the huge difficulties of getting in and out of Berlin. East Germany and West Germany were two different countries at that time and East Germany had a puppet communist government controlled by the Soviet Union.

West Berlin, although under the control of the Western Allies, was an enclave completely surrounded by East German territory and, in order to get by road from West Germany to West Berlin, it was necessary to cross the West–East German frontier and then travel over 100 miles along an East German autobahn (motorway). As hitchhiking on the autobahn was forbidden, I would have to get a lift all the way from the frontier into West Berlin.

Despite the difficulties, I decided to give it a try and, after waiting for several hours near the frontier, I at last found a friendly truck driver who took me all the way to West Berlin. The only problem was that we arrived in the city well after midnight and the truck driver deposited me in a part of the city which was completely deserted and had little, if any, street lighting.

I took out my street map to find the location of the nearest youth hostel and stumbled along, not at all sure that I was heading in the right direction. Half an hour later I had to admit that I was completely lost. There was not enough light to read the map and I could not even make out the names of the streets.

Nevertheless, I decided to keep walking as it was getting cold and I thought it would not be too long until dawn. After walking for what seemed several miles, I at last managed to decipher the name of a street. On checking the map, I saw that, if I walked along to the end of that street and took a left, I would be heading in the direction of the youth hostel. I felt elated but it was short-lived. Halfway along the street, I almost collided with a high concrete construction stretching across the road and the pavement in such a way that access beyond that point was impossible. I looked up and, when I saw the barbed wire, it dawned on me what it was. That was my first encounter with the Berlin Wall.

For nearly 30 years afterwards, that wall would be a symbol of the Cold War and the division of Europe, but my first impression of it was the way it divided streets, families and communities. The communist authorities must have been pretty stupid not to have foreseen that the Berlin Wall would become a powerful propaganda weapon against the oppression of their regime. When President John F. Kennedy came to view the wall, he gave his famous rallying cry: 'Ich bin ein Berliner!' It was a brilliant piece of oratory expressing the solidarity between the Western world and the people of Berlin.

According to official records, 136 people lost their lives trying to cross the wall to freedom. The East German Volkspolizei (Vopos) were ordered to shoot anyone trying to go over the wall. Nobody, of course, tried to escape from West to East and even some of the Vopos eventually defected to the West.

On the day after my near-collision with the Berlin Wall, I became increasingly curious as to what life was like on the other side. Armed with only my passport and a few West German marks, I went along to Checkpoint Charlie, the main crossing point between West and East. I had no problem getting through with my British passport but, on my return, I was kept waiting by the Vopos for what seemed like hours. I am not sure whether it was simply a bureaucratic delay or whether it was meant to discourage people from visiting East Berlin.

At first it was difficult to believe that East Berlin and West Berlin were part of the same city. West Berlin was a vibrant, bustling, modern city with bright lights, advertisements and shop windows displaying all the haute couture and other products of Western capitalism. East Berlin by comparison was drab and dreary. Some of the streets looked as if they had been in a time warp since the 1930s. In other streets, the buildings had been completely razed to the ground by allied bombing and had been replaced with grotesque concrete Stalinist architecture. There was almost an eerie silence about the place and then I realised what it was. There were hardly any motor vehicles apart from an occasional bus or truck. After a while, I began to appreciate the atmosphere because the air was fresher and there was much less noise pollution than any other city I had visited. Nevertheless, my over-all impression was that East Berlin was a sad place and the people did not look happy. I could understand why some of them were prepared to risk their lives by escaping over the wall, especially if they had friends or relatives on the other side.

Little did I think that, 30 years later, I would be sitting in Bonn discussing the fall of the Berlin Wall with the man who became the first chancellor of a reunited Germany. Helmut Kohl had the reputation of being a right-wing Christian Democrat who got on very well with Margaret Thatcher. I first met him when I was a member of the Foreign Affairs Committee of the House of Commons. When we visited other countries, it was not every head of government who had time to meet us, but Kohl always made time and he was good value. He would seat us round his Cabinet table, ask his civil servants to leave and sometimes spend over an hour with us talking ad lib about any subject we wanted to raise with him. He was an enormous, gregarious person with a love of conversation and a great sense of humour.

He never could understand the British Eurosceptics' hostility to federalism because it had worked well in Germany, and the written constitution of the Federal Republic of Germany had facilitated the reunification of his country. After the fall of the Berlin Wall, Kohl had taken a big gamble by offering the East Germans an exchange rate of a mark for a mark, despite the fact that the Ostmark, the East German currency, was worth only a fraction of the Deutschmark, the West Germany currency. For the East Germans, it was a bargain and a big incentive for reunification, but Kohl risked the wrath of many of his own supporters in the West, because of the negative impact on the economy. But Kohl was a man of vision who seized the moment, and sometimes political leaders have to take risks instead of always playing it safe. Kohl's political reputation was later tarnished by allegations of corruption but, despite that, history will record him as the father of a united Germany.

However, even Kohl would admit that all his efforts would have been in vain if it had not been for the work of President Mikhail Gorbachev, the last president of the Soviet Union. It was Gorbachev's twin strategies of *glasnost* (openness) and *perestroika* (restructuring) which brought about a wind of change which swept through the USSR with implications throughout Eastern

Europe and further afield. The world would never be the same again.

In my youth, I had more than a smidgeon of admiration for some of the Communist Party members in Fife but I could never understand how any thinking person could defend the old Soviet system and its foreign policy. I remember refugees from Hungary arriving in Cowdenbeath in 1956 after Russian tanks had brutally quashed the Hungarian people's uprising. The local Communists were embarrassed by it all. Some resigned from the party in disgust and others, who tried to justify the use of tanks against innocent civilians, came to be known as 'tankies'. I do not know where Gorbachev stood in 1956, but 30 years later he was no 'tanky'. He was a liberator.

I was first introduced to Gorbachev by John Major, when he was prime minister. I was having a drink with some colleagues on the terrace at the House of Commons when Major called out: 'Dennis, come and meet the president.' I could hardly believe it. I shook hands with Gorbachev, expressed the hope that his visit to Britain would be a success, and then jokingly warned him that he should watch some of the company he was keeping. Major laughed but maybe my attempt at a joke was lost through the interpreter's translation. Gorbachev gave a very serious reply to the effect that a new era had arrived when dialogue between people of different political beliefs was essential. I could not argue with that.

The Foreign Affairs Committee had a formal discussion session with Gorbachev and some of his delegation, including Eduard Shevardnadze, Minister for Foreign Affairs, who later became the first president of the independent state of Georgia after the break-up of the Soviet Union. We discussed a whole range of issues including Afghanistan, the future of Europe, nuclear weapons and human rights.

Gorbachev was like a breath of fresh air compared with most of the politicians I had met on visits to Moscow or at the Soviet Embassy in London. The latter would simply regurgitate the same old Communist Party line on everything and, when asked an awkward question, they would just try to defend the indefensible. They reminded me of the 'tankies'. With Gorbachev, on the other hand, there was real engagement and exchange of ideas. There was also a gravitas, an honesty and a humanity about him.

I could never understand how Gorbachev, despite his international stature, was never given due recognition within his own country. He deservedly received the Nobel Peace Prize for ending the Cold War and helping to make the world a safer place to live in. But at home he was undermined by Boris Yeltsin, a drunken populist who was not fit to lace Gorbachev's boots.

One of the few Communist leaders who managed to survive into the twenty-first century was President Fidel Castro of Cuba, who had been in power for over half a century before illness forced him to hand over power to his brother Raúl in 2006.

I met Fidel in Havana in 1982 as a member of a visiting delegation from the House of Commons Foreign Affairs Committee. We were doing an inquiry into British foreign policy in Central America and the Caribbean region. Thatcher and Reagan were both obsessed with anti-communism and Reagan seemed convinced that the Castro regime was intent on exporting revolutionary communism throughout the entire region, thereby posing a threat to the security of the USA. The CIA was already involved in helping anti-democratic forces in places like Nicaragua, Guatemala and El Salvador and, as a result, there was widespread violation of human rights throughout the region. In the eyes of the Americans, however, Castro was Public Enemy Number One.

During our visit, we discovered that Cuba's main exports were not armed revolutionaries but doctors, nurses, teachers, engineers and technicians, who had been sent to help other countries, particularly in the Caribbean and Africa. There was a happy-go-lucky Latin atmosphere about Havana, compared with most cities in the Communist world, but the British ambassador told us to be wary of spies and seductive women who might use their charms to blackmail us.

Castro was famous for his lengthy speeches at party rallies and, when we met him, he immediately launched into a rant about Reagan and his ally, Thatcher, whom he kept on referring to as 'your leader'. When I pointed out to him that Thatcher was not my leader and that I profoundly disagreed with many of her domestic and foreign policies, Castro upbraided me. He told me that, when I was in the British parliament, I could criticise the prime minister as much as I wanted but, when I was abroad, protocol dictated that I should not criticise her. I thought that was a bit rich coming from the leader of a one-party state.

After the meeting, Sir Peter Mills MP, a Tory member of our delegation chided me: 'You are a disgrace, Canavan. Even Fidel

Castro thinks you are such an extremist that he had to give you a dressing-down for maligning our prime minister!'

On the way back from Cuba, I stayed overnight at the British High Commission in Barbados. The High Commissioner told me that I would be sleeping in Princess Margaret's bed, although he hastily added that I would have the bed all to myself as she had just left. He explained, or rather complained, that she frequently used the High Commission as a staging post on her way to the romantic island of Mustique, a favourite trysting place for the Princess and her boyfriend, Roddy Llewellyn. Maybe the High Commissioner thought that leaking that information would put an end to such abuse of free accommodation at the tax-payer's expense. Yet, when I described Princess Margaret in the House of Commons as a 'parasite', the Speaker, George Thomas, exploded with rage and threatened to kick me out. During a subsequent TV interview, I pointed out that even respectable dictionaries define a 'parasite' as a creature that lives at others' expense without making any useful return. But freedom of speech in the House of Commons does not extend to criticism of royalty. I wonder what Fidel Castro would think of that!

CHAPTER FIFTEEN

──── ◆ ────

Real war

When I was elected to the House of Commons in 1974, I never dreamt that Britain would be engaged in another war, but less than a decade later came the Falklands conflict. I was one of the 33 MPs who opposed the war. I strongly disapproved of the Argentinian invasion of the Falklands, but I felt that military intervention by Britain would lead to the loss of many lives and I thought that Britain's claim to the Falklands was a bit dubious to say the least. Even 'Rambo' Reagan's administration initially favoured diplomacy rather than military action, but Thatcher was hell-bent on a destructive war which cost billions of pounds and, more importantly, over 900 lives.

Shortly after the end of the war, the Foreign Affairs Committee embarked on an inquiry about the future of the Falklands and we decided to visit the islands in order to take evidence. It was a long, arduous journey, starting with a flight from RAF Brize Norton to Dakar in Senegal. The next leg of the journey was from Dakar to Ascension Island, where we camped overnight in portakabins.

In the morning, we boarded a Hercules aircraft for what we hoped would be the final leg of our journey. There was an element of uncertainty about it all because the Hercules had to be refuelled in mid-flight. If anything went wrong with the refuelling operation or if we happened to be buzzed by the Argentinian airforce, we would have to do a U-turn and possibly an emergency landing somewhere, but the options for that were rather limited in the middle of the South Atlantic.

It was the most uncomfortable journey I have ever experienced. Not knowing how long the flight would last was nerve-racking and the noise of the aircraft engine made conversation virtually impossible. The aircraft was more suitable for transporting large military cargo rather than human beings. When we were told that Margaret Thatcher had undertaken the same journey a few weeks previously, I had a sneaking admiration for her endurance, even though the pilot later explained that a caravan had been brought on board to accommodate her.

The refuelling operation went very smoothly and we arrived at Port Stanley airport on schedule. As we travelled into the town, Union Jacks and pictures of Margaret Thatcher were everywhere. I also noticed some welcoming graffiti: 'God Save the Queen', 'Well done, Maggie', 'Foulkes, fuck off!' Before leaving the UK, George Foulkes, a member of our delegation, had issued a press statement criticising the British Government's policy on the Falklands. Although I basically agreed with the contents of George's statement, issuing an advance press release was not a smart move because it gave the impression that we were pre-judging the outcome of our inquiry. But George was always desperate for publicity and the graffiti indicated that the contents of his press release had reached the Falklands before us.

Despite the fact that we were absolutely shattered after such a long journey, we were taken to Government House for a reception, hosted by Sir Rex Hunt, Governor of the Falkland Islands. He was a pompous little man, a very minor diplomat who would have remained in obscurity if the Argentinians had not had the stupidity to invade the Falklands. Rex Hunt suddenly became an international figure, although some of his photographs made him an object of ridicule, with his governor's dress uniform, complete with plumed hat. He looked a complete anachronism, a remnant of a previous imperial era, but perhaps that was appropriate, since he ruled over one of the last outposts of the British Empire.

The welcome reception was packed with Foreign Office diplomats, Falklands government officials and military top brass, the latter in dress uniform. At one stage, I got involved in a conversation with a man in a dog collar who turned out to be the local prelate, a Catholic monsignor. He started lecturing me about what an evil lot the Argies were. I might have put up with it if he had confined his remarks to the Argentinian government but he seemed to imply that the entire Argentinian people were collectively guilty and he kept going on about their lack of respect for human rights. I asked him what, in his opinion, was the most fundamental of all human rights and, as expected, he replied: 'The right to life.' I then asked him: 'What then was the biggest violation of human rights during the Falklands War?' He was stuck for an answer. I rephrased my question: 'What incident led to the biggest loss of life in the war?'

'I suppose you mean the *Belgrano*,' was the reply.

The *Belgrano* was an Argentinian warship which was sunk by a Royal Navy nuclear-powered submarine, HMS *Conqueror*, causing the loss of 323 Argentinian sailors. As was later confirmed, the *Belgrano*, when attacked, was outside the 200-mile exclusion zone declared by the British Government and it was actually heading back towards Argentina. Nevertheless, Margaret Thatcher personally authorised the attack.

I continued my conversation with the monsignor: 'And who was responsible for that violation of human rights?' Silence. I tried again.

'Do you not agree that Margaret Thatcher was responsible for killing over 300 people, which was the biggest violation of human rights during the Falklands War?'

By this time, my cross-examination of the monsignor was beginning to draw an audience and the verbal exchange was beginning to get rather heated. One of the military top brass came to the monsignor's rescue, growling something about scurrilous accusations and trying desperately to change the subject of conversation.

Unbeknown to me, the incident had been mis-reported by a sneaky young man called Patrick Watts, who was head of Falklands Radio but also acted as a stringer for the London-based *Daily Telegraph*.

The following day, there were banner headlines in the *Telegraph* about my confrontation with the monsignor. The day after that, some of the tabloids copied the story and embellished it to such an extent that the monsignor and I had allegedly been involved in a punch-up which had to be broken up by a brigadier. So much for journalistic licence. I later got an apology from Sir Rex Hunt, who admitted that he should have taken steps to avoid such inaccurate media coverage of a private event which he had hosted. The person responsible for leaking the 'story' was actually a Falklands government employee!

During our visit to the Falklands we stayed at the Upland Goose Hotel in Port Stanley. 'Hotel' was too grandiose a description of the joint. The AA would not have given it a half-star rating and Egon Ronay would have slated it. It was mutton, mutton, mutton every day of the week, and not very good mutton at that. The rooms were cold and damp, with wallpaper peeling off, and the furniture and interior decor were depressing. To make matters worse, the service was absolutely appalling. The proprietor, perhaps for political reasons, seemed to think that he was doing us a favour by giving us a roof over our heads.

he Bonny Baby competition, Central Park, Cowdenbeath, 1943. That's my mum second from the left, proudly
lding the winner.

he 7-a-side football champions at the Cowdenbeath Co-operative Gala, 1953. *Back row, left to right:* Michael
yne (who went on to play for the Scotland Youth Team), Robert Dunne, Michael Jack, Dennis Canavan.
ont row, left to right: Jimmy Mulrein, John Mullen, Willie Callaghan (who went on to play for Scotland and
n a Scottish Cup Winner's medal with Dunfermline Athletic FC).

Mum, Dad, Raymond, Dennis, Kathleen and Ian on holiday at Pettycur Bay, Kinghorn, July 1947.

Dux of St Columba's High School, 1958.

St Andrew's College (Drygrange Seminary) Football Team, 1959. All of the players became ordained priests with the exception of the holy goalie and me. *Back row, left to right*: Benny McAllister, John Creanor, Francis Burns, Dennis Canavan, David McCann, Patrick Clarke. *Front row, left to right*: John Cullen, Joe McMullan, Harry Reid, Danny Boyd, Willie Gallagher.

ennis John, Ruth, Mark and Paul, 1973.

king Parliament by storm. After my election in 1974.

With Henry Dawson, Tony Benn, Caroline Benn, Naida Ferguson and John Robertson, before a public meeting in Bonnybridge, 1977.

On an underground visit to Polmaise Colliery, Fallin, 8 February 1978. *Left to right*: Tam Bone, Graham Steel, Dennis Canavan, Terry McMeel and John MacCormack.

With Mark, Elnor, Dennis John, Paul and Ruth, 1979

king the plunge with the Parachute Regiment for a charity event, Aldershot, c. 1980.

ith Yasser Arafat in Beirut, 30 November 1981.

Parliamentary charity swim at the RAC club in London, c. 1982. That's me in the front on the extreme left. The woman on the extreme right was a 'bunny girl' from the Playboy Club, who was invited along by a Tory MP. Most of the participants would probably prefer to remain anonymous but the woman in the middle is Janet Fookes MP (now Baroness Fookes), and to the right of her is George Thomas, Speaker of the House of Commons, who turned up to start us off despite the fact that the House was sitting at the time. A few weeks earlier, he declined an invitation from me to open a conference at Stirling University on the grounds that he never left the Palace of Westminster when the House was sitting.

Parliamentary line-up for the 1984 London Marathon. *Left to right*: Colin Moynihan MP, David Heathcoat-Amory MP, Dennis Canavan MP, Gary Waller MP, Alistair Burt MP, Matthew Parris MP and Dick Douglas M

Scottish Labour Party 5-a-side football tournament, 1985. *Left to right*: Michael Martin MP, Donald Dewar MP, Willie McKelvey MP, Tam Dalyell MP and Dennis Canavan MP.

Crossing the finishing line with a personal best time in the 1985 Glasgow Marathon.

With Harry Ewing MP and David Steel MP, signing the Claim of Right at the first meeting of the Scottish Constitutional Convention in the Assembly Hall, The Mound, Edinburgh, 20 March 1989.

Shaking hands with King Juan Carlos of Spain in Madrid, c. 1990. Also in the picture are, *left to right*: Ivan Lawrence MP, Jim Lester MP, Ted Rowlands MP, Michael Welsh MP and Peter Temple-Morris MP.

With Helmut Kohl (left), Chancellor of the Federal Republic of Germany, in Bonn, c. 1993. *Left to right*: Bob Wareing MP, Jim Lester MP, David Sumberg MP, David Howell MP, Chancellor Helmut Kohl, John Stanley MP, Michael Jopling MP, Mike Gapes MP and Dennis Canavan MP.

With Boutros Boutros-Ghali, Secretary-General of the United Nations, at the UN Headquarters in New York, c. 1995. *Left to right*: Peter Shore MP, Dennis Canavan MP, Bob Wareing MP, David Sumberg MP, David Howell MP, Boutros Boutros-Ghali, Michael Jopling MP, David Harris MP, Helen Irwin (Clerk to the Foreign Affairs Select Committee), John Stanley MP and Rosie Challis (Assistant Clerk to the Foreign Affairs Select Committee).

Celebrating with Camelon Juniors Football Club when they won the Scottish Junior Cup in 1995. Also in the photograph are, *left to right*: Brian Fairley, John Wardrope, George Fairley, Anne Wallace and Marilyn Anderson.

The Scotland team singing *Flower of Scotland* before playing against England in a parliamentary challenge football match at Upton Park, home of West Ham FC, in 1998. *Back row, left to right*: Michael Connarty MP, Parliamentary Clerk, Ian Gibson MP, George Galloway MP, Jim Murphy MP, Piper, Craig Brown (Scotland coach), Jimmy Wray MP, Goalkeeper, John McAllion MP, Lord Taylor of Warwick, Jim Fitzpatrick MP. *Front row, left to right*: Ian Stewart MP, Douglas Alexander MP, Des Browne MP, Dennis Canavan MP, Stephen McCabe MP, Ian Davidson MP, John McFall MP, Russell Brown MP.

DEWAR BLOW AS MARTIN IS THRASHED BY DENNIS THE MENACE

FALKIRK WEST remained Canavan Country as the fiery rebel MP fought off claims on his territory.

Go-it-alone Dennis stormed to a sensational victory in the constituency which he won with a 14,000 majority in the 1997 General Election.

This time, without the backing of the official Labour Party machine, he took on the official candidate and trounced him with a 12,000 majority.

His major opponent Ross Martin was left licking his wounds after trying to oust the local favourite.

Canavan stood as an independent – cheekily labelling himself the MP for Falkirk West on his official nomination papers – after his very public split from the official New Labour party.

Rejected Canavan wins by over 12,000 votes

Evening Times, 7 May 1999. (Reproduced with the permission of the Herald & Times Group)

HOLYROOD BOUND: THE MAN NOT CONSIDERED

LAST LAUGH

Labour's reject MP takes the applause after famous victory

By JAMIE MACASKILL

LABOUR rebel Dennis Canavan swept to a stunning victory last night.

The veteran left wing MP, rejected as a candidate by New Labour, raised his hands in triumph as the Falkirk West result was declared.

Canavan, 57, stood as an Independent candidate after being rejected by Labour's selection panel.

He romped home to a stunning majority of 12,192 over Labour but admitted: "The brilliance of my victory is tinged a wee bit with sorrow.

"Sorrow in that I'm not standing before you tonight as a member of the party in which I was virtually born and brought up.

"I hope some reconciliation may be possible but I say here that there will be no compromise on the principles and policies which I have always held dear and the Labour party used to hold dear.

"This campaign was also about right of people at local level to decide who their candidates and representatives should be without outside influence or central control."

Canavan's rejection by Labour came despite his being one of the party's most committed campaigners for devolution and publicly proclaiming that being a member of a Scottish Parliament was his great dream.

Local voters, apparently disgusted at the way the popular Westminister MP had been treated, turned out in large numbers to back him.

The turn-out of 62 per cent was one of the biggest in the country.

Labour's decision to dump him led to a mass exodus from the local party where 95 per cent of Labour members backed his selection bid.

WINNER: Canavan had overwhelming local support

ABOVE. Congratulating Donald Dewar after his election as Scotland's First Minister, 13 May 1999

LEFT. With John Knox at the Assembly Hall on The Mound, where the newly elected Scottish Parliament met for the first time, 12 May 1999.

The Scotland team which beat Ireland 3–2 in the inter-parliamentary football match at Trinity College, Dublin, November 2002. *Back row, left to right*: Duncan Hamilton MSP, Allan Wilson MSP, Frank McAveety MSP, Goal Keeper (Scottish Parliament employee), Henry McLeish MSP, Jim Murphy MP, Kenny MacAskill MSP, Tommy Sheridan MSP. *Front row, left to right*: Bruce Crawford MSP, Robin Harper MSP, Angus Mackay MSP, Dennis Canavan, MSP, Michael Matheson MSP, Russell Brown MP, Ken McIntosh MSP.

Bertie Ahern, the Irish Taoiseach, shaking hands with the team captains before the Scotland *v* Ireland inter-parliamentary football match in Dublin, 24 November 2002. The Irish captain is Jimmy Deenihan TD.

ABOVE. With Adam, after receiving an honorary doctorate from the University of Strathclyde, 4 July 2008.

LEFT. With Christine and Adam after receiving an honorary doctorate from the University of Stirling, 21 November 2008.

t the Falkirk Wheel with some young supporters – Jennifer, Kirsten and Callum – during my last election
mpaign, 2003.

t Lock 16, Forth and Clyde Canal, Camelon

With a group of pupils at Easter Carmuirs Primary School, Camelon.

With Christine and Adam, 2008.

One day, when we were visiting some of the remote areas where the worst of the fighting had taken place, I came across what I thought was just a pair of abandoned boots at the side of a track. On closer inspection, I discovered it was a shallow grave, with the feet of an Argentinian soldier protruding from the ground. The fact that this was several weeks after the cessation of hostilities did not indicate much respect for the dead.

It was a long and exhausting day, travelling by helicopter, land-rover and foot across some rough terrain. When we at last got back to the Upland Goose Hotel, we were greeted with yet another plate of ghastly mutton stew. After dinner, Sir Anthony (Tony) Kershaw, Tory MP for Stroud and Chairman of the Committee, asked me if I would like a nightcap. I immediately accepted his offer, not least because I was wanting something to wash away the awful taste of mutton. Tony went up to the bar and ordered two whiskies.

'We're closed!' was the blunt reply from the proprietor. Tony, being an absolute gentleman, just shrugged his shoulders and seemed intent on retiring to bed. I looked at my watch. It was not quite 11 o'clock and I had noticed some other customers being served just before us. I pointed out to the proprietor that we were guests but he refused to budge. I could see some of his regular cronies sniggering over their beer and I was not prepared to be a passive witness to a blatant attempt to humiliate Tony. I said in a voice loud enough to let all the customers hear: 'Are you seriously telling me that you are refusing to serve the Chairman of the Foreign Affairs Select Committee of the House of Commons, yet you were serving the Argentinian General Menendez and his men all through the night during the occupation?'

I told them that, during the course of our inquiry, we had found out that the Upland Goose had been used by senior Argentinian army officers who had been made very much at home by the hotel staff. When I suggested to the proprietor that he could be put on trial for aiding and abetting the enemy, he eventually reached for the bottle of whisky and poured out two large drams. Tony winked at me and we toasted our victory.

Although he was apparently willing to serve the occupying forces, the proprietor of the Upland Goose had no love of the Argies or South Americans in general and, in that respect, he was not atypical of Falkland islanders. They were, for the most part, an insular lot in more ways than one. There were only about 1,800 of them, and all of them appeared to be of white British ethnic origin. They seemed to be unaware that the days of the British Empire were over and, with the possible exception of some Unionist townships in Northern Ireland, I had never seen so many Union Jacks flying in one small territory. In a sense, they were more British than the British, and Margaret Thatcher was their Boadicea because she had come to their rescue and had publicly declared that the interests of the Falkland islanders were paramount. That simply encouraged the delusion that they had some absolute right of 'self-determination'. It was difficult trying to explain to them that self-determination did not mean that a population of 1,800 people had the right to determine the foreign policy and the defence expenditure of a population of 55 million people thousands of miles away. Many of the islanders refused to entertain the possibility of building closer links with mainland South America, especially Argentina, and they were very suspicious of the Foreign Affairs Committee because they thought that we might recommend something other than the status quo.

On the flight back home, Tony Kershaw was given a copy of a radio message telling us that there was considerable press interest in our visit and that a large number of media representatives were awaiting our arrival. Tony therefore suggested that we have a press conference. I feared the worst, because I had heard from phonecalls back home that the story of my altercation with the Monsignor had grown legs. I voiced my concerns to Tony that the press conference should not be diverted from the subject of our inquiry. I suggested that, if there were any questions about the Monsignor and me, I would politely say that I would deal with them after the Committee's official press conference had finished. Tony agreed.

When we touched down at RAF Brize Norton, there was a media circus. Half of Fleet Street seemed to be there, along with radio and TV teams. They were barking questions at me as soon as I arrived and the RAF press officer had difficulty in establishing some order before the press conference started. The very first question was even more aggressive than I had anticipated:

'Will Mr Canavan tell us about his punch-up with the priest?'

I politely replied: 'There was no punch-up but I shall give a fuller answer to that and any related questions after the committee's press conference, which is about our inquiry into the future of the Falkland islands.'

After a period of silence, some of the 'quality press' asked a few questions about our inquiry, which Tony dealt with in his usual efficient but noncommittal way, which was not surprising because we had not even started to write up our report. As there was nothing newsworthy in what Tony was saying, I knew that they were simply waiting for a juicy story about me and so, after the committee press conference, I made a statement:

> Shortly after our arrival in the Falklands, we attended a reception at Government House, hosted by the governor, Sir Rex Hunt. At one point, I got engaged in a conversation with a Catholic priest. We had a robust exchange of views about human rights and the sinking of the *Belgrano* but, at no time, was there any violence or threat of violence and I deplore the way in which the incident has been misreported.

I thought I dealt as well as possible with the subsequent barrage of questions but the next day's headlines were all about me and the priest, whereas the serious work of the committee scarcely rated a mention. When I apologised about that to Sir Anthony Kershaw, he replied philosophically but very naïvely: 'Never mind, Dennis. The reports of your fight with the Catholic priest might endear you to some of your Scottish Presbyterian constituents!'

Some time after our return to the UK, the committee decided to do a separate inquiry into the circumstances surrounding the sinking of the *Belgrano*. Tam Dalyell MP had doggedly pursued the issue and managed to unearth some evidence which seriously challenged the official British version of events. The UK government claimed that the *Belgrano* was sunk because it posed a threat to British forces. Tam claimed that was untrue and a suspicion grew when it was revealed that the logbook of HMS *Conqueror*, the submarine which torpedoed the *Belgrano*, had mysteriously gone missing.

When we questioned Ministry of Defence officials about the matter, reference was made to top secret intelligence documents regarding the sinking of the *Belgrano*. The documents, which were locked in a safe at the MOD headquarters, came to be known as the Crown Jewels. The committee put in a formal request to see the Crown Jewels and, to my surprise, Michael Heseltine, Secretary of State for Defence, agreed. I had assumed that there would be some kind of vetting procedure for members wishing to see the documents and that we would have to sign the Official Secrets Act. However, the only conditions were that we had to view the documents under supervision at the Ministry of Defence and that we were not allowed to copy the documents, although we could take notes. I decided that this was an opportunity not to be missed.

The main Ministry of Defence building is situated in Whitehall, a few minutes' walk from the House of Commons. When I arrived at the main door, I was escorted through myriad corridors and ushered into a small room with a table and chair. I was asked to sign a statement to the effect that I had been granted access to the documents and, to my surprise, there were no conditions attached. I was then left on my own and the MOD official who had accompanied me retired to the adjacent room.

I must have spent at least an hour poring over the documents. There were nautical maps of the area around the Falklands, including a clear indication of the 200-mile exclusion zone and the positions and directions of the *Belgrano* and HMS *Conqueror* before and at the precise time when the attack was launched. Two things were crystal clear. Firstly, the *Belgrano* was outside the exclusion zone when it was attacked and, secondly, it was heading towards Argentina.

The Tory members of the Committee, however, thought that the evidence was inconclusive. In a select committee of the House of Commons, it was traditional for the chairman to try to seek a consensus amongst members, irrespective of party loyalties. That was not always possible and sometimes there would be votes on amendments to a draft report. Unlike votes on the floor of the House, there was no whipping system in committees or, more precisely, there was not supposed to be any whipping. Sometimes Labour or Conservative members would be split on an amendment and cross-party voting was not unusual. However, during the *Belgrano* inquiry, it soon became evident that the Tory government whips were twisting arms behind the scenes.

There emerged such a fundamental difference of view between the Tory members and the Labour members that the Labour members eventually decided to take what was, for the Foreign Affairs Committee, an unprecedented step, which was never repeated during the 15 years I was a committee member. The chairman's draft report was such a cover-up that we Labour members decided to write our own minority report. For that, we had no assistance from the committee clerks and we had to do all the research and drafting ourselves. During the Christmas recess, we had our first meeting in London at the home of veteran Labour MP, Ian Mikardo, who was the senior Labour member on the committee. Some of those meetings were also attended in an advisory capacity by Tam Dalyell, who had been beavering away at the subject for ages, in his own inimitable way, and Arthur Gavshon, an investigative journalist. Gavshon, a Jewish South African, had huge respect in his own profession and amongst politicians, dating back to 1947 when he had revealed to the world that the 'cargo' on a ship called the *Exodus* on its way from France to Haifa consisted of Jewish emigrants, survivors of the Holocaust. More recently, he had been co-author of a book on the sinking of the *Belgrano*, which was hailed as a seminal work.

Each of the Labour committee members took responsibility for drafting a section of the report, which was then subjected to detailed analysis and critique by the other MPs and our two advisors. The whole painstaking process took several months. We knew of course that our report would be rejected by the committee, which had a Tory majority. Nevertheless, we felt it important to expose the official report as a whitewash which had no evidence to back it up. Our minority report was published in the same volume as the official report and, even a quarter of a century later, readers can study both reports and draw their own conclusions. One of the main functions of a select committee inquiry is to discover the truth, irrespective of any embarrassment it may cause to the government of the day. I am convinced even now that our minority report on the *Belgrano* was a genuine attempt to do that, based on the evidence available to us.

As a postscript to the Falklands conflict, I should 'fess up to profiteering from the war. I was one of about 30 Labour MPs who had voted against the Government. I did so on the grounds that I preferred diplomatic pressure and sanctions against Argentina rather than an armed conflict which would involve the loss of many lives. Shortly after the vote in parliament, the Welsh Labour MP, Leo Abse, called a meeting of all the Labour 'rebels'. He informed us that the Liberal MP, Cyril 'Fatso' Smith had gone on a local broadcasting station called Radio Trent and said that the MPs who had voted against the war were traitors and should be tried for treason. I had never heard of Radio Trent and I was not too concerned about Fatso's silly suggestion. But Leo Abse, who was a very distinguished QC, persuaded us to part with a tenner each to cover legal expenses for a joint libel claim. The result was an out-of-court settlement whereby Fatso had to stump up £100 to each of us. Leo was not amused when I asked him:

'What kind of a lawyer are you? Is my reputation worth only a hundred quid?'

CHAPTER SIXTEEN

The Middle East

My first visit to the Middle East was in 1976, under the auspices of Labour Friends of Israel (LFI), an organisation affiliated to the Labour Party and comprising supporters of the state of Israel. Many of them were descended from Jewish refugees who had fled from Eastern Europe to escape the Holocaust, and I had an instinctive empathy with them because I perceived those refugees as the underdogs and I had read a fair bit about the plight of the Jewish people and the foundation of the state of Israel.

It was Maurice Miller, Labour MP for East Kilbride, who first introduced me to the LFI. The contact was a young man called Benny, who made great efforts to befriend new Labour MPs and brief them about the situation in Israel. It was not long before Benny asked me if I would be interested in visiting Israel and I accepted his invitation.

The delegation also included Brian Sedgemore (MP for Luton West), Sid Tierney (MP for Birmingham Yardley) and the late John Mackintosh (MP for Berwick and East Lothian and Professor of Politics at the University of Edinburgh). It was a very interesting visit, during which we met various leading Israeli politicians, including Prime Minister Yitzhak Rabin, who was tragically assassinated in 1995 during his second period as prime minister. In the Israeli political spectrum, Rabin was left of centre and some people may have considered him to be a dove rather than a hawk. But, like many Israeli politicians, he had a military background and was Chief of Staff of the Israeli Defence Forces during the Six Day War in 1967.

At one stage, we were discussing the situation in Gaza and the plight of the Palestinian refugees. John Mackintosh said something like: 'Gaza is a problem which is of continuing concern to the international community.'

'Why?' asked Rabin.

'Because it's there,' said John.

Rabin immediately barked: 'Who said it's theirs?' He had obviously misheard or misunderstood John but he was visibly angry and proceeded to lecture us on how Israel was doing the international community a favour by continuing to occupy and administer the Gaza strip.

Our kibbutz visits were very enlightening. In the 1960s, some of my university contemporaries had volunteered to work on a kibbutz and such service was considered by some to be a badge of honour. Even some left-wing students thought it was a great socialist experience because of the communal living and cooperative ethos. However, in the mid 1970s, it was significant that some of the kibbutzim were almost like fortresses and seemed to have been strategically placed with a view to claiming and retaining rights of ownership over land.

I began questioning some of what was going on in Israel. We had visited the Holocaust Memorial, a very moving tribute to the 6 million Jews murdered during the Nazi regime. Even before that, for centuries the Jews had been persecuted and suffered terrible atrocities, often by misguided so-called Christians, who blamed the Jews collectively for the crucifixion of Christ. However, I was very concerned about Israeli militarism, supported by the USA, and the fact that virtually all Israeli politicians seemed content to continue occupying territories which did not belong to them. Many poor Arabs had been dispossessed as a result of Israeli expansionism, and even the Arabs within the official boundaries of Israel were treated like second-class citizens, if they had any citizenship at all.

Shortly after our visit, the LFI organised a report-back meeting at the House of Commons. The Grand Committee room was packed with LFI members and supporters. There is a large Jewish community in and around London and many of them, including some very wealthy people, voted Labour, probably because of the Labour Party's stance against fascism in the 1930s.

Each member of the delegation was given the opportunity to speak. I could have played to the audience and simply given a glowing report, but I felt compelled to voice my concerns. I began by praising some of the positive achievements we had witnessed during our visit. For example, an agricultural revolution had literally made the desert bloom (albeit with a lot of American and European assistance). I had also been impressed by aspects of the educational system and by the enthusiasm of the young people we had met. So far I had my audience with me, but when I mentioned Jerusalem I sensed some unease. I described Jerusalem as one of the world's greatest cities and the meeting place of three of the world's greatest religions. Some of the audience looked uncomfortable about that remark, possibly because they wanted Jerusalem as the capital of Israel and were not very keen on sharing it with anyone else. But it was when I mentioned the unfair treatment of the Arabs that I saw real hostility in some eyes. I sat down to a deafening silence and I never received another invitation from the LFI.

A few years later, I had quite a different experience when I visited the Middle East under the auspices of Friends of Palestine. The delegation included Hugh McCartney, Labour MP for West Dunbartonshire, Tony Marlow, Conservative MP for Northampton North, and Bob Parry, Labour MP for Liverpool Scotland Exchange.

Beirut was our main destination and, when we arrived there in November 1981, we found absolute chaos and near-anarchy. Large areas of the city were like bomb sites, and different sectors were under the control of different armies or militia groups. Outside our hotel was a military checkpoint. In fact, it was more like a small garrison, heavily fortified with sandbags and machine-guns. There was a flag flying but I could not identify it as any national standard.

During the night we heard heavy gunfire, some of it very close to the hotel. When I rose early to go out for a run, I noticed that it was a different flag flying at the nearby checkpoint. There had obviously been an overnight mini-coup and I suspect that it was not bloodless. For my own security, I decided to limit the extent of my run and I was glad to get back to the safety of the hotel for breakfast.

The highlight of our visit was a meeting with Yasser Arafat, President of the Palestine Liberation Organisation. Although we had asked for the meeting, there was no guarantee that our request would be granted. At that time, Arafat was the most wanted man in the Middle East. He would no doubt have been on the hit list of many rival Arab factions as well as Mossad, the Israeli intelligence agency. For security reasons, he was constantly on the move and only his closest confidants knew his whereabouts.

One evening, when we were just about to retire to bed, we got a message from our hosts that they would call for us in half an hour. We got into a car to begin one of the most hair-raising journeys I have ever experienced. It was like being picked up in a strange city by a taxi driver who, instead of driving you straight to your destination, takes advantage of your lack of local knowledge by doing a circuitous tour to maximise the fare. I was no expert on the geography of Beirut but even I began to notice that we were passing through the same streets sometimes two or three times. Maybe the driver was checking that we were not being followed or maybe he was trying to confuse us so that we would not be able to pinpoint our exact destination and convey the information to some enemy. I would not have been surprised if they had blindfolded us, but they must have trusted us to some extent.

After what seemed like an eternity wending our way through the boulevards and back streets of Beirut, we at last stopped in a dark, deserted area surrounded by high concrete buildings. The building we entered looked like a disused warehouse. The door was opened by an armed guard and it was very noticeable that virtually every person we saw in that building had either a revolver or a sub-machine-gun. I looked at my watch. It was 1 a.m., an abnormal time for an audience with any political leader, but we were not exactly in a normal situation. We were ushered into a waiting-room and thence to another room to see the president himself.

I thought that he would probably shake hands with us, exchange a few words and dispatch us on our way. In fact, we spent the best part of two hours with him, talking through the night about international affairs, but mainly about the Middle East. At that time, Arafat was a pariah to most of the international community and in the eyes of many people was simply a gun-toting terrorist. However, as the night went on and the conversation became more relaxed, I began to realise that this man was genuine in his quest for a peaceful and just solution to the Arab–Israeli conflict. He was a realistic enough politician to see that a two-state solution was probably the most feasible arrangement, with an independent state of Palestine co-existing peacefully with Israel. However, one of the difficulties was that the PLO would not recognise the state of Israel. Indeed, some of the Arab extremists wanted to sweep all Israelis 'into the sea'.

I therefore suggested to Arafat that it would be helpful if he could make a public announcement recognising the state of Israel, even if it were conditional upon Israel recognising a Palestinian state within agreed boundaries. He did not argue strenuously against that but I think there were two reasons why it was difficult for him to make a public statement at that time. Firstly, such a unilateral statement would surrender a very important card prematurely, as it could be vital in any future negotiations. Secondly, his public recognition of the state of Israel would be tantamount to signing his own death warrant because he would be denounced as a traitor by some of the more extremist Palestinian factions.

Far from being a mindless terrorist, Arafat struck me as a man trying desperately to keep his people united and to deliver their legitimate aspiration of a Palestinian state. Although he would not explicitly say so at the time, I think he had the political nous to realise that peaceful co-existence with Israel had to be part of the deal. It came as no great surprise to me when, about 15 years later, Yasser Arafat won the Nobel Peace Prize.

After leaving Beirut, we headed for Jordan with the intention of crossing into the occupied territory of the West Bank. This entailed traversing the River Jordan at the famous Allenby Bridge, also known to the Jordanians as the King Hussein Bridge and to the Palestinians as the Al-Karameh Bridge. The original Allenby Bridge, named after a British general, was built in 1918 but blown up in 1946 by the Palmach, a Jewish military force. It was rebuilt but destroyed again during the Six Day War. In 1968, it was replaced by a temporary truss-type structure which was still in place at the time of our visit.

As the West Bank side of the bridge was controlled by Israeli soldiers, our Palestinian hosts, who were probably PLO activists, dropped us off at a discreet distance from the checkpoint. We had to get on a battered old bus which was the only means of getting to the bridge. The bus was packed and most of the passengers looked like impoverished Arabs. We must have looked incongruous with our pale skins and Western suits – I think that wee Hugh McCartney was actually wearing a tie, despite the blistering heat.

When we got to the Israeli checkpoint at the bridge, we had to get off the bus with our luggage. When we showed our passports, we were told to step aside and wait. We noticed that all the other passengers were allowed to cross over but we were ordered to wait on the Jordanian side of the bridge until the appropriate clearance had been received.

After waiting over an hour in such a torrid temperature, my patience ran out. I crossed the bridge and asked the Israeli sentry how much longer we would have to wait. He ordered me at gunpoint to go back to the other side of the bridge. I explained that we were British parliamentarians and I asked to speak to his commanding officer. The subsequent conversation between us gave me an intriguing insight into the Zionist mindset.

'You must do as I say. Go back to the other side of the bridge and stay there. If you are a parliamentarian, you should obey the law.'

'It is you who are breaking the law by pointing that gun at me. Under international law, you have no right to be here. You are in breach of United Nations resolutions.'

'This is my land, our land.'

'Were you born here?'

'No. I was born in Iran but my family and I were persecuted because we are Jews and so we came here to our own land.'

'I am very sorry that you and your family were persecuted but that does not give you the right to come and dispossess other people by occupying their land.'

'This is not other people's land. This land belonged to the Jewish people centuries before the Arabs came here.'

'Look, my friend. My family came originally from Ireland. They had been there for centuries but that does not give me the right to go back to Ireland now and dispossess people who now own that land. If your logic were applied worldwide, it would be absolute chaos. Most of the population of North America would have to be repatriated to Europe, where their ancestors originally came from.'

'You do not understand. For the Jewish people it is different. We are God's chosen race and God gave us this land. It says so in the Bible.'

I realised then that it was pointless continuing the conversation because any believer in such religious fundamentalism was unlikely to listen to rational argument. Besides, my interlocutor had the slight advantage of being armed and I could see that his trigger finger was getting itchier by the minute.

I reported back to my colleagues and we decided that we had no option but to continue waiting. After a while, a UN official happened to be passing by in a jeep. He turned out to be our Good Samaritan. There were no mobile phones in those days but he radioed the British Embassy in Tel Aviv explaining our plight. Shortly afterwards, we were allowed to cross the bridge and proceed on our way but not until after we had been subjected to a comprehensive search of our persons and our baggage. At one point, one of the soldiers took a document from Bob Parry's briefcase, perused a few pages and took it along to his superior as if producing proof of some subversive literature. It was in fact a copy of Hansard, the official report of the House of Commons debates!

When we eventually got to Tel Aviv, we discussed our experience with some of the British Embassy officials. When they heard that we had met Yasser Arafat, they were incredulous and we came to the conclusion that Mossad had probably found out about our rendez-vous or at least knew that we had been in the company of the PLO. That could have explained why the Israeli authorities decided to give us such a hard time.

Despite that experience of being stranded at the Allenby Bridge, I was always fairly confident that we would get back home safely, but I did not have the same degree of confidence during a subsequent visit to the Middle East.

In August 1990, Saddam Hussein, President of Iraq, ordered the invasion and annexation of the neighbouring state of Kuwait. Such an act of blatant aggression by a ruthless dictator was roundly condemned by the United Nations and there were calls for action by the international community. George H.W. Bush, President of the USA, was in the forefront of demands for action, including military action if necessary, to force the Iraqis out of Kuwait. Some politicians went even further by calling for a full-scale invasion of Iraq to get rid of Saddam Hussein and his evil regime.

There were many foreign nationals, including Britons, living and working in Iraq at that time and, after the invasion of Kuwait, Saddam Hussein refused them permission to leave. The Iraqi dictator referred to them as 'my guests' but the reality was that they were hostages detained for the purpose of creating a human shield to deter missile attacks on Baghdad and other Iraqi cities. Some of the hostages were forced to appear on television stating how well they were being treated and pleading with America and Britain not to attack Iraq. Needless to say, this caused a great deal of distress to the hostages' relatives back home.

For weeks after the invasion of Kuwait, the drums of war got louder and louder but Saddam Hussein refused to budge. It seemed only a matter of time before a military conflict would take place. About mid-September, I received a phone call asking if I would be willing to join an international delegation to go to Iraq to plead for the release of the hostages. My first instinctive response was: 'You must be kidding' but, after a great deal of reflection, I decided to go. The other British members of the delegation were Bob Parry, Labour MP for Liverpool Scotland Exchange, and Ronnie Camp-bell, Labour MP for Blyth.

The media managed to find out about the mission and, the night before we left, I received a frantic phone call from Bryan Davies, Secretary of the Parliamentary Labour Party, pleading with me not to go. Bryan pointed out the irony of three Labour MPs trying to get into Baghdad while everybody else was trying to get out. I told Bryan that my mind was made up and that, if the worst came to the worst, the Chief Whip would probably be quite glad just to see the back of me.

All flights from the UK to Iraq had been cancelled and, as a result, we went via Jordan. We were handed the travel documentation for the final leg of the journey from Amman to Baghdad just before we boarded the plane. When I noticed that they were one-way tickets, I recalled my conversation with Bryan Davies, but I thought it was too late to back out.

On arriving in Baghdad, I was initially impressed by the superficial normality of a country on the brink of war. Shops and hotels were open, people were going about their daily business and there were none of the signs of abject poverty which I had seen in other parts of the Middle East. Many of the people we met seemed well-educated and articulate, but I soon detected an underlying atmosphere of apprehension and fear. I am not sure how much of this was due to the threat of war or how much it was due to the oppressive regime of a cruel despot who had butchered so many of his own people.

Some of the hostages were living in hotel accommodation which looked quite comfortable, but their freedom of movement was very limited and the thought that they might never see their loved ones again must have been mental torture. There was a consensus amongst them that Saddam Hussein was an evil tyrant. but that a full-scale attack on Iraq would make things worse instead of better.

When passing through Jordan, we had seen banners and graffiti proclaiming Saddam Hussein as a great hero because he was standing up to the American 'imperialists'. TV broadcasts showed similar scenes in Gaza and the West Bank and there was a fear that an attack on Iraq would lead to a widespread conflagration throughout the entire Middle East, thereby destabilising the region for decades.

Soon after our arrival, we visited some British hostages who were encamped in the grounds of the British embassy. They were a very resilient bunch who had been employed in a variety of skilled jobs, many of them in oil-related industries. Soon after the invasion of Kuwait, they realised that war was a very real threat and, when they heard about other expatriates being refused exit visas and ordered to report to government-approved locations, they decided to seek refuge in the embassy. They told us that the ambassadorial staff did not exactly welcome them with open arms but nevertheless they decided to squat in the embassy compound which, by international law, was akin to UK territory. Nevertheless, the squatters realised that Saddam Hussein had little, if any, respect for international law and they must have feared the worst.

Some of them were very skilled engineers with a remarkable degree of versatility and initiative. They had even sunk a well in the embassy grounds to ensure a reliable water supply without having to depend on the goodwill of the embassy staff. They had organised themselves into a fairly self-sufficient community and some had prepared elaborate escape plans in the event of an attack.

Many of those we met had Scottish connections, including Guy, husband of June Slora, owner of Wee Jimmy's pub in Cowdenbeath. I had called in to see June before leaving for Iraq and promised that I would do my best to secure Guy's release. In the event, Guy did not require anybody's intervention because he managed to escape by his own initiative, but many of the others were not so fortunate.

We explained to all the hostages we met that we would make representations to the Iraqi authorities to allow all of them to leave Iraq. However, it was agreed that there should be a priority list consisting of children, their parents and people who were elderly, sick or disabled. Most of them accepted this, although there was one man who came to see us afterwards on his own and pleaded with us to get on the priority list. There was nothing physically wrong with him but he was so stricken with terror that he almost burst into tears. We had a difficult job explaining to him that the list had already been agreed. All this came back to me years later when I saw the film *Schindler's List*.

We had asked to see Saddam Hussein to present the case for the release of the hostages. He was unable to meet us personally but he arranged for us to meet his deputy, Tariq Aziz, along with some other senior government ministers and advisors, in one of the presidential palaces. It was rather disconcerting because I had expected the meeting to take place in a private room with a relatively small group of people. In fact, the meeting was attended by at least 20 in a fairly formal session, with Tariq Aziz in the chair and a television crew filming the entire proceedings.

We stressed that we were not representatives of any government but that we were an international delegation of parliamentarians on a humanitarian mission with the aim of ensuring that all foreign nationals living in Iraq should be free to return to their own countries. We were careful not to use the word 'hostage' because the Iraqi authorities did not accept that term and any argument about terminology would be a distraction from the main object of the exercise. After I made my contribution, I watched Tariq Aziz closely while other members of our delegation spoke. I was looking for some reaction, friendly or hostile, but I soon came to the conclusion that Tariz Aziz would make a good poker player. He certainly did not give much away.

After we had finished speaking, we handed over the priority list containing the names of the children, their parents and people who were elderly, sick or disabled. Tariq Aziz then spoke, informing us that Iraq did not want a war but that if America and Britain attacked Iraq, then Iraq would fight back and defeat the imperialists. Regarding the matter of foreign nationals being allowed to leave Iraq, he informed us that he would convey our request to Saddam Hussein. We had not really expected an absolute commitment there and then, but I was hopeful that serious consideration would be given to our request.

When we came out of the meeting, John Simpson of BBC TV was waiting to interview us. I have always had a great respect for John. Over the last 20 years or so, he has covered events in many of the world's trouble spots, often displaying great personal courage and always demonstrating a high regard for the truth. He certainly treated us on that occasion with respect, which is more than I can say about some of the other media representatives we met.

During our stay in Baghdad, we did not have access to British newspapers, radio or TV and it was only when we got back home that we realised what negative press coverage our mission had received, especially from some of the tabloids. We were portrayed as a bunch of left-wing nutters who had been used as propaganda pawns by Saddam Hussein. We had let our country down by sucking up to the enemy. We were pilloried, discredited and ridiculed.

One paper even went so far as to claim that we had suggested some kind of exchange whereby we would arrange for volunteers, including ourselves, to stay indefinitely in Iraq in return for the release of the hostages. Bob Parry and I each later received a four-figure sum as an out-of-court settlement from the newspaper involved.

It was rather ironic that the press coverage was mostly supportive of Ted Heath when he went to Iraq a few weeks later on a similar mission. As a former prime minister, Heath of course had a bit more political clout than us. He actually met Saddam Hussein himself, who agreed to release a considerable number of the hostages. The TV and newspapers were full of pictures of a beaming Ted flying back to Britain with a planeload of people who had been released. When Bob Parry saw the photos, he said: 'That's typical, Dennis. We did all the spade-work and Ted Heath gets all the credit!'

Shortly after my return from Iraq, I attended the Labour Party conference, where I gave a very strong anti-war speech, but it fell on deaf ears. I am not an absolute pacifist. I believe that individuals and nations have the right to defend themselves from unjust aggression, but the indiscriminate nature of modern warfare means the inevitable killing of innocent people as well as active combatants. For war to be justified, there have to be clearly defined and attainable objectives which will help the cause of peace. In that respect, George H.W. Bush's war in Iraq made things worse rather than better and, a decade later, his son George Dubya waged another war against Iraq with even less justification than his father's. Bush Senior could at least have argued that he was responding to an illegal invasion of Kuwait, but Bush Junior's invasion of Iraq was a clear breach of international law and his excuse for doing so was based on information which at best was poor intelligence and at worst a tissue of lies. Saddam Hussein's 'weapons of mass destruction' were never found and the fact that Tony Blair aided and abetted George Bush in such an act of criminal folly is one of the most shameful episodes in British history. It has also critically damaged the quest for peace in the Middle East.

CHAPTER SEVENTEEN

Africa

Mother, why am I so hungry?
Hush, my babe, I'm doing my best
She sighs from an empty, arid breast.

In distant parliaments
They glorify arms
And men at arms
Not babes in arms
The arms race victims with us now.

Mothers sigh
And children die
Who's hushing whom?
And why?

In the early 1980s the Foreign Affairs Committee of the House of Commons visited Sudan as part of our inquiry into famine in the Horn of Africa, particularly Ethiopia. We had visited some camps near the Sudan–Ethiopian border, where the plight of the refugees was horrendous. Many of them were fleeing from Eritrea and Tigray, where drought and warfare had brought destitution and starvation on an almost unprecedented scale. It was a combination of natural disasters and human conflict which uprooted hundreds of thousands of people who fled from their homes, searching desperately for some means of survival for themselves and their families.

There was a stench of disease and death about those refugee camps. Some of the people we met were cadaverous and the medical staff told us they had only hours to live. I found it an appalling indictment of the so-called developed world. We could and did organise task-forces in next to no time for the purpose of waging war but we seemed incapable of organising enough trucks and helicopters to transport emergency supplies to stop people starving to death.

A task-force for destroying life seemed easier to organise than a task-force for saving life.

The border between Sudan and Ethiopia was not clearly marked at that point. It seemed like one continuous desert and we were pleasantly surprised to find that the Sudanese authorities were fairly relaxed about people from Ethiopia crossing the border to find refuge in Sudan, where the government and non-governmental organisations already had a huge refugee problem, even before the advent of people from another country.

After leaving the refugee camps we headed for a 'guest house' where we were to stay overnight. The accommodation was spartan and I noticed that we had some giant cockroaches for company. In the morning, I went along to the bathroom with the intention of having a shower, only to discover that there was not enough water to brush our teeth. My first instinct was to curse in frustration and then I remembered the men, women and children we had seen in the refugee camps the previous day. I felt ashamed at my own selfishness and an adage of my mother's came to mind: 'You never miss the watter till the well runs dry.' There was I feeling sorry for myself because I could not have a shower or brush my teeth, while people were dying a few miles away because of the lack of a clean water supply.

Sudan at that time was ruled by President Gaafar Nimeiry, who had been in power since 1969 as the result of a military coup. In 1983, he announced a revision of the penal code to accord with his version of Sharia Law and, before our departure from London, we had been briefed by Amnesty International about his deplorable record on human rights. When we met Nimeiry in Khartoum, he made us very welcome and the committee chairman, Sir Anthony Kershaw, thanked him effusively for his hospitality and congratulated him on adopting a very generous open-door policy to refugees from Ethiopia and Chad. Nimeiry explained that, in Africa, many of the tribal people did not comprehend the concept of national frontiers. Before the imperial powers came to Africa, nomadic tribes had been wandering through territories which now traversed the borders between neighbouring countries. There was therefore a kinship which transcended national boundaries and the Sudanese government felt obliged to recognise that, especially when people were in dire straits. Nimeiry's explanation seemed like an African version of 'We're all Jock Tamson's bairns.'

I expressed my admiration for such philanthropy but, mindful of the Amnesty International reports, I felt obliged to ask Nimeiry about human rights and particularly the penal system under Sharia Law.

'Mr President, we have been informed that many people in your country have been sentenced to death and many more have had their limbs cut off for relatively minor offences such as pilfering. Why do you tolerate such a barbaric practice?'

His reply was an eye-opener.

'Mr Canavan, capital punishment is used by many other governments, including your friends, the Americans. We must have law and order and people must be taught the difference between right and wrong. If they do something wrong, they must be punished so that they will learn a lesson and other people will also see that, if they steal, they too will have only one hand and, if they steal again, they will have no hands. But it is not a barbaric practice, as you claim. You seem to have been misinformed. We always use anaesthetics and a qualified surgeon for such amputations. So you see, it is not barbaric at all. We are very humane.'

His response made me feel sick, but it also made me ponder over the fact that American society, in some respects, is just as barbaric, with people being fried to death in an electric chair or strapped to a bed and given a lethal injection. Not a great example to set other countries on respect for human rights.

I love Africa and the African people and I firmly believe that the colonial exploitation of Africa is something which should shame Britain and the other imperial powers. But it is tragic that, in more recent times, parts of that great continent have been governed by some of the most ruthless despots, including Nimeiry in Sudan, Idi Amin in Uganda and Robert Mugabe in Zimbabwe.

I remember Robert Mugabe and Joshua Nkomo addressing the Parliamentary Labour Party in 1979 during the Lancaster House talks which led to Zimbabwean independence. Mugabe was the more impressive of the two leaders and there were high hopes that he would lead the way in the struggle for liberation and genuine democracy in post-colonial Africa. What a tragedy that he turned out to be a megalomaniac who has caused unmitigated disaster for his people and his country. Thirty years ago, he had the potential to do for his country what Nelson Mandela did for South Africa.

I first met Mandela during a visit by the Foreign Affairs Committee to South Africa in 1990. It was shortly after his release from prison and we met him in his house in Soweto. When we arrived at the house, we found it well fortified with a high wall and fencing. We were told later by Robin Renwick, the British ambassador, that he personally had authorised the expenditure for the protection of Mandela because he knew that he was a potential target for many a would-be assassin and his survival and leadership were absolutely essential for progress to democracy. I lauded the ambassador for his foresight but I was nevertheless intrigued as to how he personally could authorise expenditure on protecting a foreign political leader. He explained that he had persuaded Prime Minister Margaret Thatcher that the British embassy should have a special fund for certain projects, most of them small-scale community development projects, and that he alone should have complete discretion as to how that money was spent, without reference to anyone else in the British Government. He virtually admitted to me that Margaret Thatcher had had no idea that some of that money was being spent on the protection of Nelson Mandela, whom she had previously tried to dismiss as a terrorist.

Mandela made us very welcome in his home. He came across as a very charismatic person and his whole life is a testament to his courage and integrity. During that particular conversation, however, the qualities which impressed me most were his humility and his willingness to forgive. This was a man who had been in prison for over a quarter of a century because of his beliefs, yet there was no anger or rancour towards his captors. At the time of our meeting, he did not even have a vote and neither did any of his black brothers and sisters. But, instead of wasting time and energy on recriminations over what happened in the past, he was focused entirely on his vision for the future.

During our discussion, I asked Mandela what he thought of President de Klerk's plan for a referendum on the new constitution, including a universal franchise which would give black people the right to vote for the first time. Voting in de Klerk's referendum would be restricted to the existing electorate, which meant that black people would have no say on whether they should have the right to vote. I judged from Mandela's response that he had every confidence in de Klerk's ability to deliver the vote.

I later raised the same question when we met de Klerk. I put it to him that he was running a risk by restricting the referendum vote to those who already had a vote, because many of them, possibly the majority, would vote 'No' out of self-interest. De Klerk replied that sometimes politicians have to take risks but I knew from his body language that he was confident of winning. He was a realistic enough politician to know when the game was up. Apartheid was finished for economic as well as democratic reasons. Even many of the South African industrialists and foreign investors in South Africa could see that.

My fears about the result of the referendum proved to be unfounded. De Klerk won the vote, apartheid was ended, the African National Congress swept to victory at the subsequent election and Nelson Mandela became the first black President of South Africa. De Klerk and Mandela were jointly awarded the Nobel Peace Prize in 1993. I feel very privileged to have met them both.

The next time I met Mandela was a few years later, when he made a state visit to London as president of South Africa. John Major was prime minister at the time and Mandela was invited to address both houses of parliament in Westminster Hall. That was a rare privilege extended to only a small number of visiting heads of state, and the invitation required a cross-party consensus.

A few years earlier, there had been a suggestion that a similar invitation be extended to Ronald Reagan, when he was president of the USA, but nothing came of it because there were too many Labour MPs opposed to Reagan's militarism. But there was no such problem with Mandela. He had well-nigh unanimous support and the only problem was that Westminster Hall was not big enough to accommodate all those wanting to attend. Admission to the event was by ticket only and I was very fortunate to receive one, probably because I was a member of the Foreign Affairs Select Committee.

I arrived about ten minutes before the proceedings were due to begin and I was lightly reprimanded by a doorkeeper who told me that I should have been there half an hour before the start. He explained that my allocated seat near the back had been given to someone else and the only vacant seats left were near the front. It was the first and only time in my life that I was rewarded for arriving late.

The friendly doorkeeper ushered me to the second row from the front and, to my astonishment, I found myself sitting immediately behind Margaret Thatcher. I could not resist the temptation to be mischievous. I tapped her on the shoulder and said: 'I'm surprised to see you here.'

'Why?' was the stern response.

'Well, I distinctly remember you describing Nelson Mandela as a terrorist and saying that anyone who believed that the ANC would form a democratic government in South Africa must be living in cloud cuckoo land.'

To her credit, she did not deny it. Her feeble retort was: 'Well, Mr Canavan, we're all entitled to make one mistake.'

I was about to reply that she had far exceeded her entitlement but, just at that moment, the trumpeters sounded a deafening fanfare to signal the arrival of the president and his retinue.

It was a day to remember. I heard Thatcher confessing to her fallibility, and then I had a grandstand seat for my hero's address.

CHAPTER EIGHTEEN

—— ◆ ——

Ireland

Before the Troubles erupted again in the late 1960s, there was a convention in the House of Commons that the domestic affairs of Northern Ireland were never mentioned, because Northern Ireland had its own parliament at Stormont. It was a silly convention, because Northern Ireland became the UK's dirty little secret and the violation of human rights was ignored.

At local government elections, many of the Catholic population did not even have a vote because only householders were allowed to vote, and many Catholics in places like Derry had no chance of becoming householders because they could not afford to buy a house, and they had little, if any, chance of getting a council house because of blatant discrimination by the Unionist-controlled council.

The coat of arms of Derry city comprises a skeleton beside the city wall, depicting the historic siege of Derry in 1689, when many of the city residents faced the threat of death by starvation. However, in the 1960s, a different interpretation was given to the city's coat of arms, when the skeleton was referred to as a Catholic outside the Guildhall (the council headquarters) waiting for a council house. It was a joke, of course, but it was no laughing matter for homeless people.

Throughout Northern Ireland, there was also blatant discrimination in terms of employment opportunities, to such an extent that Catholics found it virtually impossible to find a job with some of the major industrial employers such as Harland and Wolff, the shipbuilders, and Short Brothers, the aircraft manufacturers.

In 1972 the Stormont Parliament, which Lord Carson had famously described as a Protestant parliament for a Protestant people, was suspended and direct rule from Westminster was introduced. When I was elected to parliament there were frequent debates in the House of Commons about Northern Ireland and there was a time set aside about every four weeks for questions to the Secretary of State for Northern Ireland. I was about the only Scottish MP at that time who showed any interest in the Northern Ireland situation. It was considered by many Scottish politicians to be a hot potato and there was a fear that stirring things up might lead to sectarian violence spreading from Northern Ireland to Scotland. There was also an embarrassment about religious differences, and many Scots of different religious traditions were appalled at the atrocities allegedly being committed in the name of their religion.

I could understand such feelings but I failed to understand how remaining silent was going to help us find a solution. My grandfather was born in what later came to be known as Northern Ireland. He did not have a sectarian bone in his body and I felt that I owed it to him to speak up. When Grandad was born, Ireland was one country, although it was all part of the UK. I felt that the partition of Ireland in 1920 was a monumental blunder and that the constitutional arrangements for Northern Ireland were politically, economically and morally unsustainable. I believed passionately in the peaceful and democratic reunification of Ireland, and still do. I frequently submitted questions to the Secretary of State for Northern Ireland and I sometimes took part in debates about Northern Ireland. I also joined the Northern Ireland Committee of the Parliamentary Labour Party and later chaired that committee for about a decade. I was also a member of the British–Irish Inter-Parliamentary Body, which consisted of parliamentarians from Britain, Northern Ireland and the Republic of Ireland. As a result, I frequently visited Ireland and sometimes led parliamentary delegations there.

When I was first elected to the House of Commons, Merlyn Rees was Secretary of State for Northern Ireland. Merlyn was a fair-minded man who tried hard to build bridges between the two warring communities but, when Jim Callaghan succeeded Harold Wilson as prime minister, Merlyn became Home Secretary. Callaghan appointed Roy Mason as Secretary of State for Northern Ireland. It turned out to be one of the worst appointments he ever made. Mason was a dour, thrawn little Yorkshireman who was completely bereft of political initiative and in some respects was more Unionist than Ian Paisley. His attitude was that Northern Ireland was a purely military problem requiring a military solution. Politics and political change had nothing to do with it. PIRA (the Provisional Irish Republican Army) had to be defeated, and he was the guy who was going to defeat them. He thought he was Napoleon.

I recall one particular visit to Northern Ireland as a member of a cross-party delegation of MPs. For part of the visit, we were guests of the British Army, who took us on a tour of the Markets area of Belfast. I was in an open-air army jeep, along with Michael Mates, a Tory MP, who had previously served in Northern Ireland as a British Army officer. The colonel accompanying us told us that the Markets area was a Republican stronghold. He pointed out a particular pub which he claimed was so notorious that any Brit entering it would be lucky to come out alive. When he told us that army vehicles frequently came under fire from snipers, I prayed that none of the snipers would recognise Michael Mates. Only inches separated us, the jeep had no roof and neither of us had been given so much as a flak jacket for protection. We were sitting ducks.

Nevertheless we survived to have dinner that evening at Stormont Castle. Roy Mason, as host, was in his element. He obviously loved Stormont Castle and he behaved like a governor-general in charge of a colony. If any of the MPs present dared to suggest any possibility of constitutional change or a fresh political initiative, Mason's reply was always the same. 'We must not give in to them. PIRA must be defeated!' It was like the old Unionist mantra: 'No surrender'.

I was bored with such drivel before the first course was finished and, by the time the dessert arrived, I was utterly fed up. I told Roy that I was leaving in order to visit a friend of mine who was a lecturer in Mathematics at Belfast College of Technology. I thought that Mason was going to have an apoplectic fit. At first, he tried forbidding me and then he tried dissuading me from going because he could not guarantee my safety. I told him that I was not asking him to guarantee my safety and, when he realised that I was adamant, he insisted that I go in one of his government cars, accompanied by a driver who looked like somebody from Special Branch.

When the driver dropped me off near the city centre I asked him to come back to pick me up an hour later. However, he insisted on staying, perhaps because he was under orders from Roy Mason not to let me out of his sight. When my friend, Gabriel, arrived, I explained to the driver that we were going for a drink and I think he eventually got the message that he was not wanted. He remained in the car while Gabriel and I walked along a few blocks to a rather dingy but lively pub. We had a few beers and a crack with some of the other customers, who turned out to be salt of the earth Belfast boys who seemed very pleased to meet a visitor from Scotland. It was only after leaving the pub and walking along the street that I had a strange feeling of déjà vu. Then it dawned on me that we were in the Markets, the same area which I had toured earlier in the army jeep, and the pub I had been drinking in was the same one that the army colonel had described as so notorious that any Brit entering it would be lucky to come out alive. I thanked God that I had been drinking with Gabriel and not Roy Mason!

Mason's Minister of State at the Northern Ireland Office was a huge, gruff character called Don Concannon. Like Mason himself, he came from a coal-mining background, and Jim Callaghan should have sent both of them back to the coalface instead of Northern Ireland. Concannon was so reactionary that he vehemently opposed my private member's bill to ban the use of plastic bullets by the security forces in Northern Ireland, despite the fact that 14 people, most of them children, had been killed by such 'non-lethal' weapons.

Concannon's intransigence was also evident when some detainees in the Maze Prison were involved in a protest because they wanted to wear their own clothes rather than prison clothes. These people considered themselves to be prisoners-of-war, and even legal experts had to admit that they had been detained under emergency provisions which fell far short of what were considered to be the fair principles of British justice. I had previously visited the Maze and met some of the prisoners, both Unionist and Republican. One of them was a guy called Gusty Spence, who was serving a life sentence for murder and was Commander of the Ulster Volunteer Force (UVF) in the Maze. Many years later, I met him at a Labour Party conference and discovered that he had seen the error of his ways. He had completely abandoned the armed struggle and he seemed to be well versed in the principles of democratic socialism. The Maze Prison and its predecessor, Long Kesh Internment Camp, were like universities for some of the detainees. Many British prisons are like universities of crime and I suspect that many evil things were taught in Northern Ireland's prisons too. But they also gave people on both sides of the sectarian divide the opportunity to rethink their personal philosophies of life and political attitudes and sometimes that had a positive result.

In any case, I thought that the prisoners' request to wear their own clothing was a reasonable one and I therefore asked Minister of State Don Concannon at Question Time in the House of Commons if he would allow a cross-party delegation of MPs to visit the Maze Prison to enquire into the prisoners' complaints and report back.

Concannon's response was outrageous. He virtually accused me of being used as a propaganda pawn by the IRA and he absolutely refused to concede that the prisoners had any legitimate grievance. In his view, those people were common criminals and deserved everything they got.

The prisoners' grievance about clothing was allowed to fester and some of the prisoners not only refused to wear prison clothing but also started what became known as the dirty protest at the Maze Prison. When the Tories came to power, things went from bad to worse, but even the Thatcher Government allowed a delegation of MPs, including myself, to visit the prisoners in the H blocks (so-called because of their shape).

When I first entered one of the dirty cells, I was absolutely disgusted. A young, bearded man with hair down to his shoulders and wearing nothing but a blanket was squatting on the floor. The entire walls, ceiling and floor of the cell were smeared with excrement and the atmosphere was so nauseating that I thought I was going to vomit. I tried to engage the young man in conversation and I was amazed by his response and his attitude. Despite the filthy conditions around him, there was a dignity about him and there was no way in which his spirit was going to be crushed. I was convinced more than ever that Concannon had blundered and that Thatcher was in for a long haul.

Not long afterwards, a Republic prisoner called Bobby Sands went on hunger strike. Frank McGuire, MP for Fermanagh and South Tyrone, died, and Bobby Sands won his seat in the by-election. Thatcher still refused to give in. Bobby Sands MP continued his hunger strike to the death. Nine other Republic prisoners followed suit. Thatcher thought she had won, but her intransigence made Sinn Fein an electoral force to be reckoned with.

In 1972, the deaths on Bloody Sunday had made the British Army effectively a recruitment agent for the IRA. In 1980, the deaths of the hunger strikers made the British prime minister an election agent for Sinn Fein. The two events led to a Republican twin-track strategy which came to be known as the armalite and the ballot box.

One of my most memorable visits to Northern Ireland was to the women's prison in Armagh in the early 1980s. Republican women prisoners had been complaining about being strip-searched with such frequency that it was tantamount to harassment. The matter was raised in the House of Commons and the Northern Ireland

Committee of the Parliamentary Labour Party decided to send a delegation to investigate.

The prison in Armagh was a very old stone building, surrounded by a high wall. In some respects, it resembled a medieval fortress and the conditions were very austere. Most of the women we met were in their late teens or 20s and were accused of terrorist offences including murder, conspiracy to murder, arms dealing and membership of proscribed organisations such as the IRA. However, they had never gone through the normal due process of the judicial system. They were being detained under so-called emergency provisions which required periodic appearances before a judge who would rubber-stamp a further extension of their incarceration. For the authorities, the logistics of such court appearances were fairly simple because the Court House was conveniently located almost literally across the road from the prison. In order to 'legitimise' the detention, there was a fairly constant traffic of women from the prison to the court room and back.

When we cross-examined the women about their complaint, we were told that they were strip-searched before they left the prison and strip-searched again on returning to the prison, despite the fact that they were in police custody throughout their brief court appearance and had no contact with members of the public. Sometimes the strip-searching involved vaginal and anal intrusion. The prison warders who were conducting the strip-searches were all of the Protestant Unionist tradition and the prisoners were all of the Catholic Republican tradition. Rightly or wrongly, the latter felt that they were being unnecessarily subjected to cruel and humiliating treatment by the 'enemy'.

The prison governor seemed a reasonable man in some respects, but I wondered why a women's prison had a male governor, trying his damnedest to justify the constant strip-searching of the women in his charge. He claimed that the procedure was necessary for security reasons to ensure that there was no transfer of weapons but I wondered how on earth an armalite could be secreted in a vagina or an anus. I told the prison governor that I was not convinced by his attempted justification. I also informed him that I was the Constituency MP for Cornton Vale, the only women's prison in Scotland, and that the prison authorities there felt that occasional use of strip-searching was necessary in order to prevent drug trafficking. I asked the Armagh governor if there was a drug problem in his prison and his reply amazed me.

'No, Mr Canavan, there is no drug problem in this prison. In fact, there isn't a big drug problem in Northern Ireland, thank God.'

Although drug abuse later became widespread in Northern Ireland, and terrorist organisations became involved in drug dealing, the prison governor may have been speaking the truth at that time.

I then asked him: 'Where are all the other women prisoners in Northern Ireland? What prison are they in?' He informed me that Armagh Prison was the only women's prison in Northern Ireland. I then enquired as to how many of the prisoners in Armagh were there for alleged terrorist crimes. He replied: 'All but one'. The sole exception turned out to be a woman who had attempted to murder her husband.

'Are you telling us that, if we politicians could somehow find a peaceful solution to the problem of Northern Ireland, then the total female prison population of the entire province would be one?'

'Yes sir, we're basically a very God-fearing and law-abiding people.'

During my many visits to Ireland during the troubles, I rarely felt that I was in any great danger and, in the Republic of Ireland, the authorities went to great lengths to protect British parliamentarians. On one particular visit to Dublin, I opened the door of my hotel room to be confronted by a man lying on the lobby floor holding a sub-machine gun. I rushed back into my room and slammed the door before I found out that it was a plainclothes policeman who had been assigned as my bodyguard.

After our series of political meetings in Dublin had ended, a group of us decided to go to O'Donoghue's pub to sample the Guinness and some excellent live music. The bodyguard insisted on accompanying us, posing as a musician, complete with fiddle case. Fortunately he never had to open the case, but we guessed that it contained something much more lethal than any musical instrument.

On another occasion, I was travelling to Belfast Airport in a car with some other Labour MPs, including Kevin McNamara and Martin Flannery. We were stopped at a checkpoint and a female member of the Ulster Defence Regiment, armed with a sub-machine gun, demanded that we identify ourselves. I explained that we were British MPs and we showed her our parliamentary passes for identification. Unimpressed, she ordered us out of the car to be searched and, at one stage, I overheard her joking with her colleague: 'Huh! McNamara, Flannery and Canavan. Sounds like a Celtic half-back line!'

We eventually were allowed to proceed in time to catch our flight but that experience made me realise the daily inconvenience and harassment experienced by many innocent people in Northern Ireland at that time, and the resultant disrespect for the armed forces. Indeed, the behaviour of the armed forces in some instances must have encouraged some young people to join terrorist organisations.

The village of Crossmaglen was another example. South Armagh had the reputation of being IRA bandit territory and the British Army decided to set up a military base in the area. Instead of choosing a location somewhere in the countryside, the army decided to build a fortress adjacent to the Gaelic Athletic Association sports ground near the centre of Crossmaglen. Army personnel and supplies were usually brought into the base by helicopter.

On one famous occasion, Margaret Thatcher, the Iron Lady, was hailed by the British media as a great heroine because she had dared to enter into Crossmaglen, the heartland of the IRA. The first the local people knew about her visit was on the six o'clock TV news. The prime minister had been whisked into the base by helicopter and then whisked out again before any of the locals knew that their village had been honoured by such a distinguished visitor.

Some time later, the Gaelic Athletic Association (GAA) sent a delegation to the House of Commons to complain about the continuing occupation of their sports ground by the British Army. The GAA told us that their matches were frequently interrupted by helicopters landing and taking off. I found all this difficult to believe because I did not think that the army would be so crass. I was invited to see the situation for myself and I accepted the invitation. It was an incredible experience.

I was standing on the touchline enjoying the match and the local parish priest, who was also president of Crossmaglen Rangers Gaelic Football Club, was explaining to me the difference between the rules of Gaelic football and soccer. It was a very exciting match which had me absolutely riveted when, about halfway through the second half, a helicopter suddenly approached. It flew in at such a low level over the playing field that, at one stage, I thought that it was in danger of colliding with the players. It then touched down a few yards from the touch-line and two soldiers immediately jumped out with rifles at the ready. They crouched down and pointed their weapons towards the players and spectators. For one dreadful moment, I thought that I was going to be a witness or possibly a victim of a replay of the Croke Park massacre of 1920, when the British Army fired into a crowd at the GAA national stadium in Dublin, killing 13 spectators and a player.

However, it soon transpired that the armed soldiers were simply providing cover for the safe unloading of some items from the helicopter. My curiosity got the better of me and I approached the chopper to get a closer view of their precious cargo. I could hardly believe my eyes when I saw a team of soldiers unloading beer kegs. Meanwhile, the football match had been abandoned and the players walked off the field in disgust. No wonder some of them would be inclined to join the IRA.

I reported my observations to the Ministry of Defence, remarking that it was surely in the British Government's own interests for young men to play football rather than get involved in paramilitary activities. The presence and behaviour of the British Army in Crossmaglen was counter-productive even to the army's own objectives, but the MoD refused to listen.

When the Northern Ireland Committee of the Parliamentary Labour Party sent a delegation to Ireland, we always tried to ensure that we listened to as many shades of opinion as possible.

On one such visit, we had a meeting at the headquarters of the Democratic Unionist Party. Unfortunately, Ian Paisley, the party leader, was not there but we met some of his colleagues. The conversation was utterly depressing. At one stage, I suggested the possibility of a power-sharing executive in Northern Ireland, with cabinet ministers from different political and religious traditions. The response was: 'We are the majority. Why should we share power with Catholics? How would you like to be told that you must have a black man in your cabinet?'

Martin Flannery, Labour MP for Sheffield Hillsborough, said: 'I am not a Catholic. In fact I have no religious axe to grind. I am an atheist.'

The DUP man responded: 'Aye, but are you a Catholic atheist or a Protestant atheist?'

How do you answer that one? We were getting nowhere.

As we were leaving, I had a look at some of their political propaganda. There was a cartoon on the wall with a picture of the Pope with his heel on top of some poor soul, depicting perhaps a Catholic victim of papal oppression. There was also a leaflet urging people to vote 'No' in the 1975 referendum on membership of the European Economic Community (EEC). The leaflet claimed that the Treaty of Rome was a papist plot to subjugate us all under Vatican control and it was no coincidence that some of the principal protagonists in the campaign for EEC membership were leading Roman Catholics like Shirley Williams, a Labour cabinet minister!

Martin Flannery was very critical of the EEC but the DUP propaganda might have persuaded even him to vote 'Yes' in the referendum.

Despite the obvious difficulties, I still felt it was very important to maintain some kind of dialogue with different political parties in Northern Ireland. During my eight years as chairperson of the Northern Ireland Committee of the Parliamentary Labour Party, I organised meetings with various parties and groups, including the Ulster Unionist party, the Democratic Unionist party, the Progressive Unionist party, the Alliance party, the Social Democratic Labour Party and Sinn Fein. I even invited John Hume, James Molyneaux and Ian Paisley to address meetings of our committee at Westminster. This required notice to be given to the party whip, a batch of papers sent out every week from the whips' office, informing Labour MPs of the parliamentary business for the week ahead, as well as meetings of the Parliamentary Labour Party and its committees. The whips had no problem with John Hume attending a meeting of a PLP committee because John was leader of the SDLP, which was a member of the Socialist International and therefore the Labour Party's sister party in Northern Ireland. However, the Chief Whip was not keen on a similar invitation being extended to James Molyneaux, leader of the Ulster Unionist Party, and Ian Paisley, leader of the Democratic Unionist Party. He could think of no precedent for an MP from another party addressing a committee of the Parliamentary Labour Party. He was prepared to make an exception in the case of John Hume, but not the others. I had to work hard to persuade him otherwise, pointing out the importance of the Parliamentary Labour Party maintaining contact with all the main parties in Northern Ireland. The Chief Whip eventually relented and both James Molyneaux and Ian Paisley accepted my invitations.

Paisley also came along to another parliamentary event, even though he was not specifically invited. Shortly after Basil Hume was created a cardinal, my good friend Kevin McNamara MP invited him to say Mass in St Stephen's Crypt, near Westminster Hall. It was to be a historic occasion because it would be the first Mass to be celebrated in the Palace of Westminster since the Reformation.

Kevin asked me to be an 'usher' for the occasion and I told him that I was honoured to accept. However, I soon found out that a better job description might have been 'bouncer' rather than 'usher'. On Kevin's advice, I turned up for duty half an hour before the service was due to start. St Stephen's Crypt is a beautiful chapel just off Westminster Hall, the oldest part of the Palace of Westminster. I always found it to be a haven of peace and tranquility in the hurly burly of political chicanery and back-stabbing which goes on at Westminster.

When I entered the chapel, there were only two people in it and when I identified them, I suspected that peace and tranquility were not on the immediate agenda. Sitting in the front pews were the Reverend Ian Paisley and the Reverend Robert Bradford.

Despite our political and other differences, I had a reasonable rapport with both men. On my very first day at Westminster, I was introduced to Ian Paisley by George Thomas, who was later to become Speaker of the House of Commons. Paisley seemed genuinely interested to hear that my grandfather was born in County Tyrone. At a personal level, I always found Ian Paisley to be friendly, almost avuncular, with a good sense of humour.

His Unionist colleague, Rev. Robert Bradford, was a teammate of mine in the House of Commons Football XI. We had first met in the British Universities football championships, when he played for Northern Ireland and I played for Scotland. I guessed that both the reverends were about to stage some kind of protest and I was not looking forward to the task of chucking them out. Bradford was still fairly young and fit and Paisley was a big, heavy man. I therefore decided on a diplomatic rather than confrontational approach.

'Good morning, gentlemen. It's very good of you to come along for the Mass.'

I was told in no uncertain terms that they were not there for the Mass.

I quietly suggested that, if they wanted to make a protest, they should do it in a peaceful, dignified way, but I was not confident that they would heed my advice.

Five minutes before the Mass was due to start, the chapel was heaving at the seams. It was standing-room only and there was a large number of the parliamentary lobby correspondents present with pens and notebooks at the ready.

Cardinal Hume was a very gentle, saintly person. A former abbot of Ampleforth, he had such an aura of spirituality that he sometimes seemed semi-detached from worldly matters. I do not know whether anybody had tipped him off about the Reverends Paisley and Bradford, but the cardinal dealt with the situation in admirable fashion. He approached the altar and made the sign of the cross: 'In the name of the Father and of the Son and of the Holy Spirit.' He then paused, perhaps expecting something to happen. As if on cue, Paisley rose from his seat and informed the congregation that, as a Protestant, he was protesting about the idolatrous sacrifice of the Mass being held in the Palace of Westminster, the home of the mother of parliaments. Bradford then followed suit and both of them then headed for the door. I thanked them both as they left and Cardinal Hume continued with the service as if nothing had happened.

Paisley and Bradford were probably both following their consciences and at least their protest was peaceful and fairly dignified, in contrast to the violence experienced by many of their constituents as a result of sectarian conflict. In fact, Robert Bradford himself became a victim of that conflict. Not long afterwards he was holding a surgery for his constituents where an IRA assassin shot him dead, leaving a widow and five young children. He was a brave man who literally gave his life helping others.

The people of Ireland, particularly Northern Ireland, have suffered so much over the past 40 years and, at times, they must have wondered if the troubles would ever end. At last, on 19 July 1997, the IRA declared a cease-fire. Hopes for peace were raised, but not too high, because there had been previous cease-fires which had not lasted. The one in 1997 turned out to be ground-breaking. It led to the Belfast Agreement, signed by all the major parties on Good Friday the following year.

One of my happiest days in Ireland was 22 May 1998, when the Good Friday Agreement was endorsed in a referendum by the people of all 32 counties of Ireland. I had the privilege of spending part of that historic day in Derry, in the company of John Hume, who that year was declared joint winner (with David Trimble) of the Nobel Peace Prize. John was a worthy recipient of that prestigious award because he had risked his life and his entire political career by entering into talks with Sinn Fein leaders at a time when most politicians treated them like pariahs.

On that sunny May evening, John and his wife, Pat, invited me to join them for dinner at St John's Restaurant just across the border from Derry on the shores of Lough Swilly in County Donegal. By coincidence, another diner in the same restaurant was Bishop Edward Daly, and John introduced me to him. He was just plain Father Daly when, over a quarter of a century before, he had courageously administered the last rites to the victims of the Bloody Sunday massacre in the Bogside area of Derry, when the Parachute Regiment opened fire on civil rights demonstrators. On the day after the massacre, millions of people throughout the world saw a photograph of Father Daly bravely waving a white handkerchief in an effort to stop the Paras' gunfire, while he helped to carry a dying man away from the scene of conflict. That iconic image of a pastor tending to his flock helped to alert the international community to what was happening in Northern Ireland.

It was a completely different scene that day in May 1998, although we were only a few miles from the Bogside. The sun was just beginning to sink beneath the hills of Donegal and the surface of Lough Swilly shimmered in the twilight. When I shook hands with Bishop Daly, neither of us knew the result of the referendum but we were optimistic, even confident. Sure, there would still be some difficult times ahead but Ireland was on the cusp of a new era, with an opportunity for people to live together in peace and harmony, whatever their political and religious beliefs.

———— ✦ ————

CHAPTER NINETEEN

Changing the goalposts

Constituency boundary changes are an inevitable consequence of demographic changes but, for sitting MPs, they can be a nightmare. MPs of the same political party in neighbouring constituencies can end up at each other's throats. Glasgow is notorious for Labour MPs plotting against each other and stabbing each other in the back because the shrinking population of the city has meant a reduction in the number of parliamentary constituencies over the years.

One such famous battle was between Dr Maurice Miller, who was MP for Glasgow Kelvingrove, and Tom McMillan, who was MP for Glasgow Central. Maurice and Tom were poles apart in many respects. Maurice was a graduate of Glasgow University and had been a GP in Glasgow before his election to parliament. Tom was very much a cloth-cap trade unionist, sponsored by the National Union of Railworkers.

When the Boundary Commission reduced the number of Glasgow constituencies in the early 1970s, Neil Carmichael, MP for Glasgow Woodside, was selected as Labour candidate for the re-drawn constituency of Kelvingrove and Dr Miller was left scrambling around for another seat. Tom McMillan was convinced that Maurice had his beady eye on the Glasgow Central Constituency and was naturally determined to do everything possible to stop him.

The rivalry or hostility between them reached a ridiculous stage when Tom took a bad turn one night in the House of Commons. Tom regularly shifted a fair cargo of alcohol and, when he collapsed, his colleagues thought that perhaps he was just paralytic with the drink. However, when repeated attempts to resuscitate him failed, an MP suggested that someone should call for a doctor. As soon as the word 'doctor' was uttered, Tom woke up and exclaimed: 'If youse are getting a doctor, dinnae get that bastard, Maurice Miller. He'll dae away wi' me jist to get ma seat!'

I had a good laugh when I first heard that story but little did I know that the Boundary Commission was soon going to pose a big problem for me.

From 1974 until 1979, I represented the most marginal Labour seat in Scotland. Sometimes, when I was at a public meeting, I used to count the number of people in the hall and realise that the audience was bigger than my majority of 367. All that it needed was for 184 people to switch their votes to the SNP and I would be out. Indeed there was one memorable occasion when my majority was almost toppled by a dog. Shortly after my departure to Westminster, I was persuaded that it would be a good idea for the family to have a canine friend. The children loved the dog but I did not share their affection. It had a mind of its own and, although I tried to ensure that it had adequate exercise, it would sometimes manage to escape from the house and go running wild through the streets of Bannockburn.

One evening, Henry Dawson and his wife, Bridene, were at a bingo session in Bannockburn Miners' Welfare Club. The hall was packed, all eyes were down and there was a hush of concentration as the numbers were being called. The tables were laden with pints of heavy, glasses of whisky, gin, vodka and even more exotic libations such as Bacardi, Cointreau and Sambuca. Suddenly the door burst open and a barking dog ran into the hall. It went on the rampage, louping up on to tables, spilling hundreds of pounds' worth of drinks and snatching pencils and bingo cards with its teeth. It was absolute mayhem, with punters trying to grab the dog and others shouting: 'Get that wild beast oot o' here! Whose bloody dug is it?' Henry gave Bridene a knowing look and warned her: 'For heaven's sake, dinny tell anyone that's Canavan's dug, otherwise we've lost the next election.'

Bridene must have done what she was told because, at the next general election in 1979, my majority of 10,356 was the biggest in the history of West Stirlingshire Constituency and I had the biggest swing to Labour in the entire UK. Then along came the Parliamentary Boundary Commission and literally carved the whole thing up in such a way that I became almost paranoid. West Stirlingshire was the only constituency in the UK to be split into seven different parts, and none of the new constituencies would comprise even half of my existing constituency. The new constituencies were: Falkirk West; Stirling; Clackmannan; Cumbernauld and Kilsyth; Monklands West; Strathkelvin and Bearsden; Clydebank and Milngavie.

At the public inquiry regarding the parliamentary constituencies

within the Central Region of Scotland, the Tory Party had specifically asked for the Stirlingshire villages of Fallin, Plean and Cowie
to be put into the new Clackmannan seat, despite the fact that they
were in a different local authority area and were separated from
Clackmannan by the River Forth in such a way that constituents
would be unable to travel overland from the southern part of the
constituency to the northern part without having to go through
another constituency. Fallin, Plean and Cowie were all mining
communities and were Labour strongholds. Putting them into the
Clackmannan constituency rather than the Stirling constituency
would make the Stirling seat more winnable for the Tory Party.
It was a blatant attempt at gerrymandering but the inquiry reporter
gave the Tories everything they asked for.

I smelled a rat. The inquiry reporter was Robert Richardson
Taylor QC, Sheriff Principal of Tayside, Central and Fife. When I
checked his background, I discovered that he had stood three times
as a Tory parliamentary candidate and was a former chairman of the
Central and Southern Region of the Scottish Conservative Association. He had been appointed reporter to the inquiry by George
Younger, the Tory Secretary of State for Scotland, who lived in the
Stirlingshire village of Gargunnock and therefore had firsthand
knowledge of the political implications of the new boundaries.

I tabled motions in the House of Commons to expose the gerry-
mander and crossed swords with Francis Pym, the leader of the
House, and Speaker George Thomas, who chaired the Boundary
Commission and who was outraged that I should question his
neutrality. I tried to persuade the Labour Party to make a legal
challenge to the proposals, as it had done in England, but to no avail.
I put a similar proposal to the Labour-controlled Central Regional
Council, warning them of the possibility of Stirling having a Tory
MP for the first time for decades. My plea fell on deaf ears and the
result had devastating consequences not just for Stirling but for
Scotland.

Michael Forsyth won the Stirling seat for the Tories in 1983 and
held onto it until the boundaries were yet again changed in 1997.
During those 14 years, Forsyth was a fanatical follower of Thatcher
and was largely responsible for imposing Thatcherism on the people
of Scotland. He argued strongly for the people of Scotland to be used
as guinea pigs for the poll tax. As Scottish Office Education Minister, he tried to undermine the basic principles of equal opportunities for all children by encouraging schools to opt out of local

council management, thereby hoping to create a two-tier system. As Scottish Minister for Health, he introduced market forces into the National Health Service and pursued a policy of privatisation which led to a deterioration in standards of hygiene and nutrition in our hospitals. As Secretary of State for Scotland, he behaved like a colonial governor-general but he did not eventually get his come-uppance until 1997, by which time he had done incalculable damage to the economic and social wellbeing of Scotland.

It is arguable that Michael Forsyth might never have had a start to his political career if it were not for the fixing of the Stirling constituency boundaries in 1983. But the Labour Party did virtually nothing to stop the gerrymander and events since then have made me wonder if the Labour hierarchy did not fight the Boundary Commission because they saw the new boundaries as a means of getting rid of me.

I had been approached by party members in three of the proposed new constituencies (Stirling, Falkirk West, Cumbernauld & Kilsyth) about standing as Labour candidate in their areas. My first inclination was to go for the Stirling nomination because I lived in Bannockburn, which was in the Stirling constituency. However, I was disgusted with the failure of the Labour Party to put up a vigorous challenge to the Boundary Commission's proposals to remove Fallin, Plean and Cowie from the Stirling constituency. Their exclusion meant that, of the new constituencies, Falkirk West would have the biggest chunk of my existing constituency, with about one third of the West Stirlingshire electorate, comprising Denny, Dunipace, Stoneywood, Fankerton, Head of Muir, Denny-loanhead, Bonnybridge, Allandale, Longcroft, Haggs and Bank-nock. However, the majority of the electorate in the new Falkirk West constituency would be in the town of Falkirk, where the sitting Labour MP was Harry Ewing, who had already made it clear that he wanted to stand in Falkirk West.

After discussing the matter with party members in the Bannock-burn area, I decided to go for Falkirk West. It was a difficult decision, because the Bannockburn branch of the Labour Party were my most fervent supporters, but many of them also saw the gerrymandering of the Stirling constituency as an attempt to get rid of me. I knew that, by going for the nomination in Falkirk West, I was risking a head-on collision with Harry Ewing, but Harry had another option to go for the nomination in Falkirk East, which looked like a safe Labour seat and which comprised a major part of

Harry's existing constituency, including Grangemouth. However, the matter was further complicated by the intervention of a young man called George Galloway. George was still in his 20s but had already been chairman of the Scottish Labour Party and was fiercely ambitious. He was on the Transport and General Workers Union (TGWU) list of approved parliamentary candidates and there was a huge TGWU membership at the petro-chemical complex in Grangemouth. George therefore had his eye on the Falkirk East seat, and he had assumed that Harry Ewing would go for Falkirk West and that I would go for Stirling.

When I made up my mind about going for Falkirk West, I told Harry and George because I did not want to be accused of any skulduggery. Harry looked very annoyed and muttered something about having been approached by people in the Denny area to stand in Falkirk West. I doubted that very much, because the Labour Party members in Denny were solidly behind me. However, I knew that Harry had a strong base of support in Camelon Labour Club, which was in Falkirk West, and that he would therefore be no push-over.

When I told George Galloway about my intentions, he was livid. 'I have been working on this project for years', he told me, the 'project' being his ambition to get a safe Labour seat. He realised that, if I was successful in winning the Falkirk West nomination, then Harry Ewing would go for Falkirk East and that would present a problem for George. After his initial ire had cooled down, Gallo-way tried to flatter me by telling me that I was the only Labour candidate who could possibly win the marginal seat of Stirling. He then suggested that we discuss the matter with Hugh Wyper, who was a very senior official in George's trade union, the TGWU. At first I thought that a very odd suggestion because Hugh Wyper was not even a member of the Labour Party. He was in fact a member of the Communist Party. Nevertheless, I decided to go along with George's suggestion and we met Hugh at the TGWU Scottish headquarters in Glasgow.

In retrospect, the whole thing now seems incongruous. Here was a member of the Communist Party being consulted about who should be a parliamentary candidate for the Labour Party. However, it was not unprecedented. The Scottish miners' leader, Mick McGahey, for example, was a Communist, but was very influential in the selection of Labour candidates in safe mining constituencies.

Hugh Wyper had the reputation of being an accomplished fixer and George maybe thought that Hugh could fix the Falkirk East nomination. I told Hugh that I was going for Falkirk West and that, if Harry Ewing thought that I was going to win, he would probably go for Falkirk East. George Galloway insisted that he would still challenge Harry Ewing for the Falkirk East nomination because he thought Harry was a right-wing reactionary who must be defeated. Hugh Wyper was more reflective because he saw the political difficulty of his trade union trying to undermine a sitting Labour MP who had been a government minister.

In the event, things worked out more or less as I had predicted. Harry eventually got the message and sought and won the nomination in Falkirk East. Neither the Labour Party nor the TGWU would allow George Galloway to challenge Harry so George had to put his parliamentary ambitions on hold until 1987, when he became MP for Glasgow Hillhead. I won the Labour nomination for Falkirk West unopposed, despite the fact that some of the Camelon members would have preferred Harry, because they thought that I was too left wing. However, the members in the Denny, Bonnybridge and Banknock branches were very supportive of me, as were many of the trade union delegates. If it had gone to a vote, I was fairly confident of winning but I was glad not to be involved in a head-to-head confrontation with Harry Ewing. Although we did not always see eye-to-eye, I had a great respect for Harry and he was also a second cousin of mine. Harry's grandmother was my grandfather's sister, but Harry did not shout about it from the rooftops, which was maybe just as well. If George Galloway had known, he might have thought that there was a Fife mafia conspiring against him.

Shortly after my selection as parliamentary candidate for Falkirk West, I asked Pat Burt, a member of Central Regional Council, to be my election agent. Pat lived in Camelon and represented the 'Bog' area of Falkirk. He was well placed to rally support in what for me was new territory and he organised very successful campaigns in 1983 and 1987. I was fortunate in that I was never again involved in a battle over boundary changes and I had the privilege of representing the people of Falkirk West right up until my retirement in 2007.

Part III

— ♦ —

Parting of the Ways

———— ✦ ————

CHAPTER TWENTY

Campaigning for a Scottish Parliament

In the early 1970s, home rule for Scotland was not a popular cause within the Labour Party. On the same weekend that I was selected as Labour's parliamentary candidate for West Stirlingshire, a special conference of the Scottish Council of the Labour Party was held to discuss the party's policy on devolution.

Eight weeks previously, the Labour Party's Scottish Executive Committee had met to discuss the same issue. With typical logistical skill, Labour Party managers had arranged the meeting on the same night that the Scottish football team was playing Yugoslavia in the World Cup. Around two thirds of the committee members went to the football instead of the meeting with the result that, by a margin of six votes to five, the Executive rejected devolution and supported a proposition that 'constitutional tinkering does not make a meaningful contribution to achieving socialist goals'. In political terms, the Executive scored a spectacular own goal.

When Harold Wilson, the prime minister, heard about it, he was reported to be so angry that he immediately ordered a re-play. The hastily convened special conference of the Scottish Council of the Labour Party overturned the Executive's decision, thus enabling a pro-devolution commitment to be included in the Labour Party manifesto for the October 1974 General Election.

After Labour won that general election, I was so confident of a Scottish Parliament becoming a reality that I told my Constituency Labour Party that I would like to stand for election to the Scottish Parliament and give up my seat at Westminster. I foresaw that most of the bread-and-butter issues affecting my constituents would be dealt with by the Scottish Parliament and I also thought that membership would be more conducive to a happy family life than being an absent parent at Westminster.

Immediately after the October 1974 general election, a meeting of the Scottish Group of Labour MPs was held at Keir Hardie House in Glasgow. I was the only new member of the group and, at the age of 32, I was also one of the youngest. Labour's manifesto commitment to set up a Scottish Assembly was the main item on the agenda and there was a lengthy discussion, to which I contributed. I said that it was imperative that we implement our manifesto commitment as soon as possible for two reasons. First of all, because it would help to make the governance of Scotland more accountable to the people of Scotland and secondly because, if we failed, it would play right into the hands of the SNP. I also suggested that we should use the term Scottish Parliament rather than Scottish Assembly in order to give it more status and emphasise the fact that it would have strong legislative powers.

John Mackintosh was the only MP who supported my suggestion regarding the terminology and, apart from John, Harry Ewing, Alex Eadie, Jim Sillars, John Smith, Gavin Strang and John Robertson, I do not recall much enthusiasm being expressed for the manifesto commitment on devolution. Most of the Scottish Labour MPs seemed to think that we had better go along with it in the hope of dishing the SNP, but there were some, such as Tam Dalyell, Willie Hamilton, Bob Hughes, Robin Cook and Norman Buchan who were at best sceptical and at worst absolutely opposed to the whole idea. Willie Ross was the Secretary of State for Scotland and I got the impression that he was a rather reluctant devolutionist, but he did feel that we had to stand by the manifesto commitment.

The cabinet minister in charge of the devolution legislation was Michael Foot, who was Leader of the House of Commons and Lord President of the Council. Michael was a brilliant orator but he did not have much of an eye for detail. He was fortunate in having John Smith as his Minister of State. John's legal training and debating skills made him a formidable operator and it was said that he was the only member of the House of Commons who fully understood the detail of the legislation on devolution.

The government's first attempt was a very complex bill encompassing devolution for Wales as well as Scotland, despite the fact that the devolution model for Scotland was very different from that for Wales and there did not seem to be as much support for devolution in Wales as there was in Scotland.

Shortly after the bill was introduced, it became obvious that anti-devolution MPs on both sides of the House were determined to kill it and, in an attempt to buy off Labour opponents, the government agreed that the proposals would be subject to post-legislative referenda in Scotland and Wales. At second reading, I spoke in favour of the bill but there were many Labour as well as Conservative MPs who were against it. The committee stage was taken on the floor of the House, as it was a constitutional measure, which meant that every MP was a member of the committee and could participate in the debate. The government initially took the view that there should be no timetable motion or guillotine to limit the amount of time for debate, which led to endless filibustering by the bill's opponents. When the government eventually tabled a guillotine motion, several Labour MPs combined with the Tories to defeat it.

The government was forced to go back to the drawing board and think again. They decided to proceed with separate bills for Scotland and Wales and kept to the previous commitment on referenda, in the hope of placating Labour opponents.

Enter George Cunningham, Labour MP for Islington South and Finsbury. Cunningham was a Scot, a former pupil of Dunfermline High School, but he was no friend of Scotland. He was, however, a thrawn, intelligent character with undoubted parliamentary skills. He tabled what came to be known as the notorious 40 per cent amendment, which meant that the devolution proposals would require the support of not just a simple majority of those voting in the referendum but a minimum of 40 per cent of those entitled to vote. The amendment was supported by some of Cunningham's Labour colleagues as well as the Tories, and it was approved at the committee stage of the bill. I had argued strongly against Cunningham and urged the government to try to delete the 40 per cent amendment at the next stage of the bill.

I was invited to a meeting with Michael Foot and John Smith. Harry Ewing, the Scottish Office Minister with responsibility for devolution, was also present. They suggested to me that the government would draft an amendment to delete the 40 per cent requirement and asked if I would be willing to move the amendment, which would be tabled in my name. I agreed to the suggestion but wondered why on earth the government would not table and move the amendment itself. Although the ministers did not say it in so many words, I think that they were afraid that the government would lose face if they lost the vote. It would expose the divisions within the Parliamentary Labour Party and, if the amendment was defeated, it would publicly demonstrate yet again that the government could not carry the support of the House of Commons for one of its key policies.

The amendment was therefore tabled in my name and, before it was due for debate, I set about trying to win the support of those Labour MPs who had supported Cunningham in the previous vote. Most of them were beyond persuasion and what disappointed me most of all was the lack of rational argument on their part. If they had been honest, they would have admitted their outright opposition to the devolution proposals, and they saw the 40 per cent requirement as a means of scuppering any home rule for Scotland and Wales.

During the course of the debate, I pointed out that many of those MPs supporting the 40 per cent amendment, including Cunningham himself, had been elected with the support of less than 40 per cent of their electorate. Indeed, most recent UK governments had been elected with the support of less than 40 per cent of the electorate. If the 40 per cent requirement stood, then the majority of the people who took the trouble to vote in the referendum could end up on the losing side. For example, if there were a 60 per cent turnout and 65 per cent of voters voted 'Yes', that would still be insufficient to meet the 40 per cent requirement. That was turning democracy on its head and I argued that, in trying to rig the referendum, the House of Commons was in danger of bringing parliament into disrepute.

Michael Foot spoke in favour of my amendment but, after a heated debate, the amendment was defeated, with 51 Labour MPs voting against it. George Cunningham won the day and Scotland was the loser.

The referenda in Scotland and Wales were held on 1 March 1979. Government strategists thought that St David's Day would be a good opportunity to maximise the 'Yes' vote in Wales, where the Labour Party seemed to be even more divided than it was in Scotland.

Neil Kinnock, who represented a Welsh constituency, made a name for himself by touring Britain to campaign against devolution. When he became leader of the Labour Party a few years later, he demanded unquestioning loyalty and discipline but, when Michael Foot and John Smith were working hard to steer the devolution proposals through parliament, Kinnock was frequently absent on speaking engagements, denouncing the government proposals at every opportunity.

In Scotland, some Labour Party members who were opposed to devolution even hijacked the name 'Labour' by forming a Labour

Vote No campaign. Labour punters were understandably confused when they saw Labour Party members like Tam Dalyell, Robin Cook, Brian Wilson, Adam Ingram and Eric Milligan actively campaigning against one of the Labour Party's key manifesto commitments.

In my constituency the Kilsyth branch of the Labour Party declared itself opposed to devolution and, when I visited Kilsyth on referendum day, I was dismayed to see 'Labour Vote No' posters on display throughout the town. Labour councillor Tom Barrie, ironically a great Burns enthusiast, joined a parcel o' rogues who put more effort into the 'Labour Vote No' Campaign than they had put into Labour's previous general election campaign, when I was Labour candidate. I was not sure whether they were genuinely opposed to devolution or whether they were just using the issue to get at me because they knew I was a strong supporter of home rule for Scotland.

There was also an element in the Labour Party who adhered to the politics of blind reaction. In many parts of Scotland, Labour's main challengers were no longer the Tories but the SNP. During the 1970s, the SNP had control of several local councils covering parts of my constituency, including Falkirk, Strathkelvin and Cumbernauld & Kilsyth. As a result, many Labour Party activists, especially Labour councillors, saw the SNP as the enemy and they hated everything the SNP stood for. The SNP's fundamental goal is an independent Scotland and, in 1979, they saw Labour's devolution proposals as inadequate. Nevertheless, many SNP members saw devolution as a stepping-stone to independence and were therefore campaigning for a 'Yes' vote in the referendum. That was enough for many Labour councillors and Labour activists to resort yet again to the politics of blind reaction. If the SNP was voting 'Yes', we must vote 'No'.

Some of the anti-SNP propaganda was just lies. Some Catholic voters in Kilsyth were under the misapprehension that it was SNP policy to abolish Catholic schools and that a Scottish Parliament would be 'just another Stormont'. The Stormont parliament in Northern Ireland had become synonymous with widespread discrimination against Catholics in many areas such as housing and employment. Most Scottish Catholics are of Irish ancestry and many of them, particularly in the west of Scotland, feared that a Scottish Parliament would lead to another 'Protestant parliament for a Protestant people'.

That seemed to me to be a ridiculous claim, but many older Scottish Catholics might have had memories of the General Assembly of the Church of Scotland campaigning against the 'evil' effects of Irish immigration. In 1923, its Church and Nation Committee approved a report, 'The Menace of the Irish Race to Our Scottish Nationality', which accused the Irish Catholic population of taking jobs from Scots, of being part of a papist conspiracy to subvert Protestant values, as well as being the main cause of crime, improvidence and drunkenness. That was more than half a century before the 1979 referendum. During the intervening period, the Church of Scotland had become much more ecumenical and inter-church relations had very much improved. But old memories die hard. The Troubles in Northern Ireland were ongoing in 1979 and Stormont had been abolished only a few years previously because it was seen as incapable of governing Northern Ireland in a peaceful and democratic way. That may explain why I came across many Catholics who intended voting 'No' in the referendum. I managed to convert some of them, but I think many others did vote 'No', or abstained.

I campaigned strenuously for a 'Yes' vote in every town and village in my constituency but I realised that we were up against it. One of the best attended meetings of the campaign was at Bannock-burn Miners Welfare Club, where I spoke in favour of a 'Yes' vote and Tory MP, Betty Harvey Anderson, spoke against. Betty lived a few miles along the road at Quarter Estate, near Dunipace, and had the reputation of being a doughty fighter. She put up a principled Unionist case but I do not think she convinced many of the audience on that occasion.

I was absolutely shocked when I discovered that, elsewhere in my constituency, Robin Cook had joined a leading Tory, ex-provost Laura McCaig, on a Union Jack platform, with both of them urging the people to vote 'No'. Robin did not even have the courtesy to inform me. The first I heard about it was an advertisement in the *Stirling Observer*, no doubt paid for by some Unionist umbrella group.

With all these shenanigans, it was not surprising that there was widespread confusion amongst the electorate and the 'No' campaign undoubtedly benefited from the confusion. Many voters were so perplexed that they stayed at home and some people voted 'No' in protest at the Labour Government, which seemed in a state of terminal decline. The country had just been through a winter of discontent, with widespread industrial unrest. Public services in many areas were so badly affected that there was a serious health risk caused by uncollected rubbish rotting in the streets, and people could not even bury their dead relatives because the grave-diggers were on strike. The prime minister, Jim Callaghan, had returned from an overseas visit in the middle of it all and was so out of touch with the situation that he made the infamous comment: 'Crisis? What crisis?' People were understandably angry and some of them expressed their anger with the government by voting against it in the referendum.

Despite all that, a majority of those who voted in the referendum supported the government's devolution proposals for Scotland. About 52 per cent voted 'Yes' but, as that represented only about one third of the electorate, the 40 per cent requirement was not met. George Cunningham's wrecking amendment resulted in Scotland having to wait another 20 years for its own parliament.

Shortly after the referendum, the annual Scottish conference of the Labour Party was held in the City Halls, Perth. The Chair was Janey Buchan, who later became MEP for Glasgow. Janey and her husband, Norman, who was MP for Paisley South, were both anti-devolution. They seemed to think that setting up a Scottish Assembly would be pandering to nationalism and that nationalism was irreconcilable with socialism. Norman used to say that if you scratched a nationalist you would find a racist under the skin. There were others on the so-called left of the Labour Party who were like-minded, including Robin Cook, Brian Wilson, Neil Kinnock and Eric Heffer. They were arguing that the referendum result proved that they had been right all along and that Labour should now ditch its commitment to devolution.

So the big issue at the Scottish Conference was what Labour should do in the aftermath of the referendum. Even before the conference began, I was publicly suggesting that the government should stand by its commitment to set up a Scottish Assembly, because the majority of those voting in the referendum had voted for it and because it was a Labour Party manifesto commitment. I pressed that view when I was interviewed by Andrew Neil for a pre-conference TV broadcast and it was a view shared by some other Labour Party 'Yes' campaigners who, like me, felt that we had won the referendum, albeit by a smaller majority than we would have liked.

However, when it came to the debate, no one who held that view was called to speak; Janey Buchan, in the Chair, was obviously calling her anti-devolution pals, including Brian Wilson, who had already spoken in another conference debate. I was repeatedly standing up in an effort to catch Janey's eye, but she just blanked me. Even some people who disagreed with my views on devolution thought that Janey should have vacated the Chair for that particular debate because she disagreed with party policy on the issue. Instead, she appeared to abuse her position as Chair in a partisan way in order to influence the outcome of the debate. The result was that the conference approved a rather ambiguous statement which sent out no clear message at all to the government.

After the conference, I let it be known what I thought of the decision and what I thought of the manner in which Janey had chaired the meeting. I accused Janey of reverting to her Stalinist tendencies and this was headlined in some of the press along with other lurid terms such as 'betrayal' and 'rigging'. I now regret having used such terminology. I was absolutely raging but that is no excuse. By going over the top, I was not setting a good example in comradeship and I may have alienated some potential supporters of my cause.

The following day, I was due to appear on a TV programme about the conference. The programme was to be recorded at the Grampian TV studio in Aberdeen and, when I boarded the Glasgow–Aberdeen train at Stirling, the first people I saw in the carriage were Janey Buchan, Donald Dewar and Brian Wilson! They all had faces like thunder and, after a few minutes of fruitless effort to make conversation with them, I came to the conclusion that my time would be better spent reading the papers.

When we reached the TV studio, Janey made it absolutely clear to the producer that she was refusing to participate in any TV debate with me. The result was that Brian Wilson and I went on a head-to-head confrontation, knocking verbal lumps out of one another, with Donald and Janey glowering in the background. I accused Brian of hijacking the word 'Labour' for the 'Labour Vote No' campaign, then aiding and abetting the Tories by campaigning against Labour policy. It was a well-known fact that some big business interests had financed the anti-devolution campaign but, when I asked Brian several times who exactly had bankrolled the 'No' campaign, he refused to answer but adroitly changed the subject to have a go at me for using intemperate language. Brian is no slouch when it comes to

TV debating and what followed was a ding-dong battle which nobody won. Afterwards, I overheard Donald saying to the producer: 'Well, that will no doubt make good television but it won't do the Labour Party any good!'

After the referendum, Jim Callaghan, the prime minister, did not have a clue about what to do with the Scotland Act and he ended up doing nothing. The Cunningham amendment obliged the government to lay an order repealing the Act but the amendment did not stipulate any time limit for repeal. Shortly after the referendum, the Tories tabled a motion of no confidence in the government and it soon became clear that other opposition parties, including the SNP, would back such a move. When it came to the vote, the government lost by one and Jim Callaghan had to call a general election, which was held in May 1979. There is no doubt in my mind that the referendum fiasco contributed to Labour's defeat and the advent of Thatcherism.

When Margaret Thatcher became prime minister, one of the first things she did was to repeal the Scotland Act and there began a long regime during which it was very difficult to get the home rule issue back on to the agenda. For Thatcher, Scotland was simply part of her United Kingdom and she proceeded to foist upon the people of Scotland policies which were perceived by many Scots as the diktats of an alien government. George Younger, the Secretary of State for Scotland, was like a governor-general with no electoral mandate from the people he governed. The Tories ruthlessly used their majority in the House of Commons to force through Scottish legislation on matters such as housing, health, education and local government, despite the fact that the majority of Scots and the majority of their elected representatives were opposed to such legislation.

That was a point which I made during a speech at the launch of the cross-party Campaign for a Scottish Assembly held in Edinburgh on 1 March 1980, the first anniversary of the referendum. My attack on the Tory Government was not universally acclaimed, judging by the groans from some of the 400 people present. They obviously thought that such comments would discourage Tories from joining the cross-party campaign but I considered it naïve at that time to imagine any meaningful Tory input to a campaign for a Scottish Assembly or Parliament. Activists in the Campaign for a Scottish Assembly (CSA) included members of the SNP and the Liberals, as well as people with no party affiliation. The Labour Party leadership distanced itself from the CSA but several Labour Party members, including George Foulkes, Jim Boyack and myself, were enthusiastic supporters from the outset. The formation of the CSA turned out to be the most significant home rule initiative during the 1979–83 period.

I also tried a parliamentary initiative by introducing a bill to set up a Scottish Parliament. The bill had no prospect of becoming law but I felt it was important to keep the flag flying by reminding the House of Commons that the issue had not been buried. I sent a copy of my bill to John Prescott, Labour Shadow Minister on regional affairs. Prescott was very dismissive because my bill would have given the Scottish Parliament more powers than Labour's 1978 Act. I do not think that Prescott understood or sympathised with the home rule movement in Scotland and he did not fully appreciate the difference between the demand for a Scottish Parliament and the possibility of decentralisation to the regions of England. In the event, Prescott's contribution in that respect was nil.

Meanwhile, the CSA was gaining momentum, despite the lack of support from the Labour leadership. When an invitation was extended to all Scottish MPs to attend the CSA National Convention in 1982, Donald Dewar said he doubted whether many Scottish Labour MPs would attend and said that Labour would work for devolution through the established Party system 'rather than through this pressure group' (i.e. the CSA). I profoundly disagreed with Donald and I expressed support for the Labour Party's participation in a Scottish Constitutional Convention to try to reach some cross-party agreement on proposals for a Scottish Parliament.

In the lead-up to the 1983 general election, the CSA issued a questionnaire to all candidates, asking whether they supported the establishment of a Scottish Parliament and whether they would support the establishment of a Scottish Constitutional Convention if the Tories won the election. There was no need of a crystal ball to forecast a Tory victory. Thatcher was on a high after her victory in the Falklands War and poor old Michael Foot, the Labour leader, never looked like prime ministerial calibre. The Labour Party manifesto was later described as the longest suicide note in history. The Tories won 42.4 per cent of the UK vote but in Scotland they slumped to 28.4 per cent.

A few weeks after the 1983 general election, the CSA invited all of Scotland's political parties to a conference to discuss the implications of the general election result for Scotland and also the proposal to set up a Scottish Constitutional Convention. The invitation was accepted by the Scottish Liberal Party, the Social Democratic Party, the Scottish National Party, the Communist Party and the Ecology Party. The Tories, as expected, rebuffed the invitation and I was dismayed to hear that the Labour Party would follow a similar line by not sending a delegation. Donald Dewar was by that time Shadow Secretary of State for Scotland and he seemed to be opposed to any cross-party co-operation on devolution. I probably got up Donald's nose by going along to the conference in a personal capacity and saying that there was a lack of understanding in the Labour Party about the proposal for a Scottish Constitutional Convention and that much more work would have to be done to persuade Party members of its merits.

A few weeks later, Helen Liddell, General Secretary of the Scottish Council of the Labour Party, wrote to the CSA that 'it would not be appropriate for us to affiliate to the CSA'. It was now obvious that, without the support of the Labour Party, there was not much chance of meaningful progress towards the establishment of a Scottish Constitutional Convention. I continued to support the CSA in its efforts but I also realised that more action was required by the Labour Party, both inside and outside parliament.

Among the new intake of Labour MPs from Scotland in 1983 was Gordon Brown. I had first met Gordon when he was Rector of Edinburgh University in the early 1970s. He had edited a book of left-wing essays called *The Red Paper on Scotland* (of which I still have a signed copy) and, in his rectorial capacity, Gordon invited me to join his Commission on Higher Education, which produced a radical report on improving access to universities. More recently, I had shared platforms with him in Cowdenbeath Co-operative Hall and Lumphinnans Miners' Welfare Institute during his parliamentary election campaign. I therefore knew Gordon as a genuinely committed supporter of Scottish devolution and I was hopeful of getting him to take a more radical line than Donald Dewar.

At a meeting of the Scottish Parliamentary Labour Group at Westminster, Gordon suggested that the Group should produce a Green Paper outlining Labour's proposals for a Scottish Parliament. I supported him and suggested that the Group should conduct a nationwide discussion on the Green Paper with a view to presenting a bill in parliament. This was agreed and I was given the job of drafting the Green Paper and leading the nationwide discussion, because I was convener of the Devolution Sub-Committee of the group.

The Green Paper was based on the Labour Party's proposals for a Scottish Parliament. The nationwide discussions included an open invitation to any individual or any organisation in Scotland to respond and a series of consultative meetings were held at various venues throughout Scotland. The response was generally very supportive and I enlisted the help of Jim Ross to draft a bill based on the Green Paper and the consultation. It was unprecedented for the Labour Party to produce such a bill when in opposition, and Jim was the ideal man for the job. A retired civil servant, he was an active member of the Labour Party. He also had invaluable experience as a former head of the Scottish Office Devolution Unit in the 1970s.

The bill which we produced in the 1980s was not simply a regurgitation of the Scotland Act of 1978. Our bill proposed to give the Scottish Parliament more powers, including revenue-raising powers. I was delighted when John Smith, as Shadow Chancellor, agreed to put his name to the bill, because I had tried unsuccessfully to persuade John to devolve some revenue-raising powers when he and Michael Foot were in charge of the previous Labour Government's ill-fated devolution proposals. John had argued then that it would have been technically too difficult to operate different tax rates for different parts of the UK, but he later changed his mind when the Inland Revenue became computerised.

John Smith's support for the updated proposals for a Scottish Parliament was pivotal, because he was a political heavyweight in a shadow cabinet which contained some people who were at best lukewarm or at worst downright opposed to devolution.

After Michael Foot resigned as leader of the Labour Party, Neil Kinnock soon emerged as the favourite to replace him. Neil had been one of the principal wreckers of Labour's previous devolution proposals and he showed no sign of remorse. When he announced his candidature for the Labour leadership, I sought a meeting with him to ascertain whether his views on devolution had changed. In the course of that meeting, I soon realised why some people described Neil as a Welsh windbag. He would take twenty-five minutes to say what an average person could say in five, and his response to me was so woolly and equivocal that, if I had been a doorstep canvasser, I would have put him down as 'doubtful but probably against'. He certainly showed no enthusiasm for a Scottish Parliament. After one of his subsequent addresses to the Scottish Conference as Labour leader, the media pointedly noted that he had made no mention at all of devolution. When asked about it, he arrogantly replied with the line: 'So what? I did not mention the climatic conditions in the Himalayas either.'

If it had not been for some Labour Party activists in Scotland pressurising Labour to stand by its commitment to devolution, Kinnock would have happily ditched it. Many of us worked hard to ensure that it was always on the agenda at the Scottish Conference and I often raised the matter in parliament, much to the annoyance of those of my so-called comrades in the Parliamentary Labour Party who opposed devolution as much as the Tories.

As Margaret Thatcher's second term of office drew to a close in 1987, it looked increasingly likely that she would win a third term, despite the fact that support for the Tory Party in Scotland was at an all-time low. People started asking: 'What should we do if the Tories make it three-in-a-row?' This became known as the Doomsday Scenario.

I argued strongly that the Labour Party should proceed with its plans to set up a Scottish Parliament, whatever the result of the general election. We had a draft bill virtually ready for publication and we should present it in the House of Commons. If the Westminster Parliament voted it down, then Westminster would be provoking a constitutional crisis and we should do all in our power to make Scotland ungovernable. There should be no co-operation at all between Government and Opposition, particularly regarding items of Scottish legislation which were against the interests of the people of Scotland. Our aim should be to make it impossible for the government to get its Scottish legislation through parliament until the government responded to the legitimate demands of the people of Scotland for a Scottish Parliament. In an article published in the *Herald*, I called on all Scotland's Labour MPs to rise like lions for the fight ahead.

All that must have sounded revolutionary to Donald Dewar and his colleagues, who refused to countenance any suggestion that the Tories would win a third term. But that is exactly what happened. The Doomsday Scenario became a reality. In the UK, the Tories had another landslide victory but, in Scotland, the number of Tory MPs was slashed from 21 to 10. Scotland returned a record number of 50 Labour MPs.

At one of the first meetings of the Scottish Parliamentary Labour Group after the general election, I explained, for the benefit of the new members, all the work which had been done in drafting the Green Paper and conducting a nationwide consultation on Labour's plans for a Scottish Parliament. I proposed that we should now finalise the drafting of the bill and present it in parliament. The group rewarded me by voting me out of the convenership of the Devolution Sub-Committee and replacing me with Sam Galbraith, a trusty crony of Donald Dewar's. When Sam was later promoted to the front bench as Shadow Scottish Health Minister, Ernie Ross was elected to take Sam's place as convener of the Devolution Sub-Committee. Ernie was very lukewarm on the question of devolution but he was seen by Donald as a safe pair of hands and Ernie had a pathological hatred of the SNP, which no doubt endeared him to some people in the Labour Party. I always thought it rather ironic that Ernie was a strong supporter of self-determination for the Palestinian people but not for the Scottish people.

I would not have minded being ousted and replaced by someone who had better ideas and an alternative strategy, but it soon became evident that the Scottish Parliamentary Labour Group, under Donald's leadership, was bereft of ideas and had no strategy. The SNP started taunting us with the nickname 'The Feeble Fifty' and the Westminster establishment treated Scottish parliamentary business with contempt.

The first Scottish Question Time after the 1987 general election was packed with English Tory MPs who had obviously been instructed by the Tory whips to make up for the lack of Scottish Tory MPs. The Speaker, Bernard Weatherill, took no cognisance of the fact that there were 62 Opposition MPs compared with only 10 Tory MPs from Scotland. As some of the 10 Tories had ministerial positions in other departments, there was only a handful of Scottish Tory MPs on the Government benches at Scottish Question Time.

It is a custom in the House of Commons that members who want to ask supplementary questions stand up to try to catch the Speaker's eye. The Speaker then uses his discretion to call the members. Weatherill used his discretion in such a way that he completely ignored the balance of the parties in Scotland, despite the fact that Scottish Question Time was confined to Scottish matters. The Speaker chose a member from the Government side then a member from the Opposition side then another member from the Government side and so on. The result was that Labour MPs were competing against each other to catch the Speaker's eye and it was more difficult than ever for an individual Labour MP to ask a question because there were more Labour MPs than ever before. Weatherill was actually punishing us for Labour's electoral success in Scotland. For the first time that I could remember, I did not get the opportunity to ask a question at Scottish Question Time, whereas Weatherill called some Scottish Tories on more than one occasion and, to rub salt into the wound, he also called several English Tories who had never shown any previous interest in Scotland.

Several MPs, including myself, complained about this blatant discrimination, but Speaker Weatherill was adamant. In his view, the balance of the parties in Scotland was irrelevant because the House of Commons was part of the UK Parliament and he would apply the same rules to Scottish Question Time as to 'English Question Time'. I pointed out to him there was no such thing as 'English Question Time'. If he meant Question Times to departments such as Defence, Foreign Affairs and Social Security, then those departments were UK ministries, not English ministries. The only territorial ministries were Scotland, Wales and Northern Ireland. It was an absolute disgrace that the Speaker of the House of Common seemed oblivious to such constitutional and political realities. I felt so angry and frustrated with such a perverse interpretation of the Westminster 'rules of the game' that I resorted to the use or abuse of one of Westminster's silliest rules.

In Westminster parlance, anyone who is not a member is a stranger and, if it is felt that strangers should not be present during any proceedings, a member may shout: 'I spy strangers.' The Speaker then must halt the proceedings for a vote on whether strangers should withdraw from the public gallery. I am a strong supporter of all parliamentary proceedings being open to the public, but I knew that the only way to halt the proceedings by way of protest was by 'spying strangers'. To make sure that my shouting 'I spy strangers' was not misinterpreted, I made it clear that the strangers I was referring to were not the people in the public gallery but the English Tory MPs who had invaded Scottish Question Time to try to stop Scottish MPs asking questions on behalf of our constituents.

The business of the House had to be delayed for about 15 minutes until the vote took place. Donald Dewar was furious. Instead of attacking the Tories or condemning the Speaker's unfair handling of the situation, he launched such a fierce public attack on me that the following day's newspapers were full of headlines about divisions in the Labour Party. Donald gave the Westminster establishment a clear signal that they would get away with changing the goalposts so that the Tories could continue governing Scotland, even although they had no democratic mandate from the people of Scotland. Donald strenuously argued against the 'no mandate' argument because he thought that it was an attack on the integrity of the United Kingdom. I argued that the interests of the people of Scotland were far more important than the unity of any kingdom and, if the government continued to rule Scotland like a colony, then it would be the government who would be weakening the very Union which they claimed to support. I also defended what I had done to protest about the mishandling of Scottish Question Time and argued that we should consider the use of further disruptive tactics. It was not long before another opportunity arose.

The Tories did not even have enough Scottish members to form a majority on the Scottish standing committees dealing with Scottish legislation and, when they drafted two English Tory MPs onto one of the Scottish standing committees dealing with a Housing (Scotland) Bill there was hardly a whimper of protest from Donald Dewar. Indeed, I suspect that the Labour establishment at Westminster connived with the Tories on the matter in order to keep the Unionist show on the road.

As far as I knew, it was unprecedented for MPs representing English constituencies to sit on a Scottish Standing Committee dealing with the committee stage of a bill applying to Scotland only. I was deprived of a place on the committee, despite the fact that thousands of my constituents would be affected by the bill, which was threatening the existence of affordable public sector housing. At that time about 70 per cent of my constituents lived in such accommodation, I myself was a council house tenant and there were not many other MPs who could say likewise. I had previously voted against the Tory legislation forcing councils to sell off their housing stock at massive discount prices to sitting tenants. The right to buy seemed a bargain for the sitting tenant and I recently calculated that I could have gained about £70,000 if I had bought my council house. But I foresaw that, in the long term, such a policy would lead to a massive reduction in affordable rented housing and I could not in conscience vote against such legislation then use it to line my own pockets. I therefore felt that my track record gave me more right to speak and vote on the Housing (Scotland) Bill than a couple of English Tory MPs whose constituents were not in any way affected by the bill.

In the absence of any effective protest from the Labour front-bench team, I decided that enough was enough. On the first day that the committee met, I sat on the Opposition benches alongside Labour colleagues who were members of the Committee. When the committee chairman spotted me, he ordered me to leave and I refused. The chairman then suspended the committee meeting and the Labour whips' office was informed. Don Dixon, the Deputy Chief Whip, tried to bully me into leaving the committee room and, at one stage, I actually thought he was going to try physical force. I stood my ground and eventually the committee proceedings for that day had to be abandoned.

Dixon was just about spitting blood. He said that, unless I gave a commitment not to disrupt the proceedings of the committee, I would be reported to the Speaker and a motion put before the House to suspend me. I explained to Dixon that I had not disrupted the proceedings of the committee. I had simply sat in peaceful protest about my exclusion from membership of it. I pointed out that I was being deprived of the right to speak and vote on behalf of my constituents, whereas two members of the committee were being given the right to speak and vote on a matter which did not affect their constituents at all. During the 1970s devolution debate, Tam Dalyell had asked why he, as MP for West Lothian, should have the right to vote on matters affecting the people of Blackburn in Lancashire yet be deprived of the right to vote on matters affecting the people of Blackburn in West Lothian. That came to be known as the famous West Lothian Question. My question to Don Dixon was the West Lothian Question in reverse.

Dixon, who was a fierce opponent of devolution, showed no sympathy or understanding. The former was not in his nature and the latter was beyond his cerebral capacity. I was not particularly keen to get myself kicked out of the House of Commons for a week or more, as that would temporarily deprive me of the right to speak and vote for my constituents on anything. I therefore said to Don Dixon: 'OK, I give you my word that I shall not sit in at the next meeting of the Scottish Standing Committee.'

When the Scottish Standing Committee (SSC) met again two days later, I kept my promise but I felt that I should continue my protest in some way. I made no attempt to enter the committee room where the SSC was meeting. Instead, I went along the corridor to another committee room where another standing committee was dealing with the bill to impose the poll tax on England and Wales. I entered the room and sat on the Opposition benches. It was a very large committee, much larger than the SSC, and it was some time before the Committee Clerk drew the chairman's attention to the fact that I was not a member of the committee. When the chairman asked me to leave, I refused.

There followed a period of confusion when neither the chairman nor the clerk seemed to have a clue about how to deal with the situation. At one stage, the Serjeant at Arms appeared on the scene, complete with sword, and I wondered whether they were going to drag me off to the Tower. After a while, I noticed the clerk handing the government minister a piece of paper which I found out afterwards contained the wording of a resolution to report my conduct to the House, presumably to have me expelled.

When the Tory minister rose to read out the script, the Labour front-bench spokesperson, Jeff Rooker MP, snatched the paper from his hands so that he, Rooker, could move the resolution himself. Rooker had begun his parliamentary career as a left-wing firebrand. Now he was doing the Tories' dirty work for them. I was not surprised when he later accepted a seat in the House of Lords, which at one time he would have denounced as an undemocratic farce and the British establishment's pinnacle of privilege.

When Don Dixon found out about my second sit-in protest, he went purple with rage. He accused me of breaking my word, which I strongly denied, reminding him that my previous commitment referred only to the Scottish Standing Committee. In order to avoid getting kicked out of the House of Commons, I told Dixon that I had no intention of using that particular tactic again but I reserved the right to continue peaceful protests against the unfair and undemocratic procedures at Westminster.

Donald Dewar and most of the Scottish Labour Group strongly disapproved of my guerrilla tactics but I have no regrets on that score. The media coverage helped to draw public attention to the undemocratic way in which Scottish matters were dealt with at Westminster.

The Labour Party, despite having 50 Scottish Labour MPs, seemed devoid of ideas on how to pursue an effective campaign for home rule and the SNP tried to expose Scottish Labour as impotent. Things came to a head at the Govan by-election in 1988. The sitting MP, Bruce Millan, former Secretary of State for Scotland, gave up his Westminster seat to take up an appointment as European Commissioner. Although Bruce had had an apparently unassailable majority of 19,509 at the general election, a by-election in such circumstances did not augur well for Labour, and party bosses should have heeded the warning signs. In 1967, when Tom Fraser, the sitting Labour MP for Hamilton, gave up his seat in parliament for a better-paid job as chairman of the North of Scotland Hydro-Electric Board, Winnie Ewing won a famous victory for the SNP at the resultant by-election. In 1972, when George Thomson, the sitting Labour MP for Dundee East, gave up his seat to take up a lucrative post as European Commissioner, he paved the way for Gordon Wilson to win the seat for the SNP at the February 1974 general election.

Shortly before the Govan by-election, I attended a Special Conference of the Scottish Council of the Labour Party, which was called to decide Labour's position on the poll tax. Whether by accident or design, the venue of the conference was Govan Town Hall. Everybody in the Labour Party was opposed to the poll tax, which was seen as the most iniquitous tax ever invented. It was such a regressive tax that Margaret Thatcher was described as Robin Hood in reverse, robbing the poor to give to the rich. A working-class family consisting of mum, dad, and two youngsters over the age of 18 living in a small council house would pay four times the amount of poll tax paid by a millionaire living alone in a mansion. To make matters worse, the Tory Government had decided to use the people of Scotland as guinea pigs by introducing the poll tax in Scotland before it was introduced in England, despite the fact that there had been no mention of the poll tax in the Scottish Tory Party manifesto. It was the worst of many examples of the Tory Government riding rough-shod over Scotland by imposing policies which had clearly been rejected by the majority of the people of Scotland and the majority of their elected representatives.

There was widespread opposition to the poll tax. Many people on low incomes could not afford to pay it and many others, including myself, who could afford to pay, refused to do so on conscientious grounds. Our aim was to stand shoulder to shoulder in solidarity with people who could not afford to pay. We hoped to maximise the number of non-payers so that the poll tax would become unworkable and the government would be forced to scrap it. The non-payment campaign attracted broad support from people of various political persuasions, as well as the trade union movement, the churches and community organisations. I spoke at one public meeting in West

Lothian, attended by several hundred people, where the other speakers were the local Church of Scotland minister, the local Catholic priest and Alex Salmond. Other Labour Party members were also active in the non-payment campaign, including John McAllion MP, George Galloway MP and Bill Spiers, Depute General Secretary of the Scottish Trades Union Congress.

We were completely disowned and condemned by the Labour leadership, who repeatedly came out with spurious statements such as 'even bad laws must be obeyed' and 'law-makers must never be law-breakers'. The history of our democracy contains many examples of people who campaigned against bad laws even to the extent of breaking the law in order to change the law: the Tolpuddle Martyrs, the Suffragettes, and the conscientious objectors to military conscription, to name a few. But the Labour leadership in the 1980s attacked their own party members who were using civil disobedience to defeat the poll tax.

The Special Conference held at Govan Town Hall in 1988 was a farce. The Party managers made sure that virtually everybody who was called to the rostrum to speak would toe the leadership line and the chairman turned a blind eye to my repeated requests to speak. The conference passed a wishy-washy statement opposing the poll tax but rejected all suggestions of non-payment.

Shortly afterwards, at a meeting of the Scottish Group of Labour MPs at Keir Hardie House, a plea was made for a compromise statement, whereby the position of non-payers would at least be respected, but that too was thrown out. By this time, it was clear that the SNP candidate for the Govan by-election would be Jim Sillars, former Labour MP and a formidable campaigner. At the Group meeting, I suggested that the poll tax would be the big issue during the campaign and that Labour's position would not do our candidate any good. Sillars would be telling the voters: 'Don't pay!' whereas the Labour Party would be telling the voters: 'Stump up!' My plea fell on deaf ears.

Jim Sillars won a famous and deserved victory at the Govan by-election.

The non-payment campaign continued, despite harassment by certain council officials and sheriff officers. At one point, I received a notice from sheriff officers that they had applied to the Lord Advocate for an arrestment of my wages. So much for the legal expertise of sheriff officers. Even I knew that an arrestment of earnings order had to be served on the employer, and I was certainly not employed by the Lord Advocate. I argued that my employers were the constituents of Falkirk West, who had the power to arrest all my wages at the next election if they felt that way inclined. I heard no more about the arrestment of my wages and I publicly announced that I would not pay my arrears of poll tax until the government announced its abolition.

The non-payment campaign spread to England when the poll tax was introduced south of the border and the outrage was so widespread that there were riots in the streets. I deplore assaults on police officers during the course of their duty and I condemn the smashing of shop windows, the looting and other acts of mindless violence which I saw on television. But peaceful protest and civil disobedience are justified in certain situations and there is no doubt that those who refused to pay the poll tax helped to achieve its demise, as well as that of Margaret Thatcher. Soon after John Major announced the abolition of the poll tax, I paid all my arrears to Central Regional Council, which amounted to several thousand pounds. I am convinced to this day that the poll tax would not have been defeated if we had relied on cosy parliamentary debates. There is a place for legitimate extra-parliamentary action.

Similarly, there was a need for extra-parliamentary action in the campaign for a Scottish Parliament. The imposition of the poll tax on Scotland made many more people realise the need for a Scottish Parliament, because there was no way in which any Scottish Parliament would have foisted such an evil tax on the people of Scotland. Tory Government policy was galvanising people in support of a Scottish Parliament but the Scottish Group of Labour MPs had no idea of how to take the campaign forward. It was the Campaign for a Scottish Assembly that again seized the initiative.

In July 1988, the CSA produced proposals for a Scottish Constitutional Convention, which in turn would produce proposals for a Scottish Parliament. I expressed strong support for the idea but predictably it met with a cool response from Donald Dewar and Murray Elder (now Lord Elder), General Secretary of the Scottish Labour Party. Nevertheless, leading lights in the CSA worked hard to persuade the Labour Party to support the Convention proposal. Whether it was their gifts of persuasion that did the trick or the result of the Govan by-election, only Donald Dewar could tell. But, by the end of 1988, he had changed his tune.

In January1989, Labour accepted an invitation from the CSA to participate in all-party talks on the proposed Scottish Constitutional Convention. The Tories' decision to boycott the Convention was predictable but, when the SNP also decided on a boycott, there was genuine disappointment amongst some Labour members, including myself. I publicly called on the SNP to think again but my plea fell on deaf ears. I still think that the Scottish Parliament, when it was eventually set up, would have been a stronger and better parliament if the SNP had been in there, fighting their corner in the Scottish Constitutional Convention.

Despite the SNP and Tory boycott, the inaugural meeting of the Convention was a great success. It was held in the Church of Scotland Assembly Hall in Edinburgh on 30 March 1989.

I was suffering from extreme depression at the time, because I knew that my youngest son Paul had only weeks to live. But even I was on my feet to give Canon Kenyon Wright, the Convention's Executive Chair, a standing ovation for a rousing speech, during which he raised the possibility of Margaret Thatcher's rejecting the Convention's plans:

'What if that other single voice we know so well responds by saying: *We say No, and we are the State*? Well, we say: *Yes, and we are the people!*'

That struck a chord with the audience because the Convention's plans were to be based on the previously agreed Claim of Right, which declared the sovereignty of the people of Scotland.

By the end of 1990, the Convention had agreed on the basis of a scheme for a Scottish Parliament, although some matters such as the detail of the electoral system still had to be decided. In the lead-up to the 1992 general election, the Convention organised a campaign to raise public awareness of the plans for a Scottish Parliament. There were high hopes that a Labour victory in 1992 would enable a Scottish Parliament to become a reality but Kinnock blew it and the Tories, under John Major, managed to hang on to power. Even in Scotland, the Tories tried to claim some kind of victory because their vote went up by 1 per cent from their all-time low in 1987.

Once again, the Labour leadership did virtually nothing to challenge the Tories' lack of mandate in Scotland. In the immediate aftermath of the election, I attended a meeting in Glasgow to discuss what action could be taken to further the cause of setting up a Scottish Parliament. Also present at the meeting were John

McAllion MP, George Galloway MP, Mike Russell of the SNP, as well as the popular musicians, Ricky Ross of 'Deacon Blue' and Pat Kane of 'Hue and Cry'.

We all favoured a campaign to highlight the fact that about three-quarters of Scottish voters had voted for parties committed to a Scottish Parliament. Realising that those parties had differing views about the powers of the parliament, we decided that a demand for a multi-option referendum would be a unifying factor, the three options being (1) the status quo (2) a devolved parliament and (3) independence. After racking our brains for a snappy name for the campaign, I eventually came up with the suggestion of 'Scotland United' which met with unanimous approval.

'Scotland United' served a useful purpose in the immediate aftermath of the 1992 general election because it helped to keep the flag flying for a Scottish Parliament at a critical time when the Tories wanted to bury it once and for all and even some Labour MPs such as Brian Wilson and Norman Hogg wanted Labour's commitment shifted to the back burner, if not ditched completely.

However, when Neil Kinnock resigned as leader of the Labour Party after the election, he was succeeded by John Smith, who had a long-standing commitment to setting up a Scottish Parliament which he described as 'unfinished business'. It was a tragedy that John did not live to see the fruits of his efforts and, when Tony Blair took over as leader, I never had the same faith in him as I did in John Smith.

I also thought that George Robertson, Shadow Secretary of State for Scotland, was a creature of expediency rather than a man of principle. He once famously said that a Scottish Parliament would kill the SNP stone dead. He was also very much involved in behind-the-scenes negotiations which led to a reduction in the size of the proposed parliament from 144 members to 129, with 73 members being elected under 'first past the post', and 56 elected by proportional representation (PR) on a regional basis.

There were many people in the Labour Party who were absolutely opposed to PR because they thought that it would decrease Labour's chances of winning an over-all majority. I took the view, and still do, that the choice of voting system should be based on democratic principle rather than perceived advantage for any political party. There is no voting system which is absolutely perfect but the worst of the lot is 'first past the post', because it could lead to a situation whereby a party with only about one third of the votes could nevertheless have an overall majority of seats in parliament.

I agreed with the Liberal Democrats that the single transferrable vote (STV) system would be the best in terms of ensuring a link between members and constituencies, while achieving a reasonable degree of proportionality. I can understand that, faced with people like George Robertson, the Liberal Democrats felt that they had to compromise, but the result is a hybrid system whereby MSPs are elected under two different methods, often leading to friction, if not absolute hostility, between constituency MSPs and regional MSPs.

It is also possible to get elected to a regional seat with as little as 6 per cent of the vote, and some would argue that such a low threshold could give a foothold to extremists of left or right. If it was George Robertson's aim to devise a scheme which would pay lip-service to PR yet maximise the number of Labour seats, it is rather ironic that one of the first beneficiaries was Tommy Sheridan, especially when George Robertson had spent much of his political life conducting a witch hunt against Trotskyites!

Shortly after Tony Blair became leader of the Labour Party in 1994, I had an unexpected opportunity to discuss the Scottish constitutional question with him directly. I had tabled a question to Prime Minister John Major and, by the luck of the draw, it was virtually certain to be reached for oral answer. To my surprise, I received a message from Blair's office that he wanted to see me before Question Time. I thought at first that he was going to try telling me what question to ask, because I knew that he and his team of advisors put a huge amount of preparation into Question Time and they liked to orchestrate things with the help of pliant Labour backbenchers.

When I entered the Leader of the Opposition's office, behind the Speaker's Chair, he gave me a warm welcome before asking me what subject I intended raising at Prime Minister's Question Time. I had already made up my mind to ask a question supporting the establishment of a Scottish Parliament and I told him so. When he pressed me for detail, I reminded him that, earlier that week, John Major had described Labour's proposal to set up a Scottish Parliament as 'teenage madness'. I intended pointing out to Major that previous Tory prime ministers such as Sir Alec Douglas-Home and Ted Heath had supported the principle of a Scottish Parliament, as had more recent Tory cabinet ministers such as Malcolm Rifkind and George Younger. Blair seemed surprised at this information, which revealed his lack of knowledge about the issue. He then asked me how I thought Major would respond to me.

I told him that I thought Major would attack the so called tartan tax, namely the revenue-raising powers of Labour's proposed parliament and he would emphasise that the Tories had never supported any proposal which would mean the people of Scotland paying more taxes. I also suggested to Blair that, if he were to come in on that subject at Question Time, he should remind Major that there was no meaningful parliament in the world which did not have revenue-raising powers and that even the smallest local authority in Britain had such powers.

Blair listened very respectfully to what I had to say and he seemed very thoughtful. Question Time went much as I had predicted. I reminded John Major about his reference to 'teenage madness' and asked him whether he thought that erstwhile supporters of a Scottish Parliament such as Alec Douglas-Hume, Ted Heath, Malcolm Rifkind and George Younger were all teenage madmen. My joke seemed to go down very well and I later received an award from the BBC for the best question of the year. Even the Blairites apparently liked it because Tony despatched an emissary to my office with a congratulatory message and thanking me for the pre-Question Time briefing.

Some time afterwards, I began to wonder if my briefing of Tony Blair had led to unintended consequences. He was later to make a very foolish comparison between the Scottish Parliament and a parish council. He perhaps was trying to reiterate my point that even the smallest local authority in Britain had revenue-raising powers but his words were not well chosen for the context and, as a result, the SNP seized on his gaffe. Here was the leader of the Labour Party implying that a Scottish Parliament would be akin to an English parish council.

I suspect that another unintended consequence came not long after my discussion with Blair. Without any prior consultation with the Labour Party, he suddenly announced that, before introducing the legislation to set up a Scottish Parliament, a Labour government would hold a double-barrelled referendum. The people of Scotland would be asked whether they wanted a parliament and, if so, whether they wanted it to have revenue-raising powers. George Robertson, who was Shadow Secretary of State for Scotland, meekly accepted the policy change without a whimper but some Labour MPs, including myself, smelled a rat. The second question was designed to scupper the revenue-raising power of the Scottish Parliament.

I am convinced to this day that Blair did not want the parliament to have such power and he thought that the people would reject it in a referendum. In the event, the people voted for revenue-raising. The power, which is limited to varying the basic rate of income tax by 3p per pound, has never been used, probably because it is so limited.

Within the Scottish Constitutional Convention, I had argued strongly for fiscal autonomy, whereby the Scottish Parliament would raise all revenue within Scotland and within an agreed Scottish off-shore sector for the purpose of oil revenues. I also proposed that the Scottish Parliament should have borrowing powers. In the Labour Party at that time, I was like a lone voice crying in the wilderness, but such ideas are now gaining currency and I am convinced that their day will come. In the meantime, the Scottish Parliament must be the only parliament in the world that does not have the responsibility of raising a single penny of its budget but is completely dependent on the vote of another parliament.

Nevertheless, the establishment of the Scottish Parliament is one of the most positive achievements of the Blair government, although some of the forecasts about the political implications were well off the mark. George Robertson's prediction that a Scottish Parliament would kill the SNP stone dead has already come back to haunt him.

As for Tony Blair, I never thought that he was an enthusiastic supporter of a Scottish Parliament and I do not think that he fully understood what it was all about. He inherited the policy from John Smith and he realised that he had to go along with it, albeit reluctantly. Perhaps he was hoping that the people of Scotland would vote 'No' to at least one of the questions in the referendum.

The 1997 Labour Party manifesto contained the commitment to hold a pre-legislative referendum on the proposal to set up a Scottish Parliament along the lines of that agreed by the Scottish Constitutional Convention. A few days after Labour's landslide victory at the general election, the new Parliamentary Labour Party met for the first time at Church House, Westminster. During a debate on the priorities of the newly elected government, I urged that the referendum be held at the earliest opportunity, because the people of Scotland had been waiting long enough and any further procrastination would lead to accusations of skulduggery.

To my surprise, the government did as I requested. The referendum was held on 11 September 1997 and the result was 74.3 per cent in favour of a Scottish Parliament and 63.5 per cent in favour of revenue-raising powers. Even Blair knew then that there was no going back. Donald Dewar, as Secretary of State for Scotland, piloted the legislation through the House of Commons with his usual parliamentary proficiency and the bill reached the statute book the following year.

In May 1999, the Scottish Parliament met in the Church of Scotland Assembly Hall in Edinburgh, the same hall which had housed the inaugural meeting of the Scottish Constitutional Convention a decade before. It was the first Scottish Parliament for nearly 300 years, indeed the first-ever Scottish Parliament elected on a democratic franchise.

Various politicians will no doubt try to claim the credit for setting up the parliament, but it was the people of Scotland who brought the Scottish Parliament into being and, on that unforgettable day in May 1999, the people were literally dancing in the streets of Scotland's capital. They certainly had a lot to celebrate. It had been a long, hard struggle.

◆

CHAPTER TWENTY-ONE

The birth of New Labour

On Thursday, 12 May 1994, I was on my way to the House of Commons for Question Time when I saw an *Evening Standard* billboard proclaiming: 'John Smith dies'.

It took a while before the news sank in. Making every effort to avoid the inescapable truth, I kept on telling myself that there are thousands, maybe even millions of John Smiths, but I eventually came to the conclusion that there was only one John Smith whose death would have merited such a proclamation on the streets of London. When I arrived at the House of Commons, I received confirmation of the news, if any confirmation was required. The Labour Party had lost its leader and the nation had lost its prime minister-in-waiting.

I cannot claim to have been one of John Smith's 'inner circle', but I had a huge respect for him and we had some enjoyable times together. When I was first elected to parliament, John and I represented neighbouring constituencies and I have a fond recollection of us on an underground visit to Cardowan Colliery at Stepps, in North Lanarkshire. Cardowan had man-riding conveyor belts to transport the miners from the pit bottom to the coalface, and one of the miners gave us a demonstration of how to fall onto the belt and lie belly down while the belt was still moving. The demonstrator made it look easy but there was an acquired knack to it and John was not the most slender or most nimble of people. Nevertheless, he was up for it and the miners had a good laugh at our efforts. Once we got used to it, John and I were like a pair of excited teenagers on a fairground ride.

On the day that John died, there was an eerie silence throughout the Palace of Westminster and members of all parties were in a state of shock. I went to Annie's Bar, where I saw hardened journalists with tears in their eyes. Even they were stuck for words.

The House met as usual for prayers at 2.30 p.m. but the rigid ritual of the House of Commons would not permit prayers for John or his family or even a mention of his name. Much of the official parliamentary praying is taken up with prayers for the Queen and other members of the royal family and, for some reason or other, the chaplain was not permitted to make any exceptions. There was not even a period of silence when members could pray privately.

Immediately after prayers, the Speaker, Betty Boothroyd, told a hushed House: 'I regret to have to report to the House the death of the Right Honourable John Smith QC, Member for Monklands East.' The sitting was then suspended until 3.30 p.m., when John Major, the prime minister, led the tributes to the man who had so recently been his most powerful adversary. That familiar figure was missing from the Opposition dispatch box and Major correctly judged the mood of the House in moving its adjournment, saying that he did not believe that there would have been the stomach for any other business in the House that day.

After Major finished, Margaret Beckett spoke; before John's death, she had been his deputy and so stepped into the role of acting leader until a new leader was elected. After Margaret spoke, several other members, including myself, rose to speak and I saw Donald Dewar glowering at me and indicating that I should sit down and shut up. I could not believe it. Perhaps Donald thought that tributes should be paid only by ministers, privy councillors and other members of the parliamentary establishment, or perhaps he thought that I would put my foot in it. In any case, I decided to ignore Donald. It was up to Betty Boothroyd, as Speaker, to decide whether I should be given the opportunity to pay tribute to my dead comrade and Betty called me to speak after various party spokespersons. I gave the following short speech:

John Smith was a lad o' many pairts, but perhaps his greatest gift was his ability to unite people. I suppose most of the political pundits would put John slightly to the right of me on the political spectrum of the Labour Party. But John's greatest ability was his ability to unite people, whatever their views, in the struggle against injustice and the struggle for a better life for the people we represent. It is a tragedy that our party and our country have been robbed of such a great asset.

I particularly remember his efforts many years ago, when he was in government, to get the Scottish Home Rule Bill onto the Statute Book. It is a tragedy that the architect of that legislation is no longer with us, but I trust that soon the fruits of his labours will be there to be seen.

John Smith may go down in history as the greatest prime minister we never had. I join the rest of the House in expressing our condolence to Elizabeth and their daughters on their sense of loss. We'll never see his like again.

Donald Dewar made no comment, but Elizabeth Smith later thanked me personally for what I had said about her husband.

In the immediate aftermath of John's death, it seemed that the entire nation was in mourning and there was already talk about the possibility of a state funeral. That is a measure of the widespread affection and respect for a man who was recognised as one of the greatest parliamentarians of his time, despite the fact that he had not held ministerial office for 15 years.

On the day after John Smith died, I met Gordon Brown at Heathrow Airport when we were both waiting for a flight back to Scotland. Although the Parliamentary Labour Party was officially in mourning, there was already talk amongst Labour MPs as to who should succeed John. The initial conversation between Gordon and me was all about John and the Smith family, but I eventually got round to telling Gordon to get his hat in the ring to succeed John. Gordon hummed and hawed and muttered something about stopping Prescott, because he would be a disaster. I told him: 'Prescott has no chance. Blair is the only guy who can beat you.'

Gordon then tried to turn the conversation back to the Smith family, indicating that no one should start campaigning until after the funeral. I agreed with him that it would be disrespectful and foolish to start openly campaigning at that time but I warned him that Blair and his Prince of Darkness, Peter Mandelson, had already started conspiring and would have no scruples about trying to stitch up the succession before the funeral. Gordon seemed unconvinced. Maybe he was so overcome with grief that he felt compelled to wait until his friend was buried. Or maybe he was just too decent. Or maybe he was naïve enough to trust Blair by putting too much faith in their previous understanding that Gordon would be the successor if anything happened to John. Soon after John Smith's funeral, Gordon seemed more actively interested in standing for the leadership, but by then it was too late. Mandelson had fixed it for Blair and Gordon had to wait another 13 years before becoming leader. Gordon's dithering and lack of judgement were his undoing, and he has displayed those same traits since eventually succeeding Blair.

I could not believe it when Gordon brought Mandelson back into the Cabinet in 2008, especially after Mandy had stabbed him in the back and had previously resigned from the cabinet in disgrace on two separate occasions.

Shortly after John Smith's death, a by-election was held in John's constituency of Monklands East. On the face of it, Monklands East looked a very safe Labour seat. John's majority at the 1992 general election was over 15,000 and there was no shortage of ambitious people waiting to fill his shoes.

The Labour Party chose Helen Liddell as its candidate. I first met Helen in the early 1970s, when she was a young researcher for the Scottish Trades Union Congress. Shortly afterwards, she became General Secretary of the Scottish Labour Party but was then head-hunted by Robert Maxwell, the former millionaire Labour MP and head of the Mirror Group of newspapers. She was a very close confidante of Maxwell's but, when the tycoon fell off his yacht and was revealed to be a fraudulent crook who even stole from his own workers' pension fund, Helen was cunning enough not to sink with him. The vacancy in Monklands East seemed an ideal opportunity for another career move, because Helen was born and brought up in that area, although she had long since moved up-market.

In the 1990s, Monklands was a part of Scotland which was still bedevilled by sectarianism, long after other communities in Scotland had learned to build bridges between people of different faiths. The two main towns in Monklands were Airdrie, which was largely Protestant, and Coatbridge, which was largely Catholic. During the by-election, I was knocking on doors in Airdrie and, when I said I was calling on behalf of the Labour Party, I was getting doors slammed in my face. On one occasion, the man who answered the door told me that there was no way that he would ever vote Labour but, before he could slam the door, I managed to ask him why. His reply was startling: 'I'll tell you why. Because I'm fed up with all those Fenians on Monklands Council giving everything to Coat-bridge and nothing to us in Airdrie.'

When I reported this back to the Labour campaign headquarters, I found out that such a response was not atypical and, what was more worrying for Labour, most of the disenchanted voters were intend-ing to vote for the SNP. Some Labour Party members alleged that the SNP was deliberately stirring up such discontent and the fact that Helen Liddell was a Catholic was being used against her. Helen at first defended her party colleagues on Monklands Council but later changed tack, which infuriated the Labour councillors, who saw it as a blatant attempt to save her own skin at their expense. Tom Clarke, the Labour MP for Monklands West and a former provost of Monklands, was also very unhappy with Helen's criticism of the council. Her comments had the effect of adding fuel to the flames by giving credibility to the allegations. After the by-election, the Tory government set up an inquiry under William Austin Nimmo Smith QC, now Lord Nimmo Smith, who threw out the allegations against the council but, during the by-election, many voters believed them to be true.

The Labour Party was in such a state of disarray that John Smith must have been birling in his grave. It was inconceivable that such a safe Labour seat, held by the late and much-loved leader of the Labour Party, should fall into the hands of the SNP. By polling day, canvass returns showed that Labour and the SNP were neck-and-neck and Helen Liddell just squeezed home with a much reduced majority of 1,640.

When Helen came to Westminster to take her seat, there was the usual photo-call on the steps of the House of Commons, attended by Helen's family and several Labour MPs, including Harriet Harman. There must have been an immediate bonding between Helen and Harriet when the latter remarked to Helen's children: 'You must be very proud of your grandmother.' Helen was only 43, but the by-election had obviously put years on her!

Shortly after the Monklands East by-election, Tony Blair was crowned as leader of the Labour Party and he and Mandelson launched the New Labour project. One of the first things they planned was to ditch Clause Four of the Labour Party Constitution, which aimed 'to secure for the workers by hand or by brain the full fruits of their industry and the most equitable distribution thereof that may be possible, upon the basis of the common ownership of the means of production, distribution and exchange and the best obtainable system of popular administration and control of each industry or service'.

The clause had been adopted by the party in 1918 and the Blairites argued that it was archaic and alienated many voters. However, there was a hidden agenda. Part of the New Labour project was to cosy up to big business and to continue the programme of privatisation started by Margaret Thatcher. By 1994, Clause Four was mainly symbolic, but ditching it would send out a clear signal that New Labour thought socialism was dead and that capitalism was the way forward.

There had always been a debate within Labour about the precise mix of the mixed economy, and there was no doubt that many public services needed to be modernised and made more efficient. However, most people saw a continuing role for public ownership and public enterprise. For example, the water industry in Scotland was still in public ownership and the Scottish Labour Party had successfully fought a campaign to stop the Tory government from privatising it. I thought it was very important for the Labour Party to defend common ownership, especially when successful public enterprise was being threatened by the Tories, and that was basically why I opposed the repeal of Clause Four.

A nationwide debate ensued on the merits or otherwise of Clause Four and the first big test was the Scottish Labour Party Conference in the spring of 1995. The venue was Inverness and I recall getting up early in the morning to do TV and radio interviews before the conference began. At one stage, it was almost as if the studios had revolving doors, with me coming out after defending Clause Four and Blair with his entourage going in to attack it. He had obviously wanted to avoid a direct confrontation with me.

The debate was greatly influenced by what I call the toady factor. Blair was widely perceived as the next prime minister, with huge powers of political patronage. Anyone aspiring to be a minister in his government would naturally want to suck up to the Great Leader and anyone publicly opposing him would be ostracised. MPs like Donald Dewar, Helen Liddell and Alistair Darling probably always thought that Clause Four was a load of old rubbish and they were joined by erstwhile 'lefties' like John Reid, Sam Galbraith, Lewis Moonie and, of course, Gordon Brown. On the other side were the usual suspects such as John McAllion, George Galloway and myself.

During the course of the conference debate, I quoted Harold Wilson's reply when he was questioned about Clause Four: 'I don't believe that God made the world in six days, but that does not mean I'm going to rewrite the entire Book of Genesis.' Wilson was making the point that very few people took Clause Four literally.

In the same debate, John Reid had the gall to say that some of the people quoting Harold Wilson in support of Clause Four were the very same people who had attacked Harold Wilson when he was prime minister. That was rich coming from John Reid, who had been a member of the Communist Party during the Wilson era and spent much of his time and effort denouncing Wilson as a mere reformist rather than a real socialist.

It was a very lively debate in the Eden Court Theatre, Inverness, but the toadies predictably won the day and that was that. Even comrades south of the Border realised that, if Blair could win over the party in Scotland, he would win hands down at the Labour Party Conference in the autumn. By that time, it had become a vote of confidence in Blair's leadership and even many of the trade union leaders caved in, because they did not want to risk being accused of ruining the chance of a Labour government.

I remain convinced that the day Clause Four was ditched was a huge turning-point in the history of the Labour Party. It was the day that Labour lost its socialist soul, and it has never recovered. Over-reliance on free market forces has also had damaging effects on the UK and the global economy, leading to the worst recession for decades. Ironically, even New Labour has eventually had to use public investment and, in some cases, public ownership to rescue the banking system.

Blairites still argue that the New Labour project was the cause of the party's landslide victory in 1997 but I think that, if John Smith had lived, Labour would have won by a similar margin. The truth is that, by the mid-1990s the Tories were unelectable. They were in a state of terminal decline and there was a strong stench of corruption about them. It was time for a change, and Labour's theme tune for the 1997 general election captured the mood of the country: 'Things can only get better.'

A few days after Labour's historic victory, the new Parliamentary Labour Party met for the first time. There were so many Labour MPs that we could not fit into any of the House of Commons committee rooms and we moved across the road to Church House, near Westminster Abbey. Everything was carefully stage-managed. We were all asked to take our seats before the new prime minister arrived and, when Tony entered the hall, he was greeted with a sycophantic standing ovation lasting several minutes. He then addressed us:

'It was New Labour that won and it is New Labour that will govern.'

That phrase revealed a lot about Blair's thinking. He had formed a new party and this was the beginning of a new era. The country had voted for him and we had all been elected on his back. We owed our seats not to our constituents but to him, and our first loyalty should be to him as the Great Leader, who had led us to such a magnificent victory. Blair got a rapturous reception from the Parliamentary Labour Party on that sunny May morning, but I saw storm clouds gathering.

◆

CHAPTER TWENTY-TWO

Political poodles

Shortly after the September 1997 Referendum, the Scottish Labour Party invited interested members to apply for inclusion on the list of approved candidates for the Scottish Parliament. Several Labour back-benchers at Westminster applied, including John Home Robertson, Michael Connarty, Ian Davidson and myself. There was of course no problem with Donald Dewar and his trusted cronies being approved as candidates. Donald, after all, was Secretary of State for Scotland, Sam Galbraith and Henry McLeish were in Donald's ministerial team at the Scottish Office and John Home Robertson had been in Donald's shadow team when we were in opposition.

But Connarty, Davidson and I were obviously deemed to be unacceptable right from the outset, and Dewar and his colleagues tried their utmost to discredit us even before the selection process began. Information was leaked to the Scottish media that Connarty, Davidson and I had no chance of being approved as Labour candidates for the Scottish Parliament and this caused banner headlines in the Scottish press. When I questioned one newspaper reporter about the matter, he did not, of course, reveal his source but he assured me that his information had come from 'the highest level' within the Labour Party.

If the object of the exercise was to scare us off, it worked only partially. Michael Connarty immediately withdrew his application but Ian Davidson and I decided to fight on.

The Labour Party leadership had devised a system of selection whereby applicants were interviewed at party headquarters and the interviewing board, consisting of a handful of party trusties, decided whether or not the applicants were successful. The entire panel of interviewers was chaired by Rosemary McKenna, MP for Cumbernauld & Kilsyth, who had been elected to Westminster only a few weeks previously as the result of a devious selection system invented by New Labour.

Norman Hogg, the sitting MP for Cumbernauld & Kilsyth, had

delayed announcing his resignation until after the election had been called. Party headquarters decided that there was insufficient time to follow the full selection procedure and the National Executive foisted an all-female short list on the Constituency Labour Party. Although there was general agreement that the Labour Party should have more women as candidates, the imposition of an all-female short list in that instance was perceived by many party members as a ploy to stop a radical lawyer called Ian Smart, who was a local party activist with an excellent chance of defeating Rosemary McKenna on a democratic vote. But Smart was excluded, possibly because he was seen as a potential critic of the party leadership. McKenna had no serious local challenge and was therefore the beneficiary of a system which many considered to be rigged. Norman Hogg was rewarded with a seat in the House of Lords.

Rosemary McKenna had hardly made any contribution at all at Westminster when it was announced that she would be heading the procedure for selecting Labour candidates for the Scottish Parliament. She chaired a selection process which brought the Labour Party into disrepute. Many good people were excluded from Rosemary's list, but the inclusion of her own daughter raised a few eyebrows.

Rosemary's sidekick was Ernie Ross, MP for Dundee West, who had moved from extreme left to extreme right since his election in 1979. During a parliamentary career lasting over 20 years, Ernie's main claim to fame happened in 1999, when he was exposed as an informer who had leaked the contents of a Foreign Affairs Select Committee report to the Foreign Office before the report was published. The purpose of the leak was to ensure that the Foreign Secretary, Robin Cook, would have prior knowledge of the report's contents, which were very critical of the government's involvement in the supply of arms to Sierra Leone in breach of a UN arms embargo. Ernie had to resign from the committee in disgrace and was temporarily suspended from the House of Commons. Long before that particular incident, I had considered Ernie Ross to be a snake in the grass. I had little or no respect for him and I suspect that the feeling was mutual.

When I turned up for the selection interview at the appointed time at Keir Hardie House in Glasgow, I was told to wait because the interviewing panel was not ready. While I was waiting, George Robertson MP, Secretary of State for Defence, came in the front door. He acknowledged my presence with what I thought was a smirk, but I must confess my bias. George Robertson and I never saw eye to eye. He was urging people to pay the poll tax when I was supporting a campaign of resistance. He was in favour of nuclear weapons when I was campaigning against them. I was in favour of fiscal autonomy for the Scottish Parliament but Robertson, when he was Shadow Secretary of State for Scotland, was opposed to all but minuscule revenue-raising powers and even they would be subject to a referendum. I do not know why Robertson was at Keir Hardie House that day, but I was very suspicious when his name cropped up later.

At last I was called for interview and, on entering the room, I could not believe my eyes when I saw that Ernie Ross was chairing the proceedings. When members of the Parliamentary Committee of the Parliamentary Labour Party later found out, they were so astounded that they changed the rules so that no member of the Parliamentary Labour Party should be allowed to sit in judgement on a fellow member in such a situation. Unfortunately for me, the rule was not made retrospective.

The National Executive Committee representative on the interviewing board was Maggie Jones. She was a full-time officer of my trade union, Unison, which gave financial sponsorship to Falkirk West Constituency Labour Party, but I knew from past experience that she was a New Labour hack and I could expect no favours from her. Her whole tone of questioning was extremely hostile from the outset and I suspect that she was flown up from London at the party's expense to do a hatchet job. I could not help wondering why the National Executive Committee in London should be directly involved at all in the selection of candidates for the Scottish Parliament but it was perhaps typical of the control-freakery of New Labour. The same Maggie Jones was later foisted upon Blaenau Gwent Constituency Labour Party, using the ploy of an all-female shortlist. At the next Westminster election, the people of Blaenau Gwent were so outraged that Labour lost its safest seat in Wales. Maggie was 'rewarded' with a seat in the House of Lords, where she now rejoices in the title Baroness Jones of Whitchurch. Her 'elevation' was announced in the infamous list leaked to *The Times*, which led to the cash for peerages scandal.

Maggie, however, was surpassed in her interviewing technique by the Chair, Ernie Ross, who obviously relished his role as grand inquisitor.

'Have you ever voted against the Government?'

'Have you ever asked an awkward question?'

'Have you ever said that George Robertson should resign?'

To the last question, I responded that I had never sought George Robertson's resignation as Secretary of State for Defence but that I had stood against him for the post of Shadow Secretary of State for Scotland in the shadow cabinet elections when we were in opposition. The fact that I had directly challenged him was a clear indication that I did not consider him to be the best person for the job, and even Blair eventually seemed to agree with me because he did not give Robertson the Scotland portfolio when Labour came to power.

After the interview, there was a delay of several weeks before the results were announced but the leaks to the press continued long before the official announcement. Ian Davidson and I were reported to have 'failed' the interview. Davidson had allegedly treated the interviewing board with insufficient respect because he was not wearing a tie! As for me, I had been deemed 'too aggressive'. In truth, I had bent over backwards to be as courteous as possible, when faced with the most provocative interrogation and hostile body language I had ever experienced during any interview. Rather than being aggressive, I was downright docile and, under the circumstances, I thought that I had performed well at the interview.

A few weeks later, the official notification arrived. It came as no surprise to receive the curt letter from party headquarters informing me that the selection board had decided that I was not acceptable as a candidate for the Scottish Parliament. Ian Davidson MP was also rejected and both of us decided to appeal. To assist in the preparation of my appeal, I wrote formally to party headquarters asking for some details of the reasons why I had been rejected. I was informed that I did not meet the criteria. When I asked what criteria I did not meet, I was told that that was confidential and that I should submit details in writing if I wanted to proceed with an appeal.

Despite my pessimism about the outcome, I decided to make a detailed written submission in support of my appeal, and Ian Davidson came to a similar decision. We held a joint press conference in Glasgow before formally handing in our appeal documents to Keir Hardie House. Unfortunately, Ian had not finalised his written submission but, for the purposes of a press photo-call at Keir Hardie House, he handed in a blank sheet of paper. Ian explained the situation to the Labour Party official who met us at Keir Hardie House to receive the appeal papers and he indicated that his written submission would follow shortly. I am convinced that

Ian acted in good faith, but he committed a blunder which the Labour Party exploited to the full.

That evening, Alex Rowley, General Secretary of the Scottish Labour Party, appeared on television claiming that Davidson had insulted the Labour Party by handing in a blank sheet of paper. He castigated Davidson for being flippant and treating the party with contempt. I was unaware of any precedent for an employee of the Labour Party making such a vicious public attack on a Labour MP, and Rowley's conduct made me realise more fully what we were up against.

Soon afterwards, Ian Davidson gave up. He had had enough, but I was determined to continue fighting. I had requested a hearing of my appeal, but that was refused. My appeal was considered in my absence and the result was a foregone conclusion. The only successful appellant in the whole process was Susan Deacon, who later became Health Minister in Donald Dewar's first Cabinet. The fact that someone of Susan's undoubted ability was rejected in the first place beggars belief; 'selectors' such as Rosemary McKenna, Ernie Ross and Maggie Jones were not in the same league as Susan.

Members of Falkirk West Constituency Labour Party were livid when they heard the outcome of the selection system. Some other local members had applied for consideration as candidates, including Kate Arnot and Anne Wallace. Kate was chair of the Constituency Labour Party and was a very active organiser for Scottish Women's Aid. Anne had been a very successful Convener of Central Regional Council, the only woman who had ever held such a post in any Scottish region. I do not know what Anne had done to fall foul of Comrades McKenna and Ross, but I suspect that Kate's rejection may have had something to do with her speech at the Scottish Labour Party Conference a few weeks earlier.

Falkirk West Constituency Labour Party had a resolution criticising the Blair Government's decision to cut benefits for the children of one-parent families. I had voted against the cuts in the House of Commons along with some other Labour MPs, but the government won the vote. During the course of her speech at the conference, Kate Arnot, who was herself a single parent, had condemned the cuts as morally bereft, economically illiterate and politically inept. That would be enough to disqualify her from being a Labour candidate for the Scottish Parliament. Like me, she had failed the loyalty test.

Around that time, I also discovered almost by accident that the Labour Government whips' office at the House of Commons had been asked to forward details to the selection board of the occasions when I had voted against the Labour Government. Tony Benn had gone to see Nick Brown, Labour's Chief Whip, to explain why he could not vote for the government on some issue. Tony, in his gentlemanly way, was apologetic about the frequency of his visits to the whips' office to explain why he could not support the government. In a rather flippant, off-the-cuff response, Nick Brown told Tony that it was just as well that he was not hoping to be selected as a Labour candidate for the Scottish Parliament because the whips' office had received a request from the people in charge of the selection to send them details of all the occasions when Dennis Canavan had voted against the government. When I later confronted Nick Brown with this further evidence of control-freakery, he confirmed the gist of the story and told me that he had complied with the selection board's request.

I would have had no serious complaint if details of my entire House of Commons voting record had been forwarded to the selection board. After all, the voting records of all MPs are available for public inspection and, apart from anything else, they also indicate how often an MP has been present in the House of Commons to vote. However, it seemed rather misleading to forward only selected information about the occasions when an MP had voted against the government without any information about how often he or she had actually voted for the government.

I had never made any secret of the fact that I had voted against some government measures such as abolishing student grants, introducing tuition fees and cutting benefits for children of one-parent families. I had publicly explained my reasons in the House of Commons and in my constituency and I honestly believed that I was acting in the best interests of the people I had been elected to represent. There had been no mention of such anti-socialist policies in the Labour Party manifesto and I therefore felt justified in telling the party leadership that they had got it wrong. I knew that my outspokenness had upset some cabinet ministers. For example, when the government announced the abolition of student grants and the introduction of tuition fees, I accused David Blunkett and other Ministers in the House of Commons of personally benefiting from a previous Labour Government's generous grants system, then kicking away the ladder of opportunity from future generations. Blunkett rounded on his critics for 'mouthing Trotsky-ite platitudes'.

Now I was to get my comeuppance by being publicly declared unsuitable to be a Labour candidate for the Scottish Parliament. It was either an act of petty vengeance or part of a strategy to try to ensure that the Scottish Parliament was stuffed with obedient puppets who had unquestioning blind loyalty to the Blairite agenda. I was not the only candidate who failed the loyalty test but, of the 'failed' candidates, I probably had the highest profile because I was a sitting Member of Parliament with over 20 years' experience.

In effect, the Labour Party leadership was arrogantly telling my constituents that the person for whom they had been voting all those years was not up to the job. They were also telling Falkirk West Constituency Labour Party that none of their members was fit to be a candidate for the Scottish Parliament because all those who had applied from Falkirk West had been rejected.

The General Management Committee of Falkirk West Constituency Labour Party organised a ballot in which 97 per cent of all local party members voted for me to be on the list of approved Labour candidates. Alex Rowley, General Secretary of the Scottish Labour Party, was summoned to a Constituency Labour Party Executive meeting in Falkirk to try to explain the selection board's decision. He was going round in circles trying to defend the indefensible but there was no way in which he was going to back down. He seemed incapable of grasping the political consequences of 97 per cent of local Party members being over-ruled by a handful of party hacks sitting at party headquarters, but it was not just Rowley's political judgement which was suspect.

At one stage, a bright young Executive member read out one of the rules relating to the selection procedure which seemed to indicate a degree of flexibility to enable further consideration to be given to the views of the Constituency Labour Party. Rowley replied: 'That might be how you interpretate [sic] the rule, comrade, but that's not how I interpretate [sic] it and that's it!'

Rowley was clearly out of his depth and, at one stage, he defensively tried to emphasise that he had nothing personal against me by stating that he 'came from the same neck of the woods' as me. This was probably a reference to the fact that he came from Kelty, a neighbouring village to Cowdenbeath, where I had been born and brought up. In fact, we attended the same school, St Columba's, although I was obviously of an earlier vintage. I gather from some of his former teachers that he was not the sharpest tool in the box, but he had the reputation of being a protégé of Gordon Brown. Rowley had been leader of Fife Council, and, when Gordon Brown picked him for the job of General Secretary of the Scottish Labour Party, I began to doubt Gordon's ability for talent-spotting. Rowley's main talent seemed to be hanging on to Gordon's coat-tails. The last I heard of him he was back on Fife Council and was still employed by Gordon as some kind of local fixer. With fixers like that, it's not surprising that Labour has lost safe seats in Fife which had been Labour strongholds since the days of my grandfather. As General Secretary of the Scottish Labour Party, Rowley did not last long enough to make his presence felt.

As General Secretary of the Scottish Labour Party, Rowley did not last long in the job, but he lasted long enough to do a fair bit of damage to the party. I was sometimes asked by TV or radio producers to do a live interview first thing in the morning to defend my position regarding my possible candidature for the Scottish Parliament. If I happened to be in London on parliamentary business, this meant that I had to rise sometimes about 5 a.m. to get to the studio on time. Almost invariably, the Labour Party would put up Rowley to try to defend the selection board's decision. It seemed rather incongruous to be sitting in a TV studio in London at that time in the morning watching the General Secretary of my own party sitting in a studio in Glasgow trying to discredit me. At first I found it rather disconcerting but, in retrospect, I think that Rowley added another thousand to my majority every time he attacked me.

Rowley and his colleagues at party headquarters set about coercing Falkirk West Constituency Labour Party to start the process of selecting a candidate from the Labour Party's list of approved candidates. When it was made clear that no Labour Party branch or trade union would be allowed to nominate me, all the branches at first were adamant that they would not participate in such a rigged system. This presented some difficulty for Labour Party headquarters but I realised that the resistance of the Constituency Labour Party would not last forever and, even if it did, Labour Party headquarters would probably just foist a candidate upon the constituency anyway.

The first sign of collaboration between the Constituency Labour Party and Labour Party headquarters came at a meeting of the General Management Committee of Falkirk West Constituency

Labour Party in the autumn of 1998. A strange face appeared at the meeting, someone I had never seen before. I found out afterwards that, although he was a party member, he was not a delegate to the General Management Committee and therefore had no right to speak. However, nobody challenged his credentials and he proceeded to argue the case for co-operating with Labour Party headquarters by participating in the selection process and meekly accepting the decision that I should not be considered as a candidate. He claimed to have had previous experience of being a member of Knowsley North Constituency Labour Party which, in similar circumstances, had been suspended and the Labour Party candidate, George Howarth, had been chosen by the Labour Party National Executive Committee.

In fact the Knowsley North constituency had been left in the lurch when the sitting Labour MP, Robert Kilroy-Silk, suddenly announced his resignation to pursue a media career as host of the TV show, *Kilroy*. I pointed out that such circumstances were quite different from those in Falkirk West, where the sitting MP with over 20 years' experience was being undermined by Labour Party headquarters.

I found out later that the man from Knowsley North was David Jones, a relative newcomer to the Falkirk area. As a senior local authority planning officer, he was in fact breaking the law by getting involved in political activity at that level. At all the meetings of Falkirk West Constituency Labour Party which I attended at that time, his was the only voice supporting the view of Party Headquarters.

The first sign of a serious crack in the solidarity of the constituency members came a few weeks later, when the Camelon branch of the Labour Party agreed to co-operate with Labour Party headquarters by starting the procedure for selecting a candidate. The Camelon branch was the biggest in the constituency in terms of membership, although only a minority of the members were politically active. The branch always held its meetings in Camelon Labour Club, a popular haunt for drinking, bingo and other social activities. Many of the club customers had been persuaded to join the Labour Party branch, which was very much under the influence of Dennis Goldie and his twin bother, Gerry. Dennis and Gerry were sometimes referred to as the Kray twins, which was rather unfair because I never heard any whisper of violent conduct on their part.

However, the Goldie twins, especially Dennis, had an uncanny hold over other people. They were both members of Falkirk Council and Dennis had been Provost of Falkirk as well as the driving force within Camelon Labour Club. If Dennis snapped his fingers, many of his cronies would immediately fall into line, and it was therefore not surprising that the Camelon branch became the first in the constituency to side with Party Headquarters. This led to a lot of ill-feeling and name-calling, including references to treachery and even Judas. It was not very comradely conduct.

Soon after the decision of Camelon branch, Labour Party headquarters instructed all branches to hold special meetings to start the selection procedure. Some of the branches, including Larbert, decided to boycott the selection procedure, but nevertheless Labour Party headquarters decided to go ahead, with an outcome which can only be described as farcical. All registered members were duly notified of the meeting but only one member turned up. That was Hugh Lynch, retired headteacher of St Mungo's High School, Falkirk, who at that time was a lifelong member of the Labour Party and a former Labour Party parliamentary candidate. Hugh later told me that, when he saw that he was the only local party member to turn up, he assumed that the meeting would not go ahead because it was inquorate. However, four would-be candidates had also turned up together with an official from Labour Party headquarters who told Hugh to interview each of the would-be candidates to decide which one should get the nomination from the Larbert branch. Hugh did as he was told and that was how Michael Kelly, former Lord Provost of Glasgow and former Director of Celtic Football Club, got the nomination from the Larbert branch. It was one-member-one-vote *in extremis*!

Kelly was seen by many party members as a carpet-bagger but he probably thought he was in with a good chance of using Falkirk West Constituency as a stepping-stone to becoming a Scottish Cabinet minister. However, I had enough faith in the people of Falkirk West to see through a third-rate PR man whose main claim to fame was being a member of the infamous board which brought Celtic Football Club to the verge of bankruptcy. In the event, Kelly did not pick up much support and the favourite who emerged was Ross Martin, a West Lothian councillor, who was Education Spokesperson for the Convention of Scottish Local Authorities. When Martin got the support of the Goldies, that ensured that he got the support of the Camelon branch, which virtually assured him of victory because Camelon had the biggest membership.

For a while, I had considered the possibility of a legal challenge against the Labour Party. At considerable personal expense, I sought legal advice, including counsel's opinion. The advice was that, if I sought judicial review in the Court of Session on the grounds of an infringement of the principles of natural justice, I would probably win. The Court could order the Labour Party to re-run the selection process, but no court could instruct a party to select a particular candidate and rightly so. I could have spent many thousands of pounds winning my case but, at the end of the day, the Labour Party would probably have re-run the whole process, giving me another hearing with more careful adherence to the rules of natural justice, but coming to the same conclusion that I was unacceptable as a candidate on purely political grounds.

After a great deal of reflection, I came to the conclusion that my dispute with the Labour Party leadership was more political than legal and that the solution lay therefore in the court of public opinion, where the jury would be the electorate of Falkirk West Constituency. In November 1998, I publicly announced one of the most difficult decisions I have ever made in my life. I was going to stand as a candidate for the Scottish Parliament, with or without the support of the Labour Party. I made it clear that my preferred option would be to stand as a Labour candidate but, if the Labour leadership continued to refuse to consider me, then I would stand in any case. I was reluctant to use the term 'independent' candidate because, from previous experience, I had come across many so-called independent candidates who were just Tories in disguise. I also still had a vague hope that the Labour Party leadership would see sense and back down.

In November 1998, when it became clear that Labour Party headquarters were intent on going ahead with the selection process without allowing me to be nominated, I sent out an open letter to all members of Falkirk West Constituency Labour Party, informing them of my intention to stand as a candidate for the Scottish Parliament. In my view, the local party members and the local electorate were being treated with absolute contempt and the fairest solution would be to let the people decide whether I was good enough to be their representative.

I expected to be expelled from the Labour Party immediately but, although the Party issued statements condemning me, no expulsion took place at that time. I continued to be a member of the Labour Party and I continued to receive the Labour 'Whip', a weekly notice issued by the government whips' office to all members of the Parliamentary Labour Party. I came to the conclusion that the party bosses were still hoping that I would change my mind or that they had received legal advice that expulsion might be premature, because I had merely announced my intention to stand as a candidate, but my actual candidature at that time had not yet materialised.

The announcement of my intention to stand with or without the support of the Labour Party received huge publicity. Many of my party colleagues were understandably upset and some of them pleaded with me not to stand on the grounds that I would simply split the Labour vote and allow the SNP to win. My reply was that I would not stand unless I thought I would win and the feed-back I got from the general public was very supportive, especially in my constituency. There were also expressions of support from some unlikely sources. James Molyneaux, leader of the Ulster Unionist party, even offered to be my election agent! I politely thanked him but told him I had the best agent in the business.

In December 1998, I attended a Christmas social function for senior citizens, organised by Camelon Labour Club and held in the club premises. This was an annual event and it was my custom, as the local MP, to drop in and give a few words of seasonal greetings. On this occasion, the event was also attended by Ross Martin, who by this time had been selected as Labour candidate for the Scottish Parliament. I could see that some of the senior citizens present looked a bit uneasy, almost embarrassed, because they had as guests two people who were going to be fighting a bitter election battle against each other in a few months' time.

As it was a Christmas event, it was not an occasion for a political speech. I simply wished them all a Merry Christmas and a Happy New Year and thanked them very much for their support over what had been a difficult year. I could tell from most of their faces that they were still supportive and, when I finished speaking, there was a tumultuous applause and some of the pensioners rose from their seats to shake my hand. I was very moved. Many of those people were lifelong members of the Labour Party who would not want to risk expulsion from the party by openly supporting me, but their body language said it all. Under normal circumstances, such Labour diehards would never have contemplated voting anything other than Labour and the knowledge that I still had their support made me feel very humble. I left the Labour Club to go to a similar event in the social club attached to Camelon Juniors Football Club. I received a standing ovation and I knew then within my heart that I could win.

Towards the end of 1998, I received a late-night phone call from a journalist asking for my comments about a speech made earlier that evening by Donald Dewar at a Labour Party fundraising banquet at a big hotel in Glasgow. Admission to such events cost in the region of £100 per plate and, as such, the attendance was largely confined to plutocratic business people eager to catch the ear of a Labour MP or maybe even a government minister. Social inclusion was obviously off New Labour's agenda.

The journalist told me that Donald had departed from his pre-pared script to launch a bitter attack on me. Donald said that Dennis Canavan's exclusion from Labour's list of candidates for the Scottish Parliament had nothing to do with his politics. 'He is simply not good enough', Donald announced to the gathering of bloated dinner suits.

Donald's remarks apparently went down like a lead balloon and, to this day, I cannot understand what possessed the Secretary of State for Scotland to use such an occasion to launch an attack on a fellow member of the Parliamentary Labour Party.

When the journalist asked if I had anything to say, I replied: 'I am quite content to let the people decide whether I am good enough.'

A few days later, David Dimbleby's *Question Time* was televised from Scotland with a Scottish audience and a Scottish panel. Over half of the hour-long programme was taken up by questions about my dispute with the Labour leadership. The audience was 100 per cent behind me and even the Tory on the panel, Michael Forsyth, former Secretary of State for Scotland (now Lord Forsyth of Drumlean), said that, despite his profound disagreements with me on matters of policy, he had to admit that I was a hard-working MP who served my constituents well. Forsyth was in a good position to know my work-rate because, for 14 years, he had represented the Stirling constituency and many of his constituents were former constituents of mine.

During the TV programme, the only person who tried to defend Donald Dewar's comments about me was Helen Liddell, which came as no surprise because she was in Donald's ministerial team at the Scottish Office. At one stage, Helen came out with a real howler: 'Do you think that we should pick someone as a candidate just because he's got blue eyes?' The entire audience dissolved into laughter, and it was Helen who was the object of their ridicule.

In January 1999, I received an unexpected invitation from Donald Dewar to meet him. I was naïve enough to imagine that, even at that late date, he might have had a change of heart and so I agreed to the meeting. The venue was the government's Scottish Office building in Glasgow, which I thought was rather strange as Labour Party business should not be conducted in government buildings. When I went along to the meeting, I found that Donald was accompanied by Anne McGuire, MP for Stirling, who was the government's Scottish whip.

The meeting was very brief and I still do not understand why Donald asked to see me, because his position remained unchanged. At one point, he told me that, if I gave up my quest to stand for the Scottish Parliament and decided to stay at Westminster, then 'no one would bother me'. When I asked him what he meant by that, he indicated that the Party leadership would not object to my being re-selected as candidate for the Westminster Parliament. I could not believe my ears.

'Are you telling me that I'm not good enough to stand for the Scottish Parliament but that I am good enough to remain at Westminster?'

Donald had no response to that. I wished him and Anne McGuire a Happy New Year and left.

A few weeks later, I found out how serious Donald Dewar and his colleagues were in their efforts to undermine me. They announced that the Labour Party would be opening an office in Falkirk. This was the first time that the Labour Party had ever had an office in my constituency, and the location in Falkirk town centre must have cost a small fortune. Party headquarters had never had to spend much money getting me elected or re-elected but it was now clear to me that they were prepared to spend thousands of pounds to stop me. The principal guests at the official opening of the Labour Party office in Falkirk were Donald Dewar, Secretary of State for Scotland, and Mo Mowlam, Secretary of State for Northern Ireland. Mo was probably the most popular politician in the UK at that time, and she had obviously been invited in the hope that some of her popularity would magically rub off onto the New Labour candidate.

I was still the local Labour MP but I was not even invited to the official opening of the Labour Party's office. Neither Donald Dewar nor Mo Mowlam informed me that they would be making an official visit to my constituency, despite the parliamentary convention that MPs making official visits to other MPs' constituencies should inform the local member as a matter of courtesy. I therefore raised the matter with Betty Boothroyd, Speaker of the House of Commons. Betty sent me a letter indicating that she strongly disapproved of any breach of the convention and that she had therefore written to the two members concerned informing them of her disapproval. Almost immediately, I received a hand-written letter of apology from Mo, but Donald Dewar made no response at all.

I think that Mo acted in good faith and was unaware of the local difficulties being experienced by the Labour Party. She was probably just being used by people like Donald, who knew well what he was doing and was completely unrepentant regarding the local difficulties for which he was largely responsible. It was becoming ever clearer what I was up against.

A few weeks before the Scottish Parliament elections were declared, some letters started appearing in the *Falkirk Herald* attacking me for having the audacity to challenge Labour. The letter-writers were obviously New Labour Blairites, some of whom did not even live in the constituency. One of the alleged letter-writers, who did have a Falkirk address, subsequently wrote to the *Herald* complaining that a letter had been published in his name the previous week. He vehemently denied that he was the author of the letter or that he had given permission for his name to be used. It was yet another example of the devious, deceitful tactics of New Labour.

Shortly afterwards, I attended a meeting of the Parliamentary Labour Party regarding Labour's forthcoming election campaign for the Scottish Parliament. One of the key campaign strategists was Jim Murphy, who later became Secretary of State for Scotland. Jim had won Renfrewshire East from the Tories in 1997. It was a spectacular victory and the Labour leadership therefore thought that Jim was an expert campaigner, although more seasoned parliamentarians considered that at that time he was still a bit wet around the ears. On more than one occasion, Speaker Betty Boothroyd had to put him in his place. She once ordered Murphy to resume his seat after one of his prolonged supplementary questions degenerated into an irrelevant rant against the SNP.

Nevertheless, Jim obviously had a high opinion of himself and, at the Parliamentary Labour Party campaign strategy meeting, he was waxing eloquent about the use of local media in the campaign, including the organisation of letters to editors for publication in their newspapers.

After the presentation, we were given the opportunity to ask questions of the election campaign team members. I asked if organisation of letter-writing included forging people's signatures on letters to newspapers. There was an embarrassing silence, but I think the New Labour hacks got the message. No more letters attacking me appeared in the *Falkirk Herald*.

CHAPTER TWENTY-THREE

—— ◆ ——

The people's verdict

Early in 1999, I decided to launch my campaign at a public meeting in Falkirk Town Hall. I booked the lesser town hall rather than the big one because I was not sure how many people would turn up and I did not want to risk a half-empty hall. I sent out special letters of invitation to people who had indicated their support for me and the response was overwhelming. The hall was bursting at the seams and extra seats were brought in but it was still standing room only. It was the biggest political meeting in Falkirk for decades.

There was also a good media attendance, including a TV crew from *Panorama*, who were doing a documentary about the control-freakery of New Labour. Robbie Dinwoodie of *The Herald* told me afterwards that he had to keep running in and out of the hall to phone his paper with a revised estimate of the increasing attendance. People were still coming in the door when I rose to speak.

I explained to the audience why I had decided to stand for the Scottish Parliament. I reminded them that I had campaigned all my political life for a Scottish Parliament, even when it was not a popular cause within the Labour Party. Most of the bread-and-butter issues facing my constituents would in future be dealt with by the Scottish Parliament rather than the Westminster Parliament and, in that sense, my membership of the Scottish Parliament would enable me to continue much of the work I had been doing for over 20 years. I explained that, in a one-member-one-vote ballot, 97 per cent of Falkirk West Constituency Labour Party had wanted me on the list of approved Labour candidates but that they had been over-ruled by less than a handful of people at party headquarters. I therefore had reached the conclusion that the only way out of the impasse would be to let the people decide. I received a standing ovation and then Yvonne Harley, president of the student union at Falkirk College, spoke. She was very supportive and, after she finished, David MacKenzie, a local CND activist who chaired the meeting, asked for contributions from the floor.

I recognised a few New Labour spies in the audience but none of them had the courage to speak. Every single contribution from the audience was very encouraging and what I found most moving were the words of support from constituents whom I had helped over the years. One lady, Christine Hodges, told the audience what I had done to help her disabled son. A student spoke of my support for the campaign to restore student grants and abolish tuition fees. A retired miner thanked me for the help I had given the miners during the 1984–85 strike. I actually felt embarrassed by the praise that was being heaped upon me, and my campaign launch received very positive coverage in the local and national media. However, I knew that I had a tough fight ahead of me.

The key player in any election campaign is the election agent, who has to be campaign manager as well as acting on behalf of the candidate regarding many of the legal requirements, such as ensuring that the nomination is timeously lodged and that the expenses are paid and properly recorded. I had thought about being my own agent but that would distract me from the main campaigning job.

As I half expected, Jim Lapsley came to the rescue by telling me that he was willing to be my agent. He knew, of course, that that would mean his expulsion from the Labour Party, but he said that he would resign his membership before they could expel him. I was very touched by Jim's personal loyalty to me and I immediately accepted his offer. He had done a very good job as my agent at the general elections of 1992 and 1997 but he knew that the forthcoming battle would be much harder.

Jim and I started gathering a group of supporters who would form our campaign team and we met regularly at the Cladhan Hotel in Falkirk. Some of them were disillusioned members or former members of the Labour Party, others had had no political experience at all and most of them knew next to nothing about electioneering. Jim and I had to start from basics, teaching them how to canvass on the doorstep and by telephone. Jim sometimes affectionately re-ferred to our campaign team as Dad's Army.

We did not have enough volunteers to cover the whole constitu-ency and we decided therefore to canvass a sample in each electoral ward. We soon found out that the Labour Party had already started telephone canvassing, apparently using professionally trained people in call centres outwith the constituency, because they would never get enough local volunteers. Indeed, some constituents told us they had received calls on behalf of the Labour Party from people south of the Border.

Our own canvass returns were very positive. Indeed, they were so positive that I found them incredible and I could not ignore the fact that most of our canvassers were very inexperienced and there would probably be a high margin of error.

However, I was particularly encouraged by reports from two of my former election agents, Henry Dawson and Eddie Monaghan. They both scorned the idea of telephone canvassing. They had been knocking on doors since the days when most working-class people did not have a phone and they were convinced that voters would give a more truthful response if you spoke to them on the doorstep.

Eddie and Henry had both left school at the age of 15 to work down the pit but they were both first-class graduates of the University of Life. They had an abundance of common sense and working-class nous which enabled them to make sound judgements of people as well as ideas. When it came to door-stepping people during an election campaign, they were also a couple of human lie-detectors. They knew how to eyeball punters when asking them how they were going to vote and they were probably right in claiming that the result was far more reliable than telephone canvassing. Eddie and Henry predicted the 1999 Falkirk West election result with an accuracy which no psephologist could match.

Quite early on in the campaign, I received a phone call from John Smith, a reporter working for the *Scotsman* newspaper. John explained that his editor wanted him to do a special election report about my campaign and, rather than simply interviewing me, he asked if he could accompany me one evening when I was knocking on the doors. I had known John since we were boys together in Cowdenbeath. He was my patrol leader when I joined the 46th Fife YMCA Scouts and more recently he had been in contact with me many times in his journalistic capacity. I do not always trust the media, but I knew that John would not do a hatchet job on me. So we went canvassing in Banknock one evening. John of course was merely observing rather than canvassing, but he could hardly believe his ears. The response was literally 100 per cent for me and I had a similar experience later in Dunipace, when I was accompanied by Andy Nicoll of the *Sun*. Of course I realised that Banknock and Dunipace were not typical of the constituency as a whole, but I felt elated by the response and the subsequent press coverage.

Before the campaign had officially started, Jim Lapsley and I hunted around for premises which would be suitable for use as our campaign headquarters. The Labour Party had already opened an office in Falkirk High Street and I was particularly keen to have a shop-front presence somewhere in the town centre. I remember trekking round the streets of Falkirk taking a note of any empty shop or office premises. Some of the properties would have been ideal for our purpose but, in most cases, the rental was prohibitive. Then a local businessman, Ian Ewing, came to the rescue. He had vacant shop premises in Vicar Street, less than five minutes' walk from the High Street, and he said that we could have the use of them for a few weeks. He did not want to charge us anything at all but I insisted on paying him.

We soon set up shop and a nucleus of key members of our campaign team got to work. John McAulay, a retired joiner from Denny, turned half the premises into a workshop, where he set about making wooden boards for the election posters. The result was the biggest number of vandal-proof posters I had ever seen.

John had been a stalwart supporter of mine for many years. On polling day in the 1979 campaign, he had been my chauffeur when I toured the entire West Stirlingshire constituency along with Billy Connolly, the comedian. Billy had been one of my constituents at that time and he phoned me up from his home in Drymen to offer his services. Twenty years later, I wrote to him asking if he would help me out again in my election campaign for the Scottish Parliament. He never replied but, by that time, he had become very busy as a court jester for the House of Windsor and he is now such a staunch Unionist that he tries to dismiss the Scottish Parliament as a 'pretendy' parliament.

As soon as the election was called, Tommy Canavan, his friend Eddie McAtee, my son, Dennis, and his pal, Norrie McEwan, began putting up the posters. By the final week of the campaign there was hardly a lamp-post in the constituency which did not have one of my posters and many visitors to the area, including media representatives, said that it was the best poster display in the whole of Scotland. That was encouraging, but I knew well that posters cannot vote. We were up against a well-financed machine.

New Labour had a war chest of several million pounds in the lead-up to the first elections to the Scottish Parliament in 1999. When it became obvious that they were prepared to spend many thousands of pounds to get rid of me, I had to do some serious thinking about how to raise funds for my campaign. I had only a limited sum of money in my bank account and I was reluctant to run up a huge amount of personal debt. My oldest son, Mark, lent me £6,000, which was very generous of him and also an act of faith on his part because he must have known that, if I lost the election, I might be bankrupt.

I never put out a formal appeal for funds but, following the launch of my election campaign, I started receiving letters of support, not just from constituents but from all over Scotland. Some of the letters contained donations. I think that the largest I received was a cheque for £200, but it was the smallest donation that I shall always remember. It was a fiver enclosed with a letter from an old lady with a Glasgow address.

In shaky, almost illegible handwriting, she reminded me that we had met about ten years previously when I was on holiday in rural Donegal. There was very little public transport in that area, and taxis were unheard-of at that time. It was fairly late at night and the old lady was stranded in Beedy's Bar in Dungloe, about ten miles from Crolly, where she was staying in a caravan. Fortunately I had not started drinking when I heard about her predicament, and I offered her a lift in my car. When we reached her destination, she wanted to pay for the petrol but I refused. Now, all these years later, she had heard about my predicament and she wanted to make a contribution to my fighting fund. Her words of support were more valuable to me than the fiver, but I knew that she would feel insulted if I returned it. I wrote a thankyou letter, telling her that I would never forget her kindness, and I never shall. I often think of her, and I wonder what she thinks about New Labour scandals arising from big business donations of thousands of pounds to people like Wendy Alexander and Peter Hain.

My 1999 campaign attracted more media interest than any campaign I have ever been involved in and the interest was not confined to Scotland. My battle against New Labour became a *cause célèbre* and media representatives arrived from all over the UK and even further afield. *Panorama* did an investigation into Labour's selection of candidates and, during the campaign itself, Falkirk High Street was often buzzing with journalists and TV cameras.

I recall one particularly humorous incident when BBC *Newsnight* sent Mark Mardell all the way from London to Falkirk to do an in-depth interview with me. When Mark suggested that we do the interview sitting on an open-air bench near Falkirk Steeple about one o'clock on a Friday afternoon, I expressed my doubts about the wisdom of his choice, bearing in mind the hustle and bustle of Falkirk High Street at that time of day and the possibility of being interrupted by passers-by. However, Mark insisted on his suggestion because he wanted to portray a man of the people amongst the people.

The interview got off to a good start. Then a bunch of pupils from Graeme High School, who had come up to the High Street during their lunch break, saw the TV crew and began to surround us. At first, Mark must have felt like the Pied Piper of Hamelin. More and more youngsters came to join us and some of them began to jump up and down and gesticulate in front of the camera. Mark tried to carry on regardless and I tried my best to concentrate on answering his questions. Pupils then started cheekily interjecting to 'help' me with some of the answers. Mark's face started getting redder and redder then purpler and purpler. Eventually, he lost it completely, banged the microphone onto the bench and snarled at the pupils: 'Fuck off!'

Of course, that just made matters worse. Some of the pupils started shouting back and taking the mickey and the whole situation developed into a fiasco. Fortunately it was not a live interview but we had to stop the entire show and start all over again after the school lunch break.

Since then I have seen the same Mark Mardell on TV, reporting in a cool, professional manner from some of the world's biggest trouble spots, but the BBC never sent him back to Falkirk. Maybe the Graeme High School bairns taught him a lesson!

A few months before the first elections to the Scottish Parliament, there was a televised discussion about the voting system. Under the additional member system, each voter would have two votes. Seventy-three members were to be elected on a first-past-the-post basis to represent constituencies. The remaining 56 members were to be elected on a proportional basis to represent regions. For the purposes of the election, Scotland was divided into eight regions, and my constituency of Falkirk West was in the region of Central Scotland, which consisted of ten constituencies, stretching all the way from Bo'ness through Lanarkshire to Kilmarnock.

During the TV discussion, Professor John Curtice of Strathclyde University pointed out that someone could get elected as a regional MSP with as little as 6 per cent of the vote and he went on to suggest that I would stand a much better chance of being elected as a regional MSP rather than as a constituency MSP. I therefore discussed the matter with Jim Lapsley and some other close friends. We reckoned that I would get a good vote in both the Falkirk constituencies, where I was well known, and also in the Kilsyth area, where I had been the Member of Parliament from 1974 until 1983. Tommy Canavan and his friends in Kilsyth and Croy were very keen on the idea and they persuaded me to stand. It cost me several thousand pounds for additional posters and an election address to be delivered to over a quarter of a million homes. In the Falkirk West constituency, the posters and leaflets urged people to 'Vote Canavan Twice'. In the other nine constituencies in Central Scotland region, my posters and leaflets asked people to vote for me in the second ballot. In fact, the regional leaflet explained to people that they could use the first (constituency) ballot to vote for the Party of their choice and use the second (regional) ballot to vote for me.

A few days before the election, I was absolutely enraged when I switched on the radio and heard a BBC news announcer trying to explain the voting system by telling people that the first vote was for their constituency MSP and the second vote was for their Party! I immediately phoned the BBC to complain and had the devil of a job trying to convince them that they were giving out false information. Instead of giving accurate, objective information to listeners, the BBC was actually causing confusion.

That was not the only time I crossed swords with the BBC during the campaign. I found out that they were doing a radio *Question Time* from Falkirk Town Hall, featuring various Party candidates on the panel, but I had not even been informed. When I complained about my exclusion from such an event being broadcast from my own constituency, I was informed that the panel consisted of regional candidates for the area rather than constituency candidates. When I pointed out that I was also standing as a regional candidate in Central Scotland and that the Labour Party representative on the panel was not, the BBC partially backed down.

The Labour Party representative was replaced by Bill Tynan, who was on the Party's list of candidates for Central Scotland. I was informed that, although I was not officially on the panel, I would be able to participate from the audience. The programme presenter was Colin MacKay, who very generously allowed me to make a contribution on every question. In fact, I probably got a better allocation of time than some of the panellists, but nevertheless I was far from impressed by the initial attitude of the BBC, which is supposed to be impartial, especially during election campaigns. They seemed to carve up an arrangement to suit the main political parties, which is very unfair to independent candidates.

Jim and I decided to lodge my nomination papers on Wednesday, 24 March 1999, the very first day that the law would allow it. We wanted our campaign to get off to a flying start. There was a TV crew waiting at my constituency office in Denny to accompany me to the Municipal Buildings in Falkirk. By the time we arrived at the car park, it was like a media circus. I posed for a few photographs and announced that I would be available for interviews afterwards.

Mary Pitcaithly, the Chief Executive of Falkirk Council and returning officer for the election, was expecting us and, when Jim handed over the £500 deposit, he confidently asked her how soon after the election he could reclaim it as it would be needed to pay the election expenses. We had previously sought Mary's advice about how I could be described on the nomination paper, as that description would also appear on the ballot paper. Mary explained that there was no way in which I could use the words 'Labour' or 'Independent Labour', and I was reluctant to use the word 'Independent', because I had been brought up to believe that so-called 'independent' candidates were just Tories in disguise. I therefore settled on the words 'MP for Falkirk West', as that was my current job description and it was important to get the message across that I was still a representative of the people. The Blairites could take away my party membership, but they could not take away my job. Only the people had that power.

On emerging from the Municipal Buildings, I was besieged with demands for media interviews. Some of the interviewers were very interested in the confrontation I had had with Helen Liddell at Scottish Question Time in the House of Commons on the previous afternoon. I had told Helen, who was Minister for Education at the Scottish Office, that many people in Scotland were looking forward to the new Scottish Parliament with a new Minister for Education whose priorities would be determined by the people of Scotland rather than the Westminster establishment, which had imposed tuition fees and scrapped student grants even for students from low-income families. I also reminded Helen that it is not the job of politicians to tell teachers how to teach and asked her to stop strutting round Scotland hectoring and hand-bagging Scottish teachers like some New Labour version of Margaret Thatcher. Helen looked very peeved, but I felt no sympathy for her.

On the day that I lodged my nomination papers, my mind was on more important things than Helen Liddell. I used the media interviews to point out that I was still a member of the Labour Party and that the Labour leadership could, even at that late date, solve the impasse by letting Party members in Falkirk West decide whether I should be the Labour candidate. The Labour Party responded later that day by expelling me, and the first I heard about it was from the press.

On the following day, I received a letter from the General Secretary of the Labour Party confirming my expulsion. I was not exactly surprised but, a few days later, I was rather bemused to receive the usual communication from the whips' office telling me to attend the House of Commons to vote for the government business. I was even more bemused when I received a letter from the Chief Whip, Ann Taylor (now Baroness Taylor of Bolton), demanding that I pay the Party levy imposed on all Labour MPs by resolution of the Parliamentary Labour Party! I wrote back to Ann telling her: 'You must think my head zips up the back if you seriously expect me to finance a discredited organisation which is spending a small fortune trying to get rid of me.' It was all good fun but it showed that, despite New Labour's slick and efficient image, sometimes one hand did not seem to know what the other hand was doing.

I do not recall any major bloomers being made by members of my campaign team but there was no shortage of humorous stories. Jim Dunlop, his wife, Margaret and daughter Alison, worked very hard for me. Jim and Margaret had been members of West Stirlingshire Constituency Labour Party in the mid-1970s but had left the party because of its increasingly right-wing agenda. When I phoned them up to help me out in 1999, they had no hesitation and Jim provided me with one of the most hilarious stories of the campaign.

One evening, he came back to our headquarters after some door-to-door canvassing. He referred to solid support in one particular street but he was rather perplexed by one woman who told him: 'Ah'll definitely be voting for Dennis Canavan because that MP we have the noo is absolutely useless.' Jim did not want to disillusion her by pointing out that I was the useless incumbent!

The greatest act of faith I experienced during the campaign was on the part of Tommy Canavan. Tommy and his pal, Eddie McAtee, were out one day putting up posters on lamp-posts, when they were approached by a New Labour clone who arrogantly told them:

'You're wasting your time. Canavan has absolutely no chance of winning'. When Tommy begged to disagree in his inimitable way, the New Labour man challenged him to a wager of £100. That was a lot of money for an unemployed person, but Tommy agreed to the bet. In the fullness of time, his faith was duly rewarded and he had the pleasure of collecting his winnings minutes after the result of the count was declared. The guy who had to stump up was Major Eric Joyce, who later became New Labour's MP for Falkirk West after I gave up my seat at Westminster. Joyce later made it to the top of the league for pocketing parliamentary expenses but, on that occasion, it was Tommy Canavan who pocketed the winnings.

On the Saturday morning before polling day, we had our traditional car cavalcade around the constituency before gathering at Falkirk Steeple for an open-air meeting. The Steeple was a favourite location for candidates and party activists to assemble for old-style soap-box campaigning and distribution of election literature. I always enjoyed it, although some of the shop-keepers used to complain about the amplified volume of my voice – we had a very powerful loudspeaker system which would echo from one end of the High Street to the other. It was also a great opportunity to meet people face to face for a wee chat and the feedback was usually positive.

On most Saturdays, we easily outnumbered the New Labour team, which was very dependent on imports. On one particular Saturday, the Scottish Executive of the Labour Party held its meeting in Falkirk. I do not recall the Executive ever meeting in Falkirk before or since, and it was done deliberately to enable Executive members to campaign against me after the meeting was over. Bob Thomson, who was treasurer of the Scottish Labour Party at that time, told some of my supporters that he and several other Executive members could not bring themselves to campaign against me and, as a result, there were still more people working for me than for the New Labour candidate on that particular day.

On another Saturday morning, however, I was surprised to see Falkirk High Street being invaded by a crowd of young people with Labour leaflets and stickers. I was told that it was an 'army' of New Labour students who had been bussed through from Glasgow at the Labour Party's expense. When I saw them giving out balloons and stickers, I decided to have some fun. I lifted the megaphone and began:

'Good morning, everybody. A very special welcome this morning to the balloons from Glasgow who have travelled all the way to Falkirk at great expense for this historic occasion. This must be the first time ever that students have gone to such lengths to campaign for a candidate who supports the introduction of tuition fees and the abolition of student grants.'

I could see more than a few shamefaced expressions amongst the students, and by the time I had finished my speech most of them had slunk off.

Later that day, the New Labour campaign bus arrived in Falkirk. I was at Brockville Stadium by that time but I was told that, when Donald Dewar stepped off the bus, he was greeted by a host of balloons and he spent only a few minutes in the town before stepping back onto his luxury bus and heading off.

I concluded that we also had the better of the Labour Party when it came to campaign vehicles. Despite New Labour's professed belief in transparency, Donald's posh bus had tinted windows so that nobody could see him from the outside. By contrast, my 'battle bus' consisted of a small decorated truck with a loudspeaker. When I was at the steering wheel, passing drivers would often recognise me and toot their horns, while pedestrians would wave encouragement or give me the thumbs-up.

All this made me feel more confident but I was somewhat dismayed by reports that, throughout Scotland in general, a high turn-out of voters was not expected.

When I was first elected to parliament in 1974, the turn-out was over 80 per cent of the electorate. In many constituencies nowadays, they are struggling to get 50 per cent. I suspect that part of the reason for that is because candidates and parties now rely too much on the mass media and telephone canvassing. Indeed, some candidates seem to do very little public campaigning and are very much dependent on their Party leaders winning or losing the campaign on national television. Of course, modern methods of communication are important and must be used, but there is nothing to beat face-to-face communication. I have always believed that, during the course of an election campaign, the candidate must try to meet as many constituents as possible.

People no longer turn up in huge numbers to public meetings but, at the first elections to the Scottish Parliament, the local Council of Churches in the Falkirk area organised a hustings meeting to which all candidates were invited. Most of the members of the audience were Party activists who were there to root for their own Party candidate or to heckle the Opposition. Nevertheless, I found it an enjoyable experience.

The chairman was Rev. Graham Blount, minister of Falkirk Old and St Modan's Parish Church, who later headed up the Scottish Churches Office at the Scottish Parliament. Graham began by saying that, if the *Herald* newspaper were to be believed, then four members of the panel of candidates would become Members of the Scottish Parliament. I found that difficult to understand but, on checking the *Herald* later, I discovered that they were predicting Ross Martin, the New Labour candidate, to win Falkirk West, whereas I would get the 'consolation prize' of one of the seven regional seats for Central Scotland, along with Michael Matheson of the SNP and Donald Gorrie of the Liberal Democrats. The prediction had no psephological basis whatsoever because the *Herald* had not done a poll in Falkirk West. They had merely attempted to extrapolate a result for the constituency from the result of a nation-wide opinion poll, despite the fact that even the dogs in the street knew that Falkirk West was very different from the national picture.

Maybe the *Herald* poll gave Ross Martin a false sense of security. He certainly looked very cocky, but he did himself no favours at all by simply parroting the Blairite line on every question raised.

At the end of the meeting Graham Blount told me privately with a meaningful smile that he had not heard anything at the meeting to persuade him to change his mind on how to vote. If I took that to be a 'for', I think I would be nearer the mark than the *Herald* prediction.

That was the only hustings meeting in Falkirk West during the 1999 campaign. I came away feeling that it was a great pity that the public no longer turn up to public meetings as they did 30 or 40 years ago. Hustings can be very informative and just as entertaining as live theatre.

Many years ago I reached the conclusion that, if the people would not go to the candidate's meetings, then the candidate must go to the people. In other words, I took to the streets. I did not even use a soapbox. I would deliver a short speech, using a megaphone, at the Steeple in Falkirk High Street and then go around shaking hands with people and chatting with them. That gave them the opportunity to ask questions and raise concerns or, in the case of committed supporters, give a word of encouragement. I would then walk maybe 100 yards to another location to repeat the exercise, and members of my campaign team would give out leaflets and stickers.

I did a similar exercise at the town centres in Denny and Stenhousemuir but I also attended canteen or factory gate meetings at some of the bigger work places such as Taylor's Foundry in Larbert, and Alexander's, the bus manufacturers in Camelon. I asked the management of the bingo clubs in Falkirk and Denny for permission to speak during the interval and I always kept it short and snappy, with no heavy politics. I would also visit the social clubs, the pensioners' lunch clubs, the retirement homes and sheltered houses throughout the constituency.

During the course of a three-week campaign, I must have spoken to or shaken hands with thousands of voters and, over a period of thirty years, I got to know many of them personally. In 1999, my campaign slogan was: 'Dennis Canavan Puts People First' and, for me, it worked better than any party label. By the time polling day came on Thursday, 6 May, I knew I was in with a fighting chance.

My good friend, John McAulay, volunteered to be my chauffeur on election day, just as he had done 20 years previously. He drove me in the decorated campaign truck round the entire constituency, stopping to visit every polling station and sometimes holding impromptu street meetings when I would speak through a loudspeaker system mounted on the top of the truck.

At one stage, we met up with Michael Connarty, MP for Falkirk East. I wondered why he was spying in my constituency instead of campaigning for Cathy Peattie, the Labour candidate for Falkirk East. During a brief conversation with him outside a polling station, he told me that, if I won the constituency seat, I would be helping the right wing. When I asked him to explain, he said that, if Labour lost in Falkirk West, they would gain a 'list' seat in Central Scotland and the person on top of the Labour list for Central Scotland was a right-wing trade union official called Bill Tynan. I always thought that there was something twisted about Michael Connarty's thinking, but that takes the biscuit.

As things turned out, Labour did not even get enough votes to win a 'list' seat in Central Scotland but the same Bill Tynan later became MP for Hamilton South, when George Robertson went to the House of Lords. Tynan just managed to scrape in against the SNP but I have no doubt that Michael Connarty would give him a warm welcome into the comradeship of the Parliamentary Labour Party.

By the time I had completed my tour of the polling stations, it was approaching 10 p.m. and I decided to go home to change before going to the count. My son, Dennis John, volunteered to be my driver and, as I was getting changed, he told me that BBC TV had just reported an enormous number of postal votes in Falkirk West, with 80 per cent of them for me. I thought perhaps that Dennis had mis-heard the report but the BBC phoned shortly afterwards to request an interview as soon as I arrived at the count. When I asked about the postal votes, I was told that the story had come from observers who were present for the opening of the postal votes earlier in the day. Although the actual counting of the postal votes was not due to begin until after the close of poll, anyone observing the opening of the envelopes would get a fair idea of how things were going. Nevertheless, I took the 80 per cent figure with a pinch of salt.

As soon as I arrived at Grangemouth Sports Centre for the count, I was besieged by reporters, photographers and people slapping me on the back. I thought it was all rather premature to say the least and, during my TV interviews, I expressed cautious optimism rather than taking victory for granted. However, Jim Lapsley, my agent, assured me that I was well ahead and, when I went round the counting tables, I could hardly believe my eyes. At every single table I had more votes than all the other candidates put together, and even some of my opponents were congratulating me.

However, there was one opponent who was significant by his absence. I was informed afterwards that Ross Martin, the New Labour candidate, was sitting outside in the car park, too embarrassed to show face. Maybe his counting agents had phoned him to tell him how things were going but, to be fair, he did eventually make an appearance just before the result was officially announced and he had the good grace to congratulate me in a civil manner.

After the event, I was told by some MSPs and people of various political persuasions that my result was the biggest sensation of the night. Party activists in counting venues throughout the country and people sitting at home were glued to their television screens when Mary Pitcaithly, the Returning Officer, went to the dais to announce the result. When she read out: 'Dennis Canavan 18,511 votes', the rest of her words were drowned out by an almighty cheer which seemed to reverberate throughout the whole of Scotland. Even some Labour Party members joined in the applause and one of them told me afterwards that he was threatened with expulsion if he did not stop!

It was a humiliation for New Labour, whose vote was a mere 6,319. My majority of 12,192 was the biggest in Scotland and I also had enough votes throughout Central Scotland to win a regional seat.

I should have been the happiest guy in Scotland that night but I did not feel it when I went to the microphone to deliver my victory speech. After thanking my agent, my supporters, the returning officer and staff, I expressed regret that I was no longer a member of the party in which I had been virtually born and brought up. I urged the Labour leadership to listen to the people. I deliberately avoided sounding triumphalist and I referred to the need to learn lessons and build bridges.

My appeals fell on deaf ears. Minutes after the count, I heard a radio interview in which Anne McGuire ruled out any possibility of my being readmitted to the Labour Party.

The following day, Tony Benn phoned to congratulate me and told me that he would be asking the Parliamentary Labour Party to restore my membership, but Tony's plea was presumably rebuffed because I never heard any more about it.

The Labour Party and I had parted ways, and it seemed there was no way back.

Part IV

— ◆ —

A Man o' Independent Mind

CHAPTER TWENTY-FOUR

The people's parliament

At the first elections to the Scottish Parliament in 1999, I was the only person elected who was not a member of any political party and, as a result, I was left very much to my own devices instead of being given any guidance or instructions from party bosses. In some respects it was a liberating experience, but it also meant more responsibility on my part.

Two days after the election, I had a speaking engagement in Edinburgh and, after the meeting, I took the opportunity of looking in at the Scottish Parliament's Administrative Headquarters. Construction work had not even started at Holyrood, the chosen location of the new parliament building, a project which was destined to become a national scandal because of continuing delays and escalating costs. In the interim, the parliament met in the Church of Scotland Assembly Hall at the top of the Mound and the MSPs' offices and the administration were based in the former Lothian Regional Council buildings on George IV Bridge.

The office block on the west side of the street must rank as one of the ugliest buildings in Edinburgh's history. It had been thrown up in the 1960s during what has been described as the Stalinist period of Scottish architecture, and the fact that it managed to get planning permission is an indictment of the architects and the politicians as well as the other decision-makers of that era. For half a century, the concrete carbuncle stood at the corner of the historic Royal Mile, in close proximity to some of the best architecture in Scotland's capital. I remember the eyesore being created. It caused massive disruption to pedestrian as well as vehicular traffic, because the plans included the construction of a subterranean tunnel from the new office block to the Council Chambers on the other side of the street, so that council members and officials would be spared the need or the indignity of crossing the road.

When Paul Grice, the Chief Executive of the Scottish Parliament, showed me round the building, I found the inside to be as depressing as the outside. However, I soon found out that there were some advantages in not being a member of any political party. The space in the building was so limited that most members had to share an open-plan office with several party colleagues but, because I had no party colleagues, I was given an office to myself. I was not sure whether that made me politically privileged or a political pariah.

Although the office accommodation left a lot to be desired, I was generally impressed by the temporary arrangements which had been made for the parliament's debating chamber. The Church of Scotland Assembly Hall has a spacious debating chamber with good acoustics, and there is far more room in the public galleries than there is at either Westminster or the new chamber at Holyrood. It was a pity, though, that the temporary desks and seats installed for MSPs looked as if they had been bought at MFI and did not blend well with the classic nineteenth-century wood panelling of the chamber walls.

The Assembly Hall at the top of the Mound had been the scene of many significant events. Some of the great ecclesiastical orators had spoken there during General Assembly debates. It was also there that, in May 1988, Margaret Thatcher had delivered her controversial 'Sermon on the Mound' when she had infamously claimed that Christianity is about spiritual redemption, not social reform. The Assembly Hall was also the venue of the first meeting of the Scottish Constitutional Convention in 1989. The Church of Scotland, the Sermon on the Mound and the Scottish Constitutional Convention had each played very different but significant roles in the creation of the Scottish Parliament. It was therefore very fitting that, on 12 May 1999, the Assembly Hall was home to one of Scotland's most historic events, the first meeting of the newly elected Scottish Parliament.

The very first item on the agenda was the swearing-in of the members, and this caused some controversy because members were required to swear an oath of allegiance to the Queen. That seemed rather incongruous to me, because the parliament had been founded on the principle of the sovereignty of the people rather than the sovereignty of any monarch, and we had been elected by the people to serve the people. Some other members also voiced concerns, but the form of the oath had been laid down in the Scotland Act 1998 and the Promissory Oaths Act 1868. Another example of Westminster control-freakery.

Paul Grice made it clear that any member who refused to take the oath would not be allowed to take part in the proceedings of the parliament. After having fought so hard and so long to get there, I did not want to get a red card in the first five minutes. However, I felt that I should make some kind of public protest and I had conscientious objections about swearing 'by Almighty God'. I therefore decided to make an affirmation rather than take the oath and I prefaced the affirmation with the following words:

> I want to make it clear that I believe in the sovereignty of the people of Scotland rather than the sovereignty of any monarch. My allegiance, therefore, is to the people of Scotland. However, in view of the legal requirement that must be met to enable me to represent my constituents, I shall make the affirmation.

The first meeting of the parliament was chaired by Winnie Ewing of the SNP because she was the oldest member. Winnie had been a parliamentary colleague of mine from 1974 to 1979, when she was MP for Moray and Nairn. Before that, she had been MP for Hamilton, having won the seat from Labour at a famous by-election in 1967. Winnie was a bonnie fechter and had the resilience to bounce back after defeat. Even after losing two Westminster seats, she made another parliamentary comeback as MEP for the Highlands and Islands, which she represented in the European Parliament for 20 years. In 1999, she was elected to the Scottish Parliament as MSP for the Highlands and Islands. With a track record like that, Winnie had excellent credentials to chair the first meeting of Scotland's new parliament. She certainly seized the moment and was roundly applauded on declaring: 'I want to begin with the words that I have always wanted either to say or to hear someone else say: *The Scottish Parliament, which adjourned on 25 March 1707, is hereby re-convened.*' It had taken 292 years and 48 days to get rid of the democratic deficit, and Scotland would never be the same again.

When the parliament met again the following day, the only item on the agenda was the election of the First Minister. I was asked by Tommy Sheridan, the sole MSP of the Scottish Socialist party, and by Robin Harper, the sole MSP of the Scottish Green party, to stand for election and I agreed. I knew that I had no chance of winning the vote but I thought that it would be an opportunity to make a short speech about what I thought should be the priorities of the parliament.

It was then that one of the glaring weaknesses of the new parliament was exposed. Some of the Westminster old-boy network had apparently conspired to try to stop any democratic debate about who should be First Minister and it looked like a stitch-up between Labour and their coalition partners, the Liberal Democrats. Lord David Steel, the Presiding Officer, initially told me that there would be no debate at all and it was clear that that was the wish of Donald Dewar, Labour's nominee for First Minister. When I protested to David Steel, he eventually agreed on a compromise whereby each candidate would be allowed to speak for two minutes only and he tried to justify his ludicrous decision by saying: 'We are not engaged in a political debate this afternoon; we are engaged in an election.' How on earth can you have a democratic election if you are denied a democratic debate?

It was not as if a debate was going to take up a huge amount of time, because there were only four candidates: Donald Dewar (Labour), Alex Salmond (SNP), David McLetchie (Conservative) and myself. As the candidates were to speak in alphabetical order, I was called first. My speech was very critical of the deal which had been struck between Labour and the Lib Dems to form a coalition. I was not opposed to coalition in principle, but the details of the Lib-Lab agreement had not even been published and, if the parliament voted for Donald Dewar, they would be buying a pig in a poke.

For example, it was clear that Labour was unwilling to abolish tuition fees for university students, despite the fact that the majority of MSPs had been elected on commitments to abolish such fees. Labour and the Lib Dems had agreed on a compromise to 'review' the funding of Higher Education. I described the 'review' as Westminsterspeak for a fudge and I called for cross-party action for the restoration of free education, investment in our National Health Service and improved job opportunities. Donald Dewar visibly winced when I said: 'Above all, we need a First Minister for Scotland who will speak for Scotland instead of someone who will act as Tony Blair's puppet.'

Despite Steel's ruling on two-minute speeches, I spoke for about three or four minutes. When I finished, Steel compounded his previous error by asking members who wished to vote for me to do so immediately instead of waiting to hear the other three candidates' speeches. It was only when Alex Salmond and others complained about such an undemocratic farce that Steel eventually relented. Not that it made any difference to the outcome because the party members had been told in advance how to vote. Donald Dewar topped the poll with 71 votes, Alex Salmond got 35, David McLetchie 17 and I got the magnificent total of 3. I said afterwards that the result proved that there were at least three wise men in the parliament!

Immediately after David Steel announced the result, Donald Dewar shook hands with Alex Salmond and David McLetchie but pointedly failed to shake hands with me, despite the fact that I was sitting just a few yards away from Alex Salmond. The party leaders then gave short speeches congratulating Dewar on his election and, despite Donald's attitude towards me, I decided to do likewise. I finished up by saying: 'Despite the fact that we have had profound political disagreements in the past and no doubt will have more in the future, to show that I bear him no personal malice, I would like to shake his hand.' I then walked across to the opposite side of the chamber and shook Donald's hand. Donald looked very uncomfortable, and his reciprocal handshake was very grudging.

Our exchange turned out to be the big media story of the day. I was astonished when a photograph of me shaking hands with Donald appeared on the front pages of many of the following day's newspapers. Donald maybe thought that the whole thing had been stage-managed to embarrass him but that was not my intention. I decided to do what I did on the spur of the moment and I was motivated by a desire to build bridges rather than any desire to embarrass anyone.

Donald, on the other hand, made it clear that bridge-building was not on his agenda, not with me at any rate. A few weeks later, I was walking up the Royal Mile on my way to the Assembly Hall, when I noticed Donald a few yards in front of me. As he was on his own, I quickened my pace to catch up with him in the hope of engaging him in conversation.

'How's it going, Donald?' I began but I got no further. As soon as he recognised me, Donald gave me the cold shoulder and made a mad dash to the other side of the road with such blind reaction that he was almost run over by a double-decker bus. If the bus had hit him, I would probably have got the blame for assassinating the 'Father of the Nation', because it was widely known that I did not approve of such a title being bestowed on a man who exhibited such a petty streak.

Although the bus missed him on that occasion, poor Donald tragically died of a brain haemorrhage the following year. They put up a statue of him in the pedestrian precinct in Buchanan Street,

Glasgow, because he was hailed by the chattering classes as a man of the people and they thought it would be a good idea for his image to be located amongst the people in the street. Unfortunately some of the people reacted by vandalising the statue with such frequency that the authorities had to raise the plinth in order to create a safe distance between Donald and the people.

On one occasion I was going to catch a bus at Buchanan Street when I bumped into Michael Martin, Speaker of the House of Commons, and his wife, Mary, almost within touching distance of Donald's statue, or at least the plinth. Michael was not long out of hospital and our conversation about his health was interrupted by a passing beggar. Michael gave the man a pound and, when I followed suit, I said to him: 'It's a pity that guy on the pedestal is no longer with us because he would have given you something more substantial.' The beggar replied:

'That bastard wouldnae gie ye the time o' day yet he died a millionaire. Supposed tae be a Labour man tae and a lot o' his money came from shares in privatised industries!'

Although he was wrong about Donald's parentage, there was more than a grain of truth in the beggar's words. People can see through politicians who speak and vote against Tory policies in parliament but then take advantage of the same Tory policies to line their own pockets.

I could never understand why Donald was virtually canonised by his fan club. He was not an instinctive or inspirational leader and he often had to be persuaded on the merits of a patently good cause. For example, he was very sceptical about the Millennium Project to re-unite the Forth and Clyde Canal with the Union Canal, involving the construction of what came to be known as the Falkirk Wheel. Donald did not seem to have the vision to recognise one of the most brilliant examples of 21st-century engineering, which had the potential to be an iconic tourist attraction with enormous economic and social benefits throughout Central Scotland. When a short-fall in funding became apparent, British Waterways wanted the government to bridge the gap, otherwise the entire multi-million pound project would be endangered. I was a strong supporter of the project and, as the Falkirk Wheel was to be located in my constituency, I decided to take the initiative of leading a delegation of about a dozen canal-side MPs to meet with Donald who, at that time, was Secretary of State for Scotland. Donald needed a lot of persuasion to provide the necessary funding and I am convinced that, if I had not arranged that meeting, the Millenium Project might never have seen the light of day.

Shortly afterwards, Donald emerged as leader of the Scottish Parliamentary Labour Group after an 'election' which would have done North Korea proud. He was the only candidate and, although there were three MSPs, including myself, who later challenged Donald for the First Minister's job, it was a shoo-in for Donald, who had the support of the Lib Dems as well as Labour.

After the election of the First Minister, I had to turn my attention to matters of administration and employment. My first priority was to find someone to manage my parliamentary office and assist me with research and other parliamentary work.

I already had a constituency office in Denny, where I had been based for 13 years, and I had a very reliable and efficient secretary, Anne Thomson, who had been employed by me since the constituency office was opened in 1986. However, it was clear to me that I would need an additional member of staff to assist me in my parliamentary work. Shortly after my election, I received unsolicited applications from various people offering their services but I decided to advertise the post.

I later found out that such a procedure was unusual. Many MPs and MSPs employ party colleagues and others employ friends and relatives. There is nothing wrong in principle with that but the system can be grossly abused, as was exposed in the case of Derek Conway MP, who used vast amounts of public money to 'employ' members of his family who did virtually nothing in return. I have also seen people of doubtful value appointed to well-paid parliamentary positions as a result of political patronage or cronyism.

The fact that I was not a member of any political party meant that I would have no back-up from a party machine or the research services which most political parties provide for their members. It was therefore essential for me to find someone of high calibre who was capable of doing good-quality research in a wide range of subjects, as well as being versatile enough to run an office. The Scottish Parliament Members' Support Allowance was sufficient to employ no more than two people at a reasonable salary and the best arrangement for me was to employ one person in my constituency office and another in my parliamentary office.

When I advertised the vacancy in the Scottish broadsheets, the job description was 'parliamentary assistant to a Member of the Scottish

Parliament', without mentioning me by name. I was surprised to receive about 300 replies. I thought about asking an employment agency to sift through the applications and draw up a shortlist for me. But I decided against that because I was unaware of any employment agency which specialised in that field and I wanted to be certain that I got the best person for the job. I therefore did the sift of all 300 applications myself and drew up a shortlist of about 10 candidates whom I interviewed personally. It was very time-consuming but, at the end of the process, I was satisfied that the best candidate got the job. She was Adele Brown, an Honours Graduate in Law from Strathclyde University, who proved to be a very good employee. Maybe she was too good, because she was head-hunted about a year later by a private-sector employer who was able to offer her a higher salary.

I then went through the whole process again of advertising, sifting, shortlisting and interviewing. Again, I was satisfied that the best candidate got the job and this time I was even more fortunate in that Maureen Connor stayed with me until my retirement.

Maureen had been involved in research at Glasgow Caledonian University. I have come across some people who are very good at academic research but pretty hopeless at running an office or communicating with ordinary people. Maureen, on the other hand, has a good combination of academic skills and people skills and was always able and willing to do a share of the work in the constituency office when necessary, although her main duties were in the parliament. Maureen and Anne were a formidable team. Maureen was invaluable in my parliamentary work and Anne's patience and understanding of people in need produced many satisfied punters. When I was up for re-election, I very often got the credit for all the hard work which Anne and Maureen did behind the scenes and I think that they had a lot to do with the fact that we got the highest majority in Scotland. Cynics tried to dismiss it as a one-off in 1999 but we repeated the feat four years later. I say 'we' because you need a good team and, if the team works hard for the people, then the people will respond.

CHAPTER TWENTY-FIVE

Lord of the manor

When I first stood for election to the Scottish Parliament, I publicly announced that, if I was elected, I would give up my seat at Westminster in order to concentrate my efforts on representing my constituents in the Scottish Parliament. All of the other Westminster MPs who were elected to the Scottish Parliament decided to hang on to their Westminster seats until the next general election because their parties did not want to run the risk of a by-election. For me, there was no such problem because I was not a member of any party, and I was very reluctant to wait until the next general election which might have meant continuing to be a Westminster MP for another three years. I found it impossible to do two jobs, and my priority obviously lay with the Scottish Parliament, where most of the bread-and-butter issues affecting my constituents were decided. Besides, most of the votes at Westminster were a foregone conclusion because of the size of the government's majority.

I was therefore inclined to give up my Westminster seat sooner rather than later but I did not want to leave Falkirk West Constituency Labour Party completely in the lurch. After all, 97 per cent of them had voted for me to be a Labour candidate for the Scottish Parliament and my dispute was with the Labour Party leadership rather than Falkirk West Constituency Labour Party. I still had friends who were active in the Constituency Labour Party, and some of them pleaded with me not to give up my Westminster seat immediately because that would cause a by-election and the Labour Party did not even have a candidate in place. Under those circumstances, the Constituency Labour Party members would be deprived of the opportunity of a democratic selection process. Labour Party headquarters would almost certainly foist a candidate upon them or instruct them to choose from a shortlist of three or four New Labour trusties.

I therefore accepted an invitation to meet with some of my comrades in the local Labour Party and, as a result of our discussions, I agreed to a compromise whereby I would not give up my seat at Westminster until the Constituency Labour Party had been given the opportunity to select a candidate. Some of my Labour Party friends obviously wanted me to be readmitted to the Labour Party and, at that point, I was still open to persuasion. But the party bosses were not interested. In fact, there was continuing arrogance and disdain on the part of Tony Blair.

When I wrote to Blair about the possibility of being readmitted to the Labour Party, he simply passed the buck by telling me that party membership was not a matter for him and that my letter had been passed to Margaret McDonagh (now Baroness McDonagh), General Secretary of the Labour Party. She did not even bother to reply.

After my election to the Scottish Parliament, I attended the House of Commons infrequently but I asked my good friend, Jimmy Dobbin, Labour MP for Middleton and Heywood, to table questions on my behalf to the Prime Minister. Jimmy and I had been good friends since our schooldays. He and his wife, Pat, had been in my class at St Columba's High School and, although they had been living in Lancashire for many years, they still kept in touch and I was delighted when Jimmy joined me in the House of Commons in 1997.

Under the Westminster system of random selection, it is pot luck whether a question to the prime minister is called for oral answer but, after persevering for several months, I eventually got a phone call from Pat telling me that my lucky number had come up. I had landed Question No. 4 to the prime minister and it was therefore virtually certain to be called for oral answer.

I decided that this was a chance not to be missed. When the Speaker called me, I asked Blair: 'What lessons have the government learned from the people of Falkirk West, who elected their Member of the Scottish Parliament with the biggest vote and the biggest majority in Scotland?'

I thought that New Labour might have learned the most basic lesson in politics: never take the people for granted. But Blair arrogantly replied: 'People will return loyal Labour Members of Parliament at the next election.' It was clear that he had learned nothing from the people of Falkirk West.

By the summer of 2000, I had had enough of Westminster and

realised there really was no future for me in the Labour Party. I had asked Falkirk West Constituency Labour Party for an opportunity to address their members to explain my situation and to listen to their views. My request was refused, possibly because there had been a coup at the previous Annual General Meeting and some of my strongest supporters had been ousted from key positions and re-placed by Blairites. The party membership was reduced to a rump, making it very easy for Councillor Dennis Goldie and his cronies to take over. It was also a simple job for them to fix the selection process so that Eric Joyce emerged as the candidate to succeed me at Westminster.

When he was a senior high school pupil, Joyce had been convicted of assaulting a young female teacher, but that did not seem to reduce his standing in the eyes of the New Labour establishment. The result of the selection process was a foregone conclusion. It was a two-horse race between Eric Joyce and Jim Devine, who later became Labour MP for Livingston. I was reliably informed that, if the result had been determined on the votes of those who turned up at the selection conference, Devine would have won hands down. But Joyce had accumulated a massive number of postal votes from people who did not even attend the selection conference. Postal votes are justifiable in the case of party members who are ill or working away from home. If, however, postal votes are extended to people who simply cannot be bothered to turn up to the selection con-ference to listen to and question the candidates, then the system becomes wide open to manipulation and it reduces democracy to a farce.

Towards the end of September 2000, I announced my intention to give up my seat in the House of Commons. Shortly afterwards Donald Dewar died and I could not believe the reaction on the part of the Labour Party bosses. For over two years, they had pretended that I did not exist and any approach from me was met by a deafening silence. Then suddenly all sorts of Labour bigwigs started making overtures to me and the flurry of activity increased after Donald's death.

John Lambie, Chairman of the Scottish Labour Party, door-stepped me at the Scottish Parliament and pleaded with me to re-join the party. John seemed genuinely surprised when I told him about my previous letter to Blair. Within days, Margaret McDonagh phoned me to plead for a meeting. I told her that I had no intention of going to London and that, if she wanted to meet me, she would have to come to my constituency office in Denny. She agreed but asked for an assurance that, if she went to Denny, she would not be surrounded by a media circus. I politely told her that that was not the way I operated and assured her that it would be a private meeting on a one-to-one basis.

During the course of our meeting, Margaret offered to recommend to the Labour Party National Executive Committee that I be reinstated as a Labour Party member but the timescale seemed very elastic and a pre-condition was that I continue my membership of the House of Commons until the next general election. It seemed to me that the Labour Party simply wanted to avoid a by-election at all costs. At one point, Margaret had the audacity to say: 'You see, Dennis, the public does not like by-elections.' She would have been nearer the mark if she had said 'party' rather than 'public'.

The Labour Party was running scared of a by-election in Falkirk West. I thanked Margaret for coming to see me and I told her that I would think about what she had said.

On 23 October I made one of my then rare visits to the House of Commons. The occasion was the election of the Speaker. Betty Boothroyd had announced her resignation and there was no shortage of applicants for her job. The archaic voting procedure in the House of Commons meant that the debates and votes could drag on until late in the evening. Normally sittings of the House of Commons begin with prayers and, at intervals along the back of each bench, there are little brass frames for holding prayer cards. If a member puts his or her name on a prayer card and inserts the card in the frame, then the member is entitled to occupy that seat for that particular day, provided the member turns up for prayers. I was always in the habit of putting in a prayer card early in the morning in order to secure a seat on the front bench below the gangway and eventually even some of my atheistic comrades copied my example in order to get a good seat. On the morning of 23 October 2000, I arrived in the Commons Chamber to discover that there were no prayer cards available. I then remembered that there would be no prayers on that day because, by the weird theological reasoning of the House of Commons, there was no Speaker and therefore no Speaker's chaplain to lead the prayers. I therefore inserted my Scottish Parliament business card, instead of a prayer card, into the brass frame.

The House was due to meet at 2.30 p.m. and, when I went to the Chamber about 2.15 p.m. in order to take my seat, I noticed that someone had pinched my Scottish Parliament card and that the front bench below the gangway was occupied by a phalanx of Labour heavyweights, including Jimmy Hood, MP for Clydesdale, and Ken Purchase, MP for Wolverhampton Northeast, who between them must have weighed about forty stone. I also noticed Anne McGuire MP, the Government's Scottish Whip, standing nearby with a smug smirk on her face. I do not know who had hatched the plot, but it was a rather puerile attempt to deprive me of my usual seat on the front bench below the gangway.

Not to be outdone, I tried to perch myself on a tiny patch of green leather bench between Dennis Skinner and Jimmy Hood, but Dennis and Jimmy closed ranks and I found myself sitting with one buttock on Dennis' right knee and the other on Jimmy's left. I could not believe that former comrades would treat me in such a childish manner, especially if they were acting under orders from Anne McGuire, an arch-Blairite.

My discomfort lasted only until the first vote, when members had to leave their seats in order to enter the voting lobbies. I made sure that I got back to my seat in double-quick time in order to claim a more spacious area.

As I expected, the debate on the election of the Speaker was very prolonged, with votes taking place throughout the afternoon and evening. At about eight o'clock, after one of many votes, I was sitting on the front bench below the gangway, when Gordon Brown, who was then Chancellor of the Exchequer, approached me. He asked if he could have a talk in private and we went to my office which was close at hand, above the Star Chamber Court.

When Gordon raised the possibility of my rejoining the Labour Party, I reminded him that, about two years previously, when I was in the throes of a bitter dispute with the Labour leadership about the rigged selection of candidates for the Scottish Parliament, he had suggested that we meet up to discuss the situation. I had followed that with a written request for a meeting with him but received no reply. I therefore told Gordon that, if he had intervened earlier, the present predicament might not have arisen. Gordon apologised and told me that, at that particular time, he had not been in a position to deliver. That made me wonder whether Donald Dewar had been the major stumbling block but the situation had changed now because Donald was no longer with us. I later formed the impression that some of the Labour high heid yins were trying to pin all the blame for my predicament on Donald Dewar simply because he was deceased, but I have never believed that Donald was the sole conspirator.

I told Gordon about my meeting with Margaret McDonagh and he assured me that, if I applied to rejoin the Labour Party, the National Executive Committee would approve it at its next meeting. Gordon was very persuasive, reminding me that we go back a long way and he made it clear that he had disapproved of the decision to reject me as a Labour candidate for the Scottish Parliament. We must have spent the best part of an hour discussing the matter and he kept trying to pin me down. Before we parted, I promised that I would reflect very carefully on our discussion.

Shortly afterwards, the debate on the election of the Speaker came to an end. After Michael Martin was declared the winner, I gave the following congratulatory speech which was punctuated by mutter-ings and rude interruptions from some of my erstwhile Labour colleagues:

> Mr Speaker-Elect, as no party leader now speaks for me, I should like to add my words of congratulation to you on your election. It is a great honour for you personally, a great honour for Mary and your family, a great honour for your native city of Glasgow and a great honour for Scotland. Much has been said about the great respon-sibilities and onerous duties to the House that accompany your new position. I hope that you will work hard to protect the rights of Members of Parliament and to ensure that the government are accountable to parliament.
>
> This may be my last opportunity to address this parliament. You, Mr Speaker-Elect, will be the fifth Speaker during my time in the House. When I was first elected in October 1974, Selwyn Lloyd was Speaker, Harold Wilson was prime minister and I was a quarter of his majority. Gradually, through the loss of by-elections, that majority was eroded and eventually there was no majority. That government was defeated on the floor of the House by a vote.
>
> That scenario is most unlikely to repeat itself during the lifetime of this parliament because of the size of the government's majority. However, a government who have a majority that is perhaps too large is not necessarily a good thing for democracy. Sometimes govern-ments with very large majorities behave arrogantly and treat parlia-ment as a mere rubber-stamp. I hope that you, Mr Speaker-Elect,

will not allow that to happen. Parliament will not do its job unless members are considered first and foremost as representatives of people rather than mere puppets of any party.

Members have a right and a duty to tell their party and their government when they have it wrong. Should it be thought that this is becoming too political, I remind the House that I am only one of three members of this parliament who is not a member of any political party. I am unique in the Scottish Parliament in that I am the only member who is not a member of any party. That is because last year I was given a free transfer from what used to be called the people's party. That was not exactly of my own volition.

I hope, Mr Speaker-Elect, that you will ensure that members of all parties and none will have the opportunity to speak up for the people whom they represent. I place on record my thanks to all members, past and present, whom I have had the pleasure of knowing and working with over the past 26 years. I have had the privilege of representing my constituents for more than a quarter of a century in this place and I hope that I will have the privilege of continuing to represent them for many years in the Scottish Parliament.

It turned out to be my last speech in the House of Commons. As promised, I did reflect very carefully on my discussion with Gordon Brown. In fact, I agonised over my decision and, at one stage, I was minded to rejoin the Labour Party and said so publicly. However, part of the deal on offer was that I would have to appear personally before the Labour Party National Executive Committee or one of its sub-committees, who would ask me for some kind of promise of allegiance. That stuck in my craw. I felt no loyalty at all to Tony Blair as leader, especially when I found out that he personally was involved in the plot to stop me being a candidate for the Scottish Parliament and he was largely responsible for the control-freakery which permeated the party.

Henry McLeish, who succeeded Donald Dewar as First Minister of Scotland, phoned to invite me to meet him. The venue was Henry's constituency office in Glenrothes, the same office which later led to Henry's downfall after a series of damaging revelations about his sub-letting parts of the office to other people or organisations. Although it was a breach of the regulations on House of Commons expenses, Henry described it as a muddle rather than a fiddle, but he eventually fell on his sword. I have always got on well with Henry and I think that he asked to see me at his constituency office rather than Edinburgh because he wanted, in the first instance, to have a frank discussion with me, without fear of being interrupted by civil servants or ministerial colleagues. It was apparent from our discussion that Gordon Brown had had a word with Henry, who made it very clear that he wanted me back into the Labour Party. He continued trying to persuade me at a subsequent meeting in his First Minister's office at St Andrew's House.

Marilyn Livingstone MSP, Convener of the Scottish Parliamentary Labour Group, also told me that I would be very welcome but Tom McCabe MSP, Labour's Chief Whip at Holyrood, did not seem very welcoming at all. Quotes such as 'Canavan will have to toe the party line if he joins our group' were attributed to some anonymous Labour MSPs in press reports, and even Henry McLeish publicly said that I would have to accept party discipline like every other Labour MSP. I felt as if they were trying to put me into a political straitjacket and I told Tom McCabe forcibly that there was no way that I could vote against commitments which I had given to my constituents on matters such as the abolition of tuition fees and the reintroduction of student grants.

As the day approached for the meeting of the National Executive Committee, I felt increasingly as if I were being summoned to party headquarters in London like some errant schoolboy to be vetted because of some wrongdoing on my part. I also worried about how my constituents would react. Many of the people who had voted for me in 1999 were traditional Labour voters, some of whom actually thought I was still the 'real' Labour candidate. For them, my rejoining the Labour Party would be no problem and some of them told me so. But there were other people who had voted for me in 1999 for the first time in their lives, precisely because I was an 'independent' candidate and they might feel let down if I gave up that independent status. I had received a massive mandate from my constituents, the biggest majority in Scotland, and that mandate was partly due to my 'independence'.

After a great deal of heart-searching, I eventually came to the conclusion that I would be in a better position to serve my constituents if I continued as an independent and I wrote to Margaret McDonagh telling her so.

I do not know to this day whether the Labour Party headquarters orchestrated the press reaction to my decision, but it was vitriolic.

'Hero becomes zero' was one of the more benign headlines, and I was accused of everything from prevarication to treachery. Tom Brown, a loyal Labour columnist, even accused me of deliberately trying to sabotage Labour's campaign in the Glasgow Anniesland by-election, caused by the death of Donald Dewar. Whatever decision I took on whether or not to rejoin the Labour Party, there was no pleasing some of the media. I was damned if I did and damned if I didn't. When I announced that I would not be rejoining the Labour Party, there was no shortage of false prophets predicting that I was walking into the political wilderness and stood no chance of ever being re-elected. When I had previously indicated the possibility of my rejoining the Labour Party, some of the same people had accused me of lining my pockets because I would get over £40,000 in severance allowance by hanging on to my Westminster seat until the next general election. David McLetchie MSP, the then Tory leader at Holyrood, had the gall to accuse me in the Scottish Parliament of accepting a so-called golden handshake, while he himself was making expenses claims which led to his downfall as party leader.

I am content to let the people decide whether my motives could ever be described as mercenary. I had actually experienced a wage-cut in 1974 when I first entered the House of Commons and I experienced another wage-cut by moving to the Scottish Parliament in 1999. Not exactly smart career moves for someone on the make.

The truth was that I was literally agonising over the decision whether or not to rejoin the Labour Party. Hard-nosed journalists may find this difficult to understand, but my leaving the Labour Party was like a family rift because I had been virtually born and brought up in the party. I spent many sleepless nights pondering over the matter and, when I eventually announced my decision, I was not even certain that it was the correct one. Now I am. New Labour was a different party from the one in which I had been raised and, if I had re-joined Blair's party, I would be wrestling with my own soul. Nowadays, when I am asked whether I shall ever rejoin the Labour Party, I usually reply: 'Never say never but I would have to see a radical change in direction.'

When I decided not to rejoin the Labour Party in 2000, I also firmly decided to give up my seat at Westminster and that is how I became Steward of the Manor of Northstead. According to the great British constitution, a Member of Parliament cannot resign but must use a quaint procedural device leading to disqualification from membership of the House of Commons. Under the Act of Settlement, any Member of Parliament accepting an office of profit under the Crown must give up his or her seat. In recent times, the two offices used for this purpose are Steward of the Manor of Northstead and Steward of the Chiltern Hundreds. As appointees to the two offices are alternated, I would become Steward of the Manor of Northstead, because Betty Boothroyd had been made Steward of the Chiltern Hundreds a few weeks earlier, when she announced that she would be quitting the House of Commons.

I had to write to Gordon Brown, as Chancellor of the Exchequer, formally telling him that I wanted to give up my seat and asking him to effect the appropriate procedure. I then received a letter from the Treasury formally telling me that I had been appointed Steward of the Manor of Northstead. To this day, I fail to understand why it is described as an office of 'profit', because there is no financial gain. At one stage, I thought about visiting the Manor of Northstead to see what I was supposed to be stewarding but I was informed that the manor house, near Scarborough in Yorkshire, had fallen into such a state of dereliction that, by the beginning of the seventeenth century, it was used as a shepherd's bothy. Which does not say much for the stewardship of some of my early predecessors.

After a while, I completely forgot about the Manor of Northstead until, nearly four years after my appointment, I received another letter from the Treasury telling me that my stewardship had been transferred to Peter Mandelson, who wanted to give up his Commons seat to become a European Commissioner. Now there is a real office of profit!

Almost as soon as I became Steward of the Manor of Northstead, the Labour Party announced that the resultant Falkirk West by-election would be held on 21 December. The Labour Party bosses obviously thought that a quick campaign might catch the SNP on the hop and, if Labour lost the seat, then the bad news would be buried in the Christmas festivities. Holding a by-election so close to Christmas, to my mind, was treating the democratic process with contempt. The turn-out of 36 per cent was less than half of what it was at the previous general election and Labour just managed to scrape in with a majority of 705.

The greatest beneficiaries of the Falkirk West by-election turned out to be a group of about 12,000 pensioners who were former employees of the Scottish Transport Group. Some of them had spent virtually all their working lives employed as bus drivers, conductors, cleaners, engineers and ferry crew in various parts of Scotland. When the Scottish Transport Group was privatised by Margaret Thatcher's government, the Treasury tried to pocket the entire surplus of the workers' pension fund and there was no sign of a change of heart when the Blair regime took over. One of the pensioners, Alex Anderson from Falkirk, came to see me as his local MSP and I raised the matter in the Scottish Parliament. The total surplus in the pension fund turned out to be about £250 million and the pensioners had not received a penny from it. I lodged a motion in the Scottish Parliament demanding justice for the pensioners, and it managed to attract the support of a record number of MSPs from all political parties. Even Lord James Douglas-Hamilton, who had been the Scottish Office Transport Minister at the time of the Scottish Transport Group privatisation, expressed support for the pensioners and I led a debate on the matter in the Scottish Parliament. My campaign in parliament was supplemented by a series of campaign meetings throughout Scotland, organised by Alex and Irene Anderson, Anne Marshall and Chick Hulston, a retired trade union official.

We had meetings at various venues, including Falkirk, Stirling, Kirkcaldy, Inverness, Kilmarnock, Greenock and Wishaw. I found some of the meetings so well attended and so lively that they were reminiscent of some of the campaign meetings which the Labour Party used to organise in the 1970s. There was a great deal of anger expressed at those meetings, but it was justifiable anger. I knew within my gut that these people were suffering a grave injustice and I was determined to fight and win their case. But initially there was no sign of a positive response from either the Scottish Executive or the UK Government.

Then suddenly, on the very first day of the Falkirk West by-election campaign, Gordon Brown and Henry McLeish made a joint announcement that the Scottish Transport Group pensioners were to receive £100 million in *ex gratia* payments from their pension fund surplus. It was no coincidence that a large proportion of the pensioners lived in Falkirk West. That was the location of the former Scottish Bus Group Engineering Workshops as well as the former administrative headquarters of Alexander's, the bus operators.

I publicly welcomed the announcement but pointed out that £100 million was only a fraction of the total surplus. The campaign therefore continued and the Scottish Executive was eventually forced to concede an additional £26 million. That worked out at an average payment of over £10,000 per person. I still think that the pensioners were shortchanged, but they would probably not have received a penny were it not for Alex Anderson's nationwide campaign and, of course, the Falkirk West by-election.

— ◆ —

CHAPTER TWENTY-SIX

Holyrood *v* Westminster: a comparison

A parliamentary mace is a symbol of authority, but whose authority?

The head of the House of Commons mace is like an ornate crown, which is very fitting for a symbol of royal authority. By contrast, the simple design of the Scottish Parliament mace makes it more like a symbol of the sovereignty of the people rather than the sovereignty of the monarch. The head of the mace is inscribed with the words 'Wisdom, Justice, Compassion, Integrity', to represent the aspirations of the people for their representatives in the Scottish Parliament. Fine words, but do the members of either parliament live up to those aspirations?

Parliamentarians, like any other human beings, have faults and failings. They are not always wise, just or compassionate and, when it comes to integrity, they often fall far short of the standards which their constituents deserve. In terms of trustworthiness, an increasing number of people would put politicians at the bottom of the league along with all the other hoods and crooks.

The scandalous abuse of parliamentary expenses has probably done more than anything else to undermine the reputation of parliamentarians. Many people now perceive politicians as a bunch of chancers on the take. There is a tendency to tar them all with the same brush, which is rather unfair because there are still some politicians who abide by the highest principles which used to be the hallmark of public service. What has happened to bring about such a change?

When I started in the House of Commons, expenses for MPs were fairly minimal. The secretarial allowance was barely enough to employ one person for 20 hours per week, and the living away from home allowance was barely enough to pay for bed and breakfast in a London boarding house. During the severe wage restraint of the mid

1970s, MPs were expected to set a good example to the rest of the nation and, when some of them complained to Bob Mellish, the Government Chief Whip, that they were finding it difficult to make ends meet, Mellish bluntly told them: 'Bump up your travel expenses!' At that time no receipts were required. The word of an honourable member had to be trusted, even though some of the members were far from honourable.

Over the years, there have been substantial increases in MPs' allowances, some of them justifiable. For example, the erstwhile secretarial allowance has been replaced by a much more generous office costs allowance to enable MPs to have a constituency office and to employ full-time staff to help with constituency and parliamentary work. The living away from home allowance has also been increased to enable MPs to meet the additional costs of a second home required for parliamentary duties.

Unfortunately, the increased allowances have not been accompanied by increased transparency and accountability. There have also been rule changes which have encouraged more members to get their snouts in the trough. In the 1970s, MPs were allowed to use the living away from home allowance to rent a flat or to pay for digs or hotel accommodation. They were not allowed to use it to buy a house. When that rule was changed, many MPs saw it as a licence to use public money get rich on the booming London property market.

I recall a casual conversation with Mike Watson (now Lord Watson, who was jailed for arson), shortly after he was elected to the House of Commons. Mike was looking around London for a suitable house to buy and, when someone suggested renting a house, he expressed incredulity.

'But why on earth would someone want to buy rather than rent?'

The future Baron Watson of Invergowrie probably thought that people like me were naïve or soft in the head for living in humble rented bedsitters, when we could have used the expenses system to line our pockets out of the housing market. Thatcher's obsession with property-owning had obviously infiltrated the new intake of MPs, including some on the Labour benches. Buying second homes led to a practice called 'flipping', whereby MPs switched the designation of their second homes from one property to another in order to maximise the take and the capital gain, funded out of the public purse.

I was unaware of any 'flipping' in the Scottish Parliament, but there were a number of MSPs who made a fat profit out of the second homes allowance before the rules were changed to stop the allowance being used to buy property.

The system of expenses in the Scottish Parliament is not perfect but I found it to be light-years ahead of Westminster in terms of transparency and accountability. If Westminster had adopted the Holyrood system, it would have avoided one of the biggest scandals in parliamentary history, which turned the Palace of Westminster into the Augean stables.

When the *Daily Telegraph* lifted the lid on the abuse of MPs' expenses, it exposed a culture of secrecy and greed which brought parliament into disrepute. It also brought down Speaker Michael Martin, the first Speaker of the House of Commons to be forced out of office for 300 years. I used to share an office with Michael before he was elevated to the office of Speaker. He struck me as a basically decent guy, but he himself would probably admit that he made some serious mistakes and he eventually made the right decision to quit. On the expenses fiasco, he was left trying to defend the indefensible.

Some of Michael's closest friends and supporters claim that he was the victim of a prolonged conspiracy against him because of his working-class background but I do not go along with that conspiracy theory. There certainly were some Westminster snobs who did not like Michael's Glasgow accent and thought he was not polished enough for the job. Michael was the son of a school cleaner and a merchant seaman but he was not the only Speaker from humble origins. Betty Boothroyd, who was the best Speaker in all my time at Westminster, was the daughter of textile workers and was a former member of the Tiller Girls dancing troupe. She was very proud of her Yorkshire accent and had the aplomb to put any arrogant snobs in their place.

Even the Tories produced a Speaker of relatively humble origins. At the age of 17, Bernard Weatherill was apprenticed to the family tailoring firm in Savile Row and was managing director of the firm when he was elected as Tory MP for Croydon North-East. Bernard used to tell a story about a conversation which took place a few days after his first election to parliament in 1964. He was sitting in a toilet cubicle in the House of Commons when he overheard two MPs chatting at a nearby urinal. He recognised one of the voices as belonging to a former customer of his, a Tory toff, who was talking in scathing terms about the new intake of Tory MPs. The voice exclaimed:

'I don't know what's become of this place. Would you believe it? My tailor has actually become a member!'

I wonder what the Tory toff would have thought if he had been told that, less than 20 years later, his tailor would be Speaker of the House of Commons.

Despite his background, Bernard Weatherill did not try to impose sartorial standards on other members. I cannot say the same about his predecessor, George Thomas. On one particularly blistering-hot summer day, I was not wearing a tie in the Commons Chamber. When a Tory MP raised a point of order to complain about my attire, Speaker Thomas indicated that, although he did not have the power to dictate what members wore in the Chamber, any member not wearing a tie would find it difficult, if not impossible, to catch his eye. In Westminster lingo that meant that he would not call any tieless member to speak. I immediately rose to seek clarification:

'Does your ruling also apply to the Prime Minister?'

As the Prime Minister at the time was Margaret Thatcher, Speaker Thomas suddenly realised that his ruling was unsustainable and he quickly moved on to the next business.

I crossed swords with George Thomas on several other occasions. During one particularly rowdy Question Time, a Tory government minister was reading a quotation from the *Daily Mail*, when I shouted out: '*Daily Mail* lies!'

Speaker Thomas immediately stopped the proceedings to bark out the order: 'The Honourable Member for Stirling must withdraw!' I sat in silence, much to the Speaker's fury.

'The Honourable Member for Stirling must withdraw that remark', said the Speaker. 'He must not accuse the minister of lying.' I rose to my feet.

'If you're speaking to me, Mr Speaker, can I first of all point out that I am not the Honourable Member for Stirling. I am the Honourable Member for West Stirlingshire. Secondly, I did not accuse the minister of lying. I accused the *Daily Mail* of lying, and that goes without saying.'

Speaker Thomas was furious, but he knew that he could do no more about it.

In the Scottish Parliament, the occupant of the Chair is called the Presiding Officer rather than the Speaker. Unlike the Speaker of the House of Commons, who wears special robes of office, the Presiding Officer wears ordinary civvies, although I did hear that the first

Presiding Officer, Lord David Steel, had suggested some kind of regalia but was knocked back. Such a suggestion coming from Steel would not surprise me, because he could be rather full of his own importance. He also got the parliament off to a bad start by kowtowing to party leaders.

For example, the allocation of time to party leaders at First Minister's Question Time is a travesty of democracy. For half an hour every Thursday during the parliamentary session, the First Minister answers questions from MSPs, but well over half of that time is taken up by questions from party leaders with sometimes only about ten minutes being left for questions from 'backbenchers'. The first question is always allocated to the leader of the largest Opposition party, the second question is always allocated to the leader of the second largest Opposition party and so on. That is even worse than the Westminster version of democracy, where the order of questions is decided by random selection and even the most humble backbencher may have the first question to the prime minister. An industrious MP can improve the odds by taking the trouble to table questions at every available opportunity but there is not much incentive for an MSP to be so diligent. Any party hack, not necessarily another member, can lodge questions on behalf of an MSP as long as the MSP designates the hack so to do. This leads to a situation where a paid party researcher can compose and lodge questions on behalf of an unlimited number of compliant MSPs who are either too indolent or too incompetent to lodge questions themselves. If the questions come up for oral answer, the party researchers then provide the supplementary questions, which means that the party machine is able to dictate the agenda and back bench MSPs are reduced to the status of party pawns.

When I complained to Lord David Steel about the disproportionate amount of Question Time allocated to party leaders and referred him to a standing order of the Scottish Parliament which states that 'in exercising any functions, the Presiding Officer shall act impartially, taking into account the interests of all members equally', his trite response was: 'Some members are more equal than others.' He was rather miffed when I told him that such a riposte might go down well in his House of Lords, but it was not appropriate in a twenty-first-century democratic parliament.

Lord Steel seemed to think that the allocation of time in the Scottish Parliament should be decided on a party basis, and this allowed the party bosses to control the parliament through the

Parliamentary Bureau. I used to refer to it as the Politburo because the way in which it operated was at times like the oxymoronic democratic centralism of the Soviet Union. The bureau meetings were held in secret and were attended only by the party business managers or whips along with senior clerks of the parliament. Even the allocation of time for members' debates was decided on a party basis and, when I challenged that, the 'justification' was D'Hondt. The D'Hondt method, named after Belgian mathematician Victor D'Hondt, was designed for the allocation of seats to each party in a parliament or a committee on a proportional representation basis. It was never meant to determine the allocation of parliamentary time.

Even in the House of Commons, the allocation of private members' time is outwith the control of the party whips but, in the Scottish Parliament, the party control-freaks can reward pliant party hacks with a debate or stop any rebellious member from raising an issue which might embarrass the establishment.

I deplored the control-freakery at Westminster and I hoped that the Scottish Parliament would be more open and transparent. But in some respects, the Scottish Parliament was even worse than Westminster. With only 129 members at Holyrood, compared with over 600 at Westminster, it was easier for the party whips to control their members. I can see the justification for the whips advising or even trying to instruct members how to vote on party manifesto commitments. After all, a manifesto is like a contract or potential contract between the elected and the electors. If a candidate stands on a party ticket, then the electors are entitled to expect that candidate, if elected, to vote for commitments contained in that party's manifesto unless, of course, the candidate has made it clear that he or she disagrees with some particular item of party policy.

But the party whips, both at Westminster and Holyrood, tell their party members how to vote on nearly every issue, and that reduces the elected member to the status of a stooge and, in the case of a government with an overall majority, it can reduce parliament to a mere rubber-stamp. Part of the job of any parliament is to make the government accountable to the people through the elected representatives of the people. If Members of Parliament are not allowed to use their judgement, then accountability suffers and democracy is undermined.

There is sometimes tension and hostility between Westminster and Holyrood, and often tension and hostility between individual MPs and MSPs. Since devolution, the role of MPs representing

Scottish constituencies has been greatly diminished and some MPs choose to ignore the fact that the Scottish Parliament is now responsible for matters such as health and education. This can lead to confrontation. For example, I was very much in the forefront of the campaign for a new hospital to serve all the people of Forth Valley and I was the first politician to express publicly a preference for the new hospital to be located on the site of the former Royal Scottish National Hospital at Larbert. Sylvia Jackson, MSP for Stirling, later expressed a preference for the new hospital to be built in her constituency, as she had every right to do. Then Anne McGuire, MP for Stirling and a member of the Westminster Government at the time, entered the fray and publicly tried to rubbish the case for the Larbert location, using information which was factually incorrect. During a debate in the Scottish Parliament, I pointed out that it was totally inappropriate for a member of the Westminster Government to interfere in such a deceitful manner on a devolved issue. Anne was not a happy bunny, but I had no obligation to keep MPs happy, especially those who had tried to undermine me. I won my case and Larbert was chosen as the location for the new hospital.

When the Scottish Parliament first started, it was a rather docile institution and the presiding officer had no problem in keeping order. After a while, the debates became livelier and sometimes there were very heated exchanges. There were some demonstrations, like the occasion when four members of the Scottish Socialist Party were suspended for disrupting the proceedings and refusing to leave the Chamber. But that was very contrived and relatively tame compared with the night when Michael 'Tarzan' Heseltine brandished the mace in the House of Commons after a vital vote on the Labour Government's bill to nationalise the aircraft and shipbuilding industries. The Tories thought that they had won the vote but it turned out to be a tie. When the Speaker used his casting vote in favour of the bill, the Labour benches erupted with glee and some of us started singing 'The Red Flag'. For Heseltine, it was like a red rag to a bull. He lost the rag completely and, in a fit of rage, grabbed the mace with one hand and swung it above his head. As I was sitting amongst a group of Labour MPs on the front bench below the gangway, I was able to see the mad gleam in Heseltine's eyes and, for one awful moment, I thought that he was going to club our heads with the mace. It was absolute mayhem and the Speaker had no option but to suspend the sitting. That was away back in the 1970s before the proceedings of parliament were televised, which is a pity because it was high drama and the action replay would still have been in demand today.

Another memorable Commons rumpus came at the end of a debate on a Public Expenditure White Paper, when Denis Healey was Chancellor of the Exchequer in 1976. A number of Labour MPs, including myself, had said that we could not support the White paper because it proposed severe cuts in essential services such as health and education. We could not possibly vote with the Tories, because they wanted even more cuts. So we decided to abstain and I did so ostentatiously by sitting on the front bench below the gangway while the vote was taking place. Healey, who can be a bit of a bully, approached me in obvious rage. With his purple face just inches from my nose, he hurled obscenities at me, trying to intimidate me, but I told him where to stuff his White Paper. The incident was witnessed by some members of the Press Gallery but they could not hear what was being said. I later received a substantial offer to go on TV and tell the nation what the Chancellor had said but I declined. It would not have been good family viewing but Denis himself later gave a sanitised but not entirely accurate version, claiming that he had questioned my virility and I had questioned his parentage.

Contrary to some reports, Denis and I never fell out over the incident. Not long afterwards, my young children were visiting parliament and I introduced them to Healey. My son Paul, who was only four at the time, said later: 'Daddy, your friend with the big, bushy eyebrows looks just like Santa Claus.' If only he knew!

Many years later, I had another confrontation with another Chancellor of the Exchequer, Kenneth Clarke, but he was more subtle when I challenged him towards the end of a Budget debate. Along with some parliamentary colleagues, I had previously been at a reception in the Irish embassy in Grosvenor Place. The Irish ambassador traditionally hosted the best parties on the London diplomatic circuit. Irish hospitality can be almost literally overwhelming, but we dutifully left early to get back to the Commons for the vote at 10 p.m.

Ken Clarke was winding up the debate when we entered the Chamber and he was in full swing, dealing very competently with some rowdy heckling. I sat down on the front bench below the gangway, just a few yards across the Chamber from the Treasury Despatch Box, where the Chancellor was holding forth. I made what in Westminsterspeak is called a well-lubricated seated intervention, describing the Budget as absolute rubbish. Ken Clarke, who was a beer man rather than a spirit merchant, turned to me and reminded me that he had resisted the temptation to increase the duty on whisky and other spirits:

'The Honourable Gentleman for Falkirk West could at least give me credit for one measure that I took for Scottish industry. I have frozen the tax on something for which he obviously has a taste!'

I could never understand why the Tories would never elect Ken Clarke as their leader. He is very intelligent, witty and a brilliant parliamentary performer. He certainly put me in my place on that occasion.

One big difference between the Scottish Parliament and Westminster is that the Scottish Parliament has only one chamber whereas Westminster has two, the House of Commons and the House of Lords. I have always supported the complete abolition of the House of Lords, which is an affront to democracy and an absurd anachronism in the twenty-first century. When I was first elected to the Commons, most members of the Lords were hereditary peers and it seemed ludicrous to me that people should have a seat in parliament simply because their daddies were there before them.

Since then, the House of Lords has been reformed somewhat but replacing some of the landed gentry with Tony's cronies has understandably led to allegations of sleaze. Blair was quick to paint New Labour as whiter than the driven snow when there was a strong stench of corruption around John Major's Government following revelations that some Tory MPs had been accepting cash from private sector companies for asking questions in the House of Commons. The hypocrisy of New Labour has now been exposed by more recent revelations about cash for peerages and New Labour peers willing to accept cash for having bills amended. Cash for changing the law is even more corrupt than cash for asking questions, yet the peers in question showed little if any remorse and the House of Lords obviously has inadequate sanctions to deal effectively with the culprits.

There is also a complete absence of accountability. The House of Lords contains the seeds of corruption within its very essence. Despite so-called reforms, the fact remains that none of its members is directly elected by the people, and political patronage can be an even greater threat to democracy than inheritance. The prime minister of the day can use his or her powers of patronage to reward friends with peerages or get rid of enemies by 'kicking them upstairs'. To suggest that appointment to the House of Lords is on merit is preposterous. I have seen some real duffers as well as rogues in ermine robes, and the system can be used to give ministerial positions to people who would find it very difficult to get elected or re-elected. Peter Mandelson is a classic example. He is no duffer, but the fact that he previously had to resign twice from the Cabinet in disgrace does not exactly make him an electoral asset.

Defenders of the House of Lords usually trot out the same old argument that the second Chamber performs a useful function as a revision mechanism which is necessary to ensure that legislation is adequately scrutinised. People who swallow that one should take a look at the Scottish Parliament, which operates effectively with only one chamber.

Part of the reason why the Scottish Parliament does not need a second Chamber is because its committee system is superior to Westminster's. When I was at Westminster, a typical legislative committee would be established to deal with only one bill. Such committees are called standing committees, but they are in fact ad hoc committees. Once the committee finishes dealing with the bill, the committee is dissolved. The select committees in the House of Commons are more permanent than the so-called standing committees, although the present system of select committees did not come into operation until the early 1980s. The select committees tend to specialise in a particular subject area, and their role is usually investigative rather than legislative. It is the job of a select committee to bring the government to account, to conduct inquiries and to issue reports with recommendations for appropriate action by the government or other bodies.

In general, the Scottish Parliament committees 'shadow' the government departments and combine legislative and investigative roles. When a committee finishes dealing with a particular bill, the committee is not dissolved. It continues to exist and the membership remains the same unless it is changed by resolution of the parliament. That allows members to remain on a particular committee for a longer period of time, thus enabling them to specialise and gain expertise in a particular subject area.

During my eight years in the Scottish Parliament, I was a member of the European Committee, which developed into the European and External Relations Committee. It enabled me to continue my interest in international affairs and we produced some well-received reports on various subjects, including international development and the need to attract more people from other countries to live and work in Scotland. A committee of the Scottish Parliament may appoint one of its members as 'rapporteur' to conduct an investigation and produce a report on a particular subject. I was author of two such reports, one on a proposed EU Charter of Human Rights and the other on the potential for co-operation between Scotland and Ireland. Both were unanimously approved by the committee and the latter was selected for debate in a plenary session of the parliament, when cross-party support was expressed for my proposed programme of co-operation between Scotland and Ireland.

The Scottish Parliament also has a degree of pre-legislative scrutiny which I never experienced at Westminster. Sometimes the appropriate committee will issue calls for evidence on a legislative proposal even before the bill is published. The procedure gives individuals and organisations outside parliament the opportunity to feed into the legislative process, and MSPs are then able to benefit from that knowledge and experience. The evidence of expert witnesses is invaluable but, in the final analysis, it is the elected representatives of the people who vote on the legislation and that is as it should be in any democracy.

Under the Westminster system, individuals and organisations outside parliament had no formal way of feeding into the legislative process other than 'lobbying'. Sometimes the form of lobbying was very questionable on ethical grounds. For example, individual companies or interest groups could use a Member of Parliament to book a banqueting room at the House of Commons to wine and dine a group of members in the hope of influencing the legislative process. Whether they were successful or not, any attempt to buy such influence should be banned.

Another difference between the Scottish Parliament and the Westminster Parliament is in the treatment of members' bills, or 'private members' bills', as they are called at Westminster. A private member's bill at Westminster has very little chance of success unless the member proposing the bill wins a top place in the annual ballot and the bill has the support of the government. An alternative procedure is to introduce a 'ten-minute rule bill' but the chances of a ten-minute rule bill becoming law are nowadays minuscule. Nevertheless, it can be a useful way of drawing parliamentary attention to an issue because the member presenting the bill is allowed to make a ten-minute speech in prime parliamentary time.

No more than one ten-minute rule bill may be introduced on any particular day and, in order to secure this much sought-after slot, the MP must be first in the queue at the Public Bill Office three weeks prior to the date on which the bill is to be presented. It was not unknown for MPs to sleep overnight outside the Public Bill Office to ensure that they could claim the coveted slot when the office opened at 10 a.m.

Because I suffer from insomnia, I would quite often arrive at the House of Commons well before 7 a.m. and I would sometimes go to the Public Bill Office to see whether anyone was waiting. In 1985, I secured the opportunity to present a ten-minute rule bill on Budget Day. I told the Clerk of Public Bills that I wanted to introduce a bill to be called the Finance Bill. No objection was raised at the time but, later that day, the clerk informed me that my proposed title would not be allowed because the term 'Finance Bill' was reserved for the government bill containing the legislative measures included in the Chancellor's Budget Statement. I then suggested that my bill be called the Finance No. 2 Bill but that too was unacceptable, despite the fact that the clerk could not quote any standing order to justify his decision. I then suggested that my bill be called the Budget Bill and this was accepted, albeit with some reluctance.

When Budget Day arrived, the chamber was packed with members waiting to hear the Chancellor Nigel Lawson's Budget Statement. However, the order of proceedings stipulated that my ten-minute rule bill speech should immediately precede the Budget Statement. I was able to use the ten minutes to launch a ferocious attack on Nigel Lawson's appalling economic record and to propose my own alternative budget. Lawson was so intent on avoiding any embarrassment that he hid behind the Speaker's Chair for the duration of my speech, which was generally well received. Even some of the Tories such as John Biffen thought it was a great wheeze, but Nigel Lawson was not amused.

When I sat down at the end of my speech, Lawson came in to make his Budget Statement but his wait was prolonged even further when some Labour MPs shouted for a vote on my bill which would delay the proceedings for another quarter of an hour. When the vote was called, the Tory MPs were afraid to leave their benches to vote in case they lost their seats for the big Budget Statement. The result was that my bill went through unopposed, but that was just the first hurdle in the legislative process. I knew that my bill had no chance of becoming law, but it was a great chance to upstage Nigel Lawson and to prick his pomposity.

The following year I tried an action replay but, when I arrived at the Public Bill Office at about 7 a.m., I discovered a Tory MP had been sleeping there all night to stop me being first in the queue. I recognised him as a Treasury parliamentary private secretary, which is like a message-boy for a Treasury minister. He also turned out to be a dog in the manger. Having successfully won the right to move a motion to present a ten-minute rule bill, he then at the last minute obediently withdrew his motion to enable the Chancellor to make his Budget Statement without anyone upstaging him.

I do not know whether the message-boy complained about having to sleep rough all night but shortly afterwards the Tory government used its Commons majority to amend the Standing Orders to forbid the presentation of any ten-minute rule bill on Budget Day. I was the last member who ever used that opportunity and the change of Standing Orders was a typical example of the parliamentary establishment shifting the goalposts when they found that the status quo was causing them some difficulty.

When the Scottish Parliament was set up, it was supposed to provide more opportunities than Westminster for ordinary members to introduce legislation. To some extent it does, but the system is far from perfect and the Executive has a vested interest in not giving more power to 'back-benchers'. There is a Non-Executive Bills Unit to support members who want to introduce a member's bill but, when I was a member, the unit was very short-staffed and therefore incapable of helping all the members wishing to use its services. During my time in the Scottish Parliament, the vast majority of the successful bills were introduced by the Executive and the political reality was that a member's bill had no chance of success unless it had the support of the Executive. By and large, the party whips controlled the votes, even on members' bills.

Nevertheless, one of the greatest strengths of the Scottish Parliament is its degree of proportional representation, which virtually ensures that no party will have an overall majority of seats and there is of course no guarantee that the Executive will have such a majority. The SNP Government which was formed in 2007 was a minority administration and that of course strengthened the parliament and made the government more accountable to the parliament. In a democracy, part of the job of parliament is to bring the government to account. During most of my time at Westminster, parliament was just a rubber-stamp for the government, despite the fact that the government never had an over-all majority of the votes cast at any general election. Such an elected dictatorship could never happen in the Scottish Parliament and that is basically why I think it is a much better model of democracy than Westminster. But both parliaments can learn from each other and from other parliaments throughout the world.

—— ◆ ——

CHAPTER TWENTY-SEVEN

The land belongs to the people

In Scotland, we are blessed with some of the finest countryside in the world, but we should never take it for granted.

Having being born and brought up in a mining area, I did not have the good fortune to be surrounded by idyllic landscapes during my childhood. Instead of hills, we had pit bings and slag heaps and many of the burns and lochs consisted of dirty pit water pumped out of the collieries in the area. In later years, Fife Council did an excellent job in reclaiming some of the land which has been scarred by the mining industry. Probably the best example is Lochore Meadows Country Park, which comprises a freshwater loch surrounded by grassy banks and woodlands, a very popular spot for walking, horse riding, canoeing and trout fishing. It is hardly recognisable as the same place which we used to call 'the Meadies'. When I was a child, the water was so murky that the only fish I caught were perch and pike and, instead of rolling green grassland, there was just a dirty, black wasteland consisting of residue from the nearby mines.

Nevertheless, there was some fine countryside within reasonable walking distance from our home. The first hill I ever climbed was Benarty on the south side of Loch Leven and, when I joined the Scouts, the Cleish Hills were a favourite destination for some of our expeditions. In the summer, we would often cycle to the beach at Aberdour or Burntisland for a swim in the Firth of Forth. I have always loved out-door activities and still do, especially walking and cycling in the countryside.

The right of access to the countryside is now enshrined in the Land Reform (Scotland) Act 2003, one of the most radical pieces of legislation passed by the Scottish Parliament. The legislation which eventually emerged was much better than the first draft produced by the then Scottish Executive.

For example, the original text excluded access to the countryside during hours of darkness. This was probably based on the ludicrous misconception that anyone found on a country estate after nightfall is probably a poacher or a burglar. During the parliamentary debate, I pointed out that hillwalkers and climbers very often have to camp in the countryside overnight in order to reach their destination. Some remote Munros (mountains over 3,000 feet high) are several hours' walk from the nearest road and, in order to reach the base of the mountain, it may be necessary to sleep overnight in a tent or a mountain bothy. That can be an interesting experience, as I had found for myself, although you never know what the company in the bothy might be like.

On one occasion, my brother Raymond and I planned an expedition in the Cairngorms along with Raymond's son, Kevin, who is a consultant anaesthetist at Raigmore Hospital, in Inverness. The plan was for Raymond and me to walk from the Linn o'Dee, near Braemar, whereas Kevin would start from a point further north and we would meet up at Corrour bothy in the Lairig Ghru. When Raymond and I arrived at the bothy just before nightfall, we found it already occupied by a group of walkers, one of whom unfortunately recognised me. I say unfortunately because he launched into a vitriolic diatribe about politicians being just a crowd of corrupt wasters who were all on the fiddle. If he had been humorous, I could have put up with it but he went on and on in a very tedious and repetitive manner, not even pausing for breath when we eventually got into our sleeping bags and put the lights out.

Suddenly the door burst open and the moonlight revealed a figure well over six feet high framed in the bothy doorway. I heaved a sigh of relief when I recognised Kevin.

'Who the hell is that?' shouted the loudmouth.

'That's my nephew,' I said, 'he's a professional anaesthetist and he's very good at knocking people out!'

The loudmouth was silent for the rest of the night.

Such anti-social conduct is thankfully not typical of my hillwalking experience. Most of the walkers and bothy dwellers I have met are good company and some of them are great storytellers.

The Scottish Parliament passed my amendment to extend the right of access to 24 hours per day, but the Scottish Executive needed more persuasion to extend the right of access to land belonging to the Queen. The bill as originally drafted specifically excluded such land, and that would have meant no right of access to Balmoral Estate, which includes some of the most scenic countryside in Scotland. The path up Lochnagar, for example, has been enjoyed by generations of hillwalkers.

The Executive originally took the view that extending the right of access to the Queen's land would somehow pose a security threat. Although I am not a royalist, I do not want to see the personal security of the Queen or any of her family threatened in any way. But the Queen is resident at Balmoral for only a few weeks of the year, and it seemed odd for the Executive to propose that the public be deprived of the right of access for 52 weeks in the year. Besides, it is probably easier to arrange security at Balmoral than it is for some of the public events which the Queen attends in London and elsewhere.

I therefore lodged an amendment to extend the right of access to land belonging to the Queen. At first ministers resisted my amendment but, to my surprise, they later agreed to accept it. As I was not privy to any communication between ministers and the Queen about my amendment, I can only speculate about the reason for the Executive's U-turn. Maybe the Queen foresaw the potential embarrassment if she was to be the sole exception to the law, or maybe she was fairly relaxed about allowing her lieges onto her land provided they did not frighten the corgis. Whatever the reason, she did not veto my amendment and an important principle was thereby established. If the legislation is good enough for the Queen, it should be good enough for every landowner in Scotland.

Unfortunately, not every landowner in Scotland agrees. The Land Reform (Scotland) Act 2003 has generally been well received and the vast majority of landowners accept it. However, some selfish landowners have challenged the legislation, and it is interesting to note the initial challenges coming not so much from the landed gentry as from the nouveau riche, like Ann Gloag of Stagecoach, who made a mint out of the privatisation of the buses, and Euan Snowie, who literally made a killing out of foot and mouth disease in 2001–02, when his firm received £38 million from the government to dispose of dead cattle.

Some purchasers of a big country estate seem to think that the entire estate or a large chunk of it is the equivalent of their garden and is therefore excluded from the right of access. They do not even understand that buying a piece of land does not give the buyer an unfettered right to do anything he wants with that land. Many of them seem to be possessed of an urban mindset which fails to appreciate countryside customs and ways of life. As a result, fences, notices, barbed wire, gates and other obstructions appear, sometimes even without planning permission being sought. Such desecration of the countryside creates obstacles for walkers, cyclists and horse-riders seeking access.

One of the worst examples I have experienced is almost literally on my own doorstep, at Sauchieburn Estate near Bannockburn. For generations, the estate belonged to the Maitland family, who were minor landed gentry of the same clan as the Earl of Lauderdale. When the Maitlands owned the estate, there was a reasonable degree of access but, when the last of the Maitlands died and the estate was put on the market, the situation rapidly changed.

Mr Bill Roddie, a millionaire property developer from Glasgow, bought the estate and, almost as soon as he moved into Sauchieburn House, obstructions appeared, including high fences, locked gates and notices at the entrance to the estate declaring the grounds to be 'private'. There are even barricades consisting of large boulders, earth and felled trees, across some of the woodland paths and notices were placed on one stretch of fencing falsely indicating that it was electrified.

Such conduct is not only a desecration of the countryside but also a breach of the law. The 2003 Act gives a general right of access to land and water, although it does stipulate some exceptions from that general right. In the case of land adjacent to a house, the 'exclusion zone' is of sufficient area to enable the occupants of the house to have a reasonable degree of privacy and enjoyment of the house. In the case of Sauchieburn House, some of the obstructions and notices are over half a mile away from the house.

Mr Roddie tried to justify his conduct by telling me that he did not want 'perverts' coming around his house. He then behaved like a common thug by assaulting one of my neighbours who was peacefully jogging through the estate. I arranged for the victim to be interviewed by a newspaper reporter, who investigated Roddie's past and discovered that he was a fraudster who had served a jail sentence for his criminal activities. After the story received prominence in a tabloid newspaper, Roddie ordered his estate manager to deposit over two tons of dung about ten yards from my house!

I refused to be intimidated by such childish anti-social conduct and I was very pleased when the local branch of the Ramblers organised a walk through Sauchieburn Estate in which over 50 people took part. As President of Ramblers Scotland, I was invited to lead the walk and other participants included prominent members of the Ramblers Scottish Council, who were holding their AGM at Stirling over that particular weekend.

It is very important for people to exercise their right to roam and to challenge selfish anti-social landlords who try to stop them. It is also very important for local authorities to use the powers which the Scottish Parliament has given them. Under the Land Reform (Scotland) Act 2003, local authorities have a statutory duty to uphold access rights and statutory powers to enforce the removal of obstructions which prevent or deter access. Local authorities must use their powers to ensure access and to conserve the countryside for future generations.

I have always believed that our mountains, lochs and glens are not simply the property of the landed gentry or the nouveau riche. They are part of our natural heritage and we should all have the right to enjoy the countryside in a responsible way.

◆

CHAPTER TWENTY-EIGHT

A national holiday for Scotland

Scotland is one of the few countries in the world that does not have a National Holiday. The USA has Independence Day, the French have Bastille Day, the Australians have Australia Day and, of course, the Irish have St Patrick's Day.

For many centuries, the last day of November has been observed as the Feast of St Andrew. In Scotland and in many other parts of the world where Scots and their descendants are gathered, 30 November is celebrated as Scotland's National Day. St Andrew is Scotland's patron saint and the St Andrew's Cross is embodied in our national flag, the Saltire.

The history linking St Andrew and Scotland is rather convoluted. A common account is that, in the fourth century, some relics of St Andrew were being transported by a monk called St Rule when he was shipwrecked off the coast of Fife. St Rule established a settlement in the north-east of Fife which came to be known as St Andrews. It became a place of pilgrimage and later a cathedral was established as well as Scotland's oldest university.

The Saltire became the national flag by Act of Parliament in 1385 but the reason for its adoption is based on legend dating back to the Battle of Athelstaneford in 831, when an army of Scots was about to face a Northumbrian army. When the Scots King Angus saw a vision of a white St Andrew's Cross in the clear blue sky, he swore that, if he was victorious, St Andrew would be forever the Patron Saint of Scotland. The Scots went on to win the battle. St Andrew's status as Patron Saint of Scotland was formalised in the Declaration of Arbroath in 1320.

At one point, St Andrew's Day was a popular day of festivity in Scotland but, in recent years, it has been celebrated more enthusiastically by expatriate Scots and their descendants in countries such as the USA, Canada, Australia and New Zealand. There are St Andrew's societies and St Andrew's clubs in many parts of the world. If St Andrew's Day were recognised at home as a National

Holiday, it would give a huge boost to such international celebrations and help to promote Scotland on the world stage.

That was partly the reason why, in 2004, I launched a proposal to make St Andrew's Day a National Holiday. The pre-legislative process in the Scottish Parliament involves conducting a consultation on the proposed bill and I was very encouraged by the response. About 85 per cent of the respondents to my nationwide consultation were in favour of the proposal and a MORI opinion poll indicated that 75 per cent of the people of Scotland supported it. I also worked hard to get 75 MSPs of various parties to add their names to the motion, which I lodged in the Scottish Parliament.

Unfortunately, the Scottish Parliament does not have the power to legislate on employment matters, as that is reserved to Westminster. The parliament therefore cannot force employers to give their employees a day off but my researcher, Maureen, discovered that, under the Scotland Act 1998, the Scottish Parliament does have the power to create an additional bank holiday in Scotland. Bank holidays are days on which banks may close their business and banking transactions can be postponed until the next working day without incurring any financial penalty. The law does not oblige employers to give their employees a day off on bank holidays, unless of course the employees' contract of employment includes entitlement to a holiday on those days. Traditionally a bank holiday has become the nearest thing we have to a nationwide holiday as distinct from a local holiday. The list of bank holidays is contained in a schedule to the Banking and Financial Dealings Act 1971 but Maureen discovered that that particular schedule had been devolved under the Scotland Act 1998. In other words, the Scottish Parliament had the power to make St Andrew's Day a bank holiday in Scotland, thereby facilitating the recognition of St Andrew's Day as a National Holiday.

The drafting of the bill was a simple task and the entire bill took up only one side of a sheet of A4 paper. After it was published, the bill was referred to the Scottish Parliament's Enterprise and Culture Committee, which noted that the bill of itself would not ensure the recognition of St Andrew's Day as a National Holiday but unanimously recommended that the general principles of the bill be approved by the parliament.

When the bill was being considered by the Committee, the Minister giving evidence on behalf of the Executive was Tom McCabe, Minister for Finance, who made it clear from the outset that he opposed the bill but failed to give any convincing reason for his stance. I suspected then and still do suspect that the Executive did not want to offend some big business interests who were opposed to the idea of workers getting an extra day's holiday, despite the fact that, if we compare the number of public holidays in Scotland with that in other EU countries, we are at the bottom of the European League.

The business community in Scotland was divided on the matter. The Scottish Retail Consortium strongly supported my bill along with some leading business people such as Lord Macfarlane of Bearsden. On the other hand, the banks were opposed to it and the Scottish CBI made it clear that they did not want an additional bank holiday. The Scottish Licensed Trade Association even made the bizarre suggestion that a St Andrew's Day Holiday would mean a loss of trade for Scottish pubs. When I told that one in an Irish pub, everybody burst out laughing and the bartender said that if a publican cannot make a profit on St Patrick's Day, he should not be in the business. It would be preposterous to claim that St Patrick's Day is somehow bad for Irish business and bad for the Irish economy. The St Patrick's Day celebrations mean an injection of 80 million euros into the Dublin economy alone and also help to promote Ireland internationally.

The opponents of my bill were helped by the Scottish Parliament Information Centre (SPICE), which produced a briefing paper indicating that my bill could lead to a loss of output of £200 million. The figure was based on the assumption that, if a group of workers were to reduce their number of working days by X per cent, then there would be an automatic reduction of X per cent in their output. I could not believe that a researcher with a PhD could display such economic illiteracy. I had to remind him that, by his reckoning, the national output during Ted Heath's three day week in 1973–74 would have fallen by 40 per cent. In fact, it increased.

When it came to the parliamentary debate on the general principles of my bill, the Executive put down an amendment asking the parliament to refer the bill back to the Committee for further consideration. To make matters worse, Labour and Lib Dem MSPs were whipped to vote for the Executive amendment, despite the fact that many of them had previously signed the motion supporting my bill. I described the Executive's conduct as an unprecedented piece of control-freakery and skulduggery and, at the end of the debate, I quoted Edwin Morgan's poem, which had been read at the official opening of the Holyrood building:

What do the people want of the place?
They want it to be filled with thinking persons
As open and adventurous as its architecture.
A nest of fearties is what they do not want.
A symposium of procrastinators is what they do not want.
A phalanx of forelock-tuggers is what they do not want.
And perhaps above all the droopy mantra of 'it wizny me' is what
they do not want.

When it came to the vote, the fearties, procrastinators and forelock-tuggers won and the bill was referred back to the Committee. It seemed to me that the Executive was afraid to kill the bill completely because of the possibility of a public backlash. Instead it was kicking the bill into the long grass but that made me even more determined to retrieve it.

Alex Neil, Convener of the Enterprise and Culture Committee, arranged a meeting with Tom McCabe in an effort to find out what the government expected the committee to do with the bill. As sponsor of the bill, I was also invited along to the meeting. McCabe was most unhelpful. He said it was not for him to suggest to the committee what to do, yet it was he who had moved the resolution to refer the bill back to the committee. Alex and I came away from the meeting feeling very despondent.

As McCabe was a major stumbling block, I decided to go over his head and make a direct appeal to Jack McConnell, the First Minister. I had known Jack for many years, ever since he was a student at Stirling University and I was the MP for West Stirlingshire, which included the university at that time. Jack was a student activist with good leadership potential. He had a youthful flirtation with the SNP but I persuaded him to join the Labour Party. He and I were founding members of Scottish Labour Action, a home-rule pressure group within the Labour Party. Knowing Jack's background, I could not believe that he would be against the idea of making St Andrew's Day a National Holiday and I therefore sought a meeting with him to discuss the matter.

I reminded Jack that my bill had huge support throughout the country and warned him that, if his government were seen to be opposing it, then he would be playing right into the hands of the SNP in the lead-up to the next Scottish Parliament elections. I also complained about Tom McCabe's negative attitude.

Jack told me that he was not instinctively opposed to my bill and promised to have a word with Tom McCabe before Tom reappeared before the committee to give an up-date of the government's position. The committee also commissioned an independent research company to do a cost–benefit analysis of the social, economic and cultural implications of celebrating St Andrew's Day, including case studies of some countries which already had a National Holiday.

By the time McCabe reappeared before the Committee, there was a noticeable shift in the government's attitude. I could not believe it. McCabe actually mentioned the possibility of Executive funding for St Andrew's Day celebrations.

In September 2006, Jack McConnell invited me to attend a meeting in Glasgow to launch the city's bid to host the 2014 Commonwealth Games. I was invited because, as convener of the Parliament's Cross-Party Sports Group, I had helped to win parliamentary support for the bid. Jack's office told me that he would like to have a private word with me afterwards about my St Andrew's Day Bill.

At the Commonwealth Games meeting, I found myself sitting next to Jack's wife, Bridget, who was there as head of Glasgow City Council's Sports and Culture Department. Bridget very kindly asked about my family, as was her wont, and was very upset when I told her that my sons, Dennis and Mark, both had life-threatening illnesses and it looked as if their days were numbered. By the time I met Jack for our private discussion, Bridget had obviously told him, because he was visibly shocked and effusive in his sympathy. Bridget and Jack McConnell are both caring persons and their personal words of support meant a lot to me at that very difficult time.

Jack also expressed support for my bill but indicated that Nicol Stephen, the Lib Dem Minister for Enterprise, was not keen on it because of the opposition from certain business interests who did not want an additional holiday. Jack therefore suggested a compromise whereby the bill would get Executive support on the understanding that the St Andrew's Day Holiday would be a replacement for an existing holiday rather than an additional holiday. I reluctantly went along with the compromise because I was realistic enough to understand that the bill had no chance of getting parliamentary approval without Executive support.

I found it interesting that the Executive did not even try to write its compromise onto the face of the bill, which was unanimously passed by the parliament without any amendment.

During the final stage of the parliamentary proceedings on the bill, I made it absolutely clear that my preference is for the St Andrew's Day Holiday to be an additional holiday. My bill established the principle of a holiday on or around St Andrew's Day and I am confident that, in the years ahead, recognition of the holiday will grow and constructive negotiations between trade unions and employers will lead to it eventually becoming an additional holiday.

After a long, hard battle, the bill was unanimously passed by the Scottish Parliament on the eve of St Andrew's Day 2006. My hope is that it will encourage the people of Scotland to celebrate our Patron Saint, our cultural diversity and our membership of the international community. I continue working towards that goal and, when it is achieved, I think that Scotland and the whole world will be the better for it.

—— ◆ ——

Getting a life

In January 2007, shortly after the death of my second son, Dennis, I was so distraught that I came to a decision to retire from full-time politics so that I could devote more time to my family. When I made a public announcement that I would not be standing for re-election to the Scottish Parliament, I was not fully aware of the immediate reaction because, on the day of my announcement, I left for Australia to visit my oldest son, Mark, who was dying of motor neurone disease.

When I returned to Scotland a few weeks later, I read in the *Falkirk Herald* that a Labour councillor, Dennis Goldie, intended to move a resolution at the next meeting of Falkirk Council to grant me the freedom of Falkirk. He had made no effort to contact me or my office before announcing his intention to the press and some of his colleagues on the council were of the view that he was perhaps motivated by his desire to succeed me as MSP for Falkirk West. I politely told Dennis that I did not want the final few months of my parliamentary service to be marred by a petty squabble in the council chambers over whether I should be given the freedom of Falkirk. I therefore asked Dennis to desist from moving the resolution and he complied with my request.

Dennis Goldie was successful in his ambition to become Falkirk West's Labour candidate for the Scottish Parliament but was unsuccessful in his ambition to succeed me as MSP for Falkirk West. It was no great surprise when he was defeated by Michael Matheson, the SNP candidate. Having been a regional MSP for Central Scotland for eight years, Michael had been very active, particularly in the Falkirk area, and he works hard on behalf of his constituents. Michael's victory in 2007 meant that the SNP became the biggest party in the Scottish Parliament, with one more seat than Labour, and Alex Salmond became leader of Scotland's first SNP Government. That might never had happened if the Labour Party leadership had not shot itself in the foot by trying to rig the Falkirk West selection process in 1998. The chickens eventually came home to roost. Not only was a safe Labour seat lost, but Labour lost power in the Scottish Parliament.

When the results of the Scottish Parliament elections in 2007 were finally announced, my sister Kathleen pointed out that, if I had stood again and won, then Labour and the SNP would have had exactly the same number of seats. That would have put Margo MacDonald and me, as the only two independents, in a very powerful position. We might even have been the 'king makers'. Nevertheless, I still think that I made the right decision to retire. I miss parliament in some respects but not enough to want to go back to full-time politics. I have not yet reached the stage of waking up in the morning and wondering what to do with the rest of the day.

Adam keeps me very busy, but he is a joy rather than a burden. It irks me when I hear ageist comments about people being too old to be good parents. I am nearly 60 years older than Adam. Perhaps he will be the best judge of my parenting skills. I am certainly not an ideal father but I am probably a better one now than what I was in my twenties, mainly because in my retirement I have more time and so I am more patient. I remember my oldest son, Mark, gently chiding me when Adam was born that I might not be around when Adam finished high school. That was before poor Mark was diagnosed with MND and ironically that crippling disease ensured that he was the one who was not around when his own son, Tommy, was still at primary school. All of my grandchildren were very young when they lost their fathers and that makes me realise that no one can make assumptions about how long parents and children can enjoy each others' company. We never know what the future holds, and we can never take life for granted.

Nowadays I spend a lot of time with my family, but I also try to find some time for voluntary work, which I can sometimes combine with leisure activities. As President of Ramblers Scotland, I continue to enjoy walking and campaigning for the right of access to the countryside. I am also President of Milton Amateurs Football Club, a position I have held almost since the club was founded over 30 years ago by a group of teenagers in the Whins of Milton area, including Pat Griffin and his brothers, John and Kevin, who were former pupils of mine. The club is now one of the most successful amateur football clubs in Scotland and provides coaching and playing opportunities for youngsters from the age of five upwards, including Adam, who is fitba' daft.

My good friend, Anne Wallace, who is Director of the Falkirk & District Association for Mental Health, persuaded me to be patron of that organisation, which offers a very valuable range of services for people with a mental health problem. I am also patron of William Simpson's, a care home in the village of Plean, which is trying to raise funds for a multi-million pound project, including a centre of excellence for the treatment of alcohol-related problems.

When my former parliamentary colleague, Eric Clarke, suggested that I join him on the Board of Trustees of the Scottish Mining Museum, I was pleased and honoured to accept, particularly because of the mining tradition in my family and the importance of preserving Scotland's mining heritage.

I have sometimes been asked whether I would accept an honour in recognition of my public service. In the unlikely event of my being offered a peerage, I would have no hesitation in refusing because I have consistently supported the abolition of the House of Lords. As far as the 'Honours List' is concerned, I have no respect for it, although I do have respect for some of the people who have been 'honoured' in that way. When I was a Member of Parliament, I was sometimes asked if I would nominate someone for an honour but I always politely declined because I thought it would be hypocritical of me to participate in a system which I have publicly attacked. At worst it is corrupt and at best it is an anachronism. What is the point of being a Member or a Commander of an Empire which no longer exists?

I have lost count of the number of former colleagues who have accepted peerages or knighthoods or CBEs or other gongs and some of them were almost on their knees, craving such recognition by the British establishment. One of them, an ex-provost and Member of the British Empire, recently accused me of double standards for criticising the Honours system and then accepting honorary degrees, as if there were some equivalence. I am very proud of my honorary doctorates from the University of Strathclyde and the University of Stirling. Both of those institutions have done a great deal to educate people and make the world a better place, whereas the British Empire did a great deal to exploit people and make the world a worse place.

Not everybody agrees with me about honorary degrees, even some of the recipients. Step forward, Dr John Greig, former captain of Rangers Football Club, who led his team to their famous European Cup-winners Cup victory in 1972.

Over 30 years later, John was given an honorary doctorate from Glasgow University for his services to football. Shortly afterwards, I met him at the Falkirk Stadium, when Rangers were the visitors. I said: 'Congratulations, John.' John looked at me with a scowl. 'What do you mean by that?' he growled and, for one dreadful moment, I regretted not wearing my shinguards, because John looked as if he might break my legs. I wondered why he was so upset and then I remembered that, earlier that week, Rangers had been knocked out of the European Champions League by Kaunas of Lithuania. John apparently thought that, when I offered my congratulations, I was being sarcastic. I hastily explained: 'John, I'm congratulating you on your doctorate from Glasgow University.' Whereupon John said: 'Ach well, Dennis, ye ken whit it's like. They're giein' them away tae onybody these days.' I don't know whether John was having a dig at me or just being his usual modest self.

Shortly after I retired, Provost Pat Reid of Falkirk Council informed me that the council would like to recognise in some way my parliamentary service to the people in the Falkirk area. There were various suggestions but the one which most appealed to me was one which would help young people to continue with their education. The council decided to invest £10,000 to set up the Dennis Canavan Scholarship Fund in order to make an annual award to a student from the Falkirk area. That initial sum was increased to around £14,000 with contributions from individuals, businesses, trade unions and other organisations. The annual award of at least £500 is given to a young person leaving school to continue in further or higher education but I insisted that it should not simply be awarded on academic attainment. I have always believed that one of the aims of education should be to encourage young people to use their skills and talents to help others. It was therefore decided that the award should be given to the student who, in the opinion of the judges, has given the most outstanding service to other people. That could be interpreted in various ways, such as caring for the elderly or coaching children in sport or helping to raise funds for international development. I hope that the award will encourage young people to continue their education and to serve others, especially those who are most in need.

If the Dennis Canavan Scholarship gives young people such inspiration, then that for me will be the greatest recognition of all. I said at the start that I never set out to be a political careerist and, looking back, I think I was probably a better teacher than a politician. I would like to be remembered as a teacher and a politician who tried to improve educational opportunities, especially for young people.

I now try to focus on looking forward. My Grandad saw education as the key to the liberation of the working class. He had a vision of a fairer society and he worked hard to bequeath to future generations a better world where all children would get the opportunity to realise their potential. I feel absolutely gutted that three of my own children did not live long enough to reach their full potential but my wish now is for my grandad's dream to come true for my remaining two children and my five grandchildren. That is also my wish for every bairn in the world.

Index

Index Note: Throughout the index where 'Dennis Canavan' and 'Labour Party' occur in other headings they have been abbreviated to 'DC' and 'LP' respectively. 'FAC' is Foreign Affairs Committee. Names with 'Mc', 'Mac' and 'St' are sorted as spelt.